# Psychological Aspects of Developmental and Physical Disabilities

## A CASEBOOK

Edited by
**Michel Hersen**

*Western Psychiatric Institute and Clinic
University of Pittsburgh*

and
**Vincent B. Van Hasselt**

*University of California—Irvine
and Fairview Developmental Center*

**SAGE** PUBLICATIONS
*The International Professional Publishers*
Newbury Park   London   New Delhi

*For information address:*

SAGE Publications, Inc.
2111 West Hillcrest Drive
Newbury Park, California 91320

SAGE Publications Ltd.
28 Banner Street
London EC1Y 8QE
England

SAGE Publications India Pvt. Ltd.
M-32 Market
Greater Kailash I
New Delhi 110 048 India

Printed in the United States of America

Library of Congress Cataloging-in-Publication Data

Psychological aspects of developmental and physical disabilities: a
   casebook / edited by Michel Hersen and Vincent B. Van Hasselt.
        p.  cm.
     Includes bibliographical references.
     ISBN 0-8039-3191-3. — ISBN 0-8039-3702-4 (pbk.)
     1. Handicapped — Mental health.  2. Psychotherapy.     I. Hersen,
   Michel.   II. Van Hasselt, Vincent B.
     [DNLM: 1. Handicapped — case studies.   2. Mental Retardation-
   -rehabilitation — case studies.   3. Rehabilitation — case studies.
   WM 302-P974]
   RC451.4.H35P75 1989
   616.89'0087 — dc20
   DNLM/DLC
   for Library of Congress                                    89-10763
                                                                  CIP

**FIRST PRINTING, 1990**

# Contents

# Preface and Acknowledgments

In the 1980s increased psychological attention has been placed on individuals (both children and adults) suffering from a variety of developmental and physical disabilities. At least four factors have contributed to the increased clinical and research interest in this area. First, of course, is the fact that innovation in medicine has resulted in greater longevity of disabled people, thus highlighting the importance of continued psychological care throughout the various developmental stages of life. Second, as a function of the staggering financial costs involved in care and rehabilitation, greater public scrutiny of the problem has eventuated. Third, the much delayed legislative initiatives (e.g., wheelchair access in public facilities) have helped to diminish and dispel the negative stereotypes held by the public at large. And fourth, but equally important, recent societal and professional concern about the increased possibility of abuse and neglect of developmentally and physically disabled individuals (at all ages) has underscored the critical psychological features in their care.

Surprising as it may seem, no casebook details the kinds of psychological interventions applied to the spectrum of developmentally and physically disabled people could be found. Indeed, we thought that by developing such a book a gap in the literature would be filled for professionals working with disabled people, such as special educators, psychologists, social workers, rehabilitation workers, physical therapists, nurses, and psychiatrists. We feel that, as a consequence of the obvious developmental and physical disabilities, too often the psychological needs of such individuals are not given sufficient attention.

The book is divided into two parts. Part I gives an overview of the issues and their diagnostic and medical considerations. Part II comprises 14 chapters that consider many of the major developmental and physical disabilities. Each chapter follows an identical outline to enable the reader to make cross case comparisons with ease: 1. Description of the Disorder; 2. Case Identification; 3. Presenting Complaints; 4. History; 5. Assessment; 6. Selection of Treatment; 7. Course of Treatment; 8. Termination and Follow-up; and 9. Overall Evaluation.

Many people have contributed their time and expertise to this book. First, we thank our respective contributors for their willingness to share their thoughts on the clinical care of developmentally and physically disabled individuals. Second, we thank Mary Newell, Mary Anne Frederick, Jenifer McKelvey, and Karen Drudy for their technical help. And finally, we thank Terry Hendrix, our editor at Sage, for his willingness to publish and his patience.

Michel Hersen
Vincent B. Van Hasselt

# PART I

## INTRODUCTION

# Chapter 1

# Overview

Vincent B. Van Hasselt
John R. Lutzker
Michel Hersen

## Introduction

During the past decade there has been an increasing awareness of the pivotal role that psychologists may play in improving the life situation of persons with developmental and physical disabilities. This was perhaps most clearly illustrated in a May, 1984, special issue of *American Psychologist*. Specifically, this issue was devoted to a discussion of relevant issues, research strategies, and treatment approaches with disabled individuals. These articles transversed a wide range of topics, reflecting areas that warrant greater attention from psychologists and other mental health professionals who work with disabled persons. Some of these include: social functioning, attitudes toward disability, mental health problems, adjustment and family reactions to disability, the increasing prevalence of developmental and physical disability, and legal and legislative initiatives with disabled populations. These issues continue to pose unique challenges to the various professionals actively involved in evaluation and remediation efforts with the disabled. A brief overview of these salient issues is provided in the sections below.

## Social Attitudes and Adjustment

In one of the articles featured in the May, 1984, *American Psychologist*, Asch (1984) addressed the difficulties of interpersonal adjustment and social discrimination encountered by many persons with some form of disabling condition. As Asch cogently pointed out, inadequate socialization, social stigma, and stereotyping have been major factors in the acceleration of assessment and intervention activities with disabled persons, who, historically, have been viewed by many as socially incompetent, helpless, and dependent (Jackman, 1983).

The pervasive negative social attitudes of nondisabled individuals toward those with disabilities, and the problems encountered by disabled persons in social adaptation have been documented for several years now (e.g., Dion, 1972; Kleck, 1968; Van Hasselt, 1983). Indeed, in an analysis conducted over two decades ago, of attitudes of nondisabled persons toward those with disabilities, Siller, Chipman, Ferguson, and Vann (1967) found the following dimensions to be paramount: generalized rejection (unpleasant personal reactions), interaction strain, distressed identification (i.e., anxiety by the nonhandicapped regarding their own potential vulnerability), imputed functional limitations, rejection of intimacy, authoritarian virtuousness (i.e., appearing to be supportive of the disabled but actually negative in attitude), and inferred emotional consequences. The latter factor refers to the common view that a disability negatively affects the character, social valence, and/or emotional status of the disabled individual. Asch (1984) concluded that "the presence of someone who actually is or is thought to be disabled arouses in the nonhandicapped person a variety of emotions that, at the very least, hinder ordinary social interaction. Nonhandicapped people prefer to avoid social contact with the disabled or behave more formally and in distorted ways if they are forced to interact with handicapped persons" (p. 532).

Psychological research also has provided a convergence of empirical data indicating that many disabled children and adults are socially isolated (e.g., Eaglestein, 1975; Van Hasselt, 1983), receive inaccurate feedback regarding their interpersonal behavior from their environment (Richardson, Goodman, Hastorf, & Dornbusch, 1961), and have fewer and more inadequate socialization experiences than nonhandicapped individuals (Kleck, Richardson, & Ronald, 1974). It appears that Richardson (1976) was quite accurate when he contended that "no further research is needed to show that it is socially disadvantageous to be . . . handicapped in initial social encounters" (p. 32).

The heightened awareness of the need for enhanced socialization in persons with disabilities has led to a proliferation of social skills interventions targeting a wide variety of disabled groups. Some of these include the blind and visually impaired (Farkas, Sherick, Matson, & Loebig, 1981; Van Hasselt, Hersen, Kazdin, Simon, & Mastantuono, 1983), deaf (Lemanek, Willamson, Gresham, & Jensen, 1986), spinal-cord injured (Dunn, Van Horn, & Herman, 1981), mentally retarded (Matson & Zeiss, 1978; Turner, Hersen, & Bellack, 1978), as well as autistic (Strain, 1983) and multihandicapped (Sisson, Van Hasselt, Hersen, & Strain, 1985) children. Further, the goals of skills-training endeavors have varied considerably and have ranged from attempts to reduce maladaptive responses (e.g., self-stimulatory behaviors) that interfere with effective social interactions (Farkas et al., 1981) to elevating levels of molecular components (e.g., eye contact, response latency) requisite to socially skillful interchanges (Lemanek et al., 1986; Van Hasselt et al., 1983). More recently, approaches that use nondisabled peers as skill "trainers" have enjoyed success in improving the social valence and acceptability of disabled children (see Sisson et al., 1985; Strain, 1983).

## Mental Health

The psychological adjustment of disabled individuals also has been the focus of increased clinical and investigative attention in recent years. Increased activity in this area is attributable to evidence of emotional and/or behavior problems in a disproportionately large number of disabled persons. For example, psychological assessment research has revealed higher levels of psychopathology (e.g., anxiety, depression) in many visually impaired children and adults relative to nonhandicapped controls or sighted norms (e.g., Bauman, 1964; Jan, Freeman, & Scott, 1977; Van Hasselt, Kazdin, & Hersen, 1986). A similar pattern of results has been reported with hearing-impaired persons (Gentile & McCarthy, 1973; Jensema & Trybus, 1975; Vernon, 1972). In their extensive review of work with the latter group, Matson and Helsel (1986) concluded that "psychiatric problems, especially personality disorders, neurosis and behavior disorders in children and adults are reported to be particularly prevalent in the hearing impaired" (p. 23). Mental health problems of the mentally retarded also have been examined empirically (see Matson & Andrasik 1983). Some difficulties that have been the focus of psychological assessment and intervention with these individuals include depression (Matson, Senatore, Kazdin, & Helsel, 1983), self-injury (Griffin, Locke, & Landers, 1975; Matson, Stephens, & Smith, 1978), and aggression (Repp & Brulle, 1981).

## Adjustment to Disability

Of particular interest to psychologists and other mental health professionals has been the process of adjustment to serious disability by both the disabled person and family system. The stages of adjustment have been viewed as parallel to those described in the literature on trauma (e.g., Kübler-Ross, 1969). For example, Weller and Miller (1977) characterize responses to spinal cord injury as shock, denial, anger, depression, and acceptance of adjustment. *Shock* is considered a protective mechanism, which may be psychological or physical depending on the nature of the disability. This phase is usually of relatively brief duration. *Denial* is used by the disabled individual to protect him- or herself from the devastating implications of a severe impairment. While gradually relinquished as a function of accommodation to the disability, denial may be dysfunctional if it interferes with intervention or rehabilitative efforts.

As a reaction to the physical and psychological injury incurred, the perceived inequity of the impairment, and the life changes the individual is forced to make, *anger* may be observed concurrent with or following denial. While seen as a normal part of the adjustment process, anger too, may impede rehabilitation if it becomes excessively disruptive. *Depression* reflects the disabled person's feelings of hopelessness, despair, and negative expectations for the future. It may be observed at any point during adjustment. Depression also is associated with feelings of guilt related to self-perceptions of excessive or irrational expressions of anger and responsibility for the trauma or injury causing the disability. Finally, *acceptance* or *adaptation* may encompass a myriad of behaviors ranging from "optimal, positive self-actualizing, to negative, embittered retreat" (Lindemann, 1981).

## Families of Disabled Persons

The advent of a chronic disability within a family has been discussed in much the same terms used to portray reactions to traumatic injury (see Blacher, 1984; Harris, 1983). Illustrative are clinician's descriptions of the reactions of parents to the diagnosis of a visual disorder in their child. Responses often include shock, grief, disappointment, and depression (Catena, 1961; Froyd, 1973). Guilt and anger may also be experienced, usually as a result of unwarranted (and sometimes superstitious) feelings of responsibility for the impairment (Cohen, 1964). Lowenfeld (1971) and Lambert and West (1980) have commented on the frequent family denial of the existence of the disability. Although these parents have natural love for the child, they are unable to accept the realty of the impairment. And recognition and emphasis of the child's deficits and inadequacies adversely affects attachment and other aspects of the parent-child relationship (Lowenfeld, 1971).

Of more recent concern are preliminary findings showing that a disproportionate number of disabled children, particularly those with additional handicapping conditions, are at greater risk for physical abuse and family abandonment (see review by Ammerman, Van Hasselt, & Hersen, 1988). An initial investigation in this area by Gil (1970) indicated that 29% of 6,000 confirmed cases of child abuse had some form of developmental disability. In a study of the incidence and characteristics of maltreatment in psychiatrically hospitalized and multihandicapped children, Ammerman, Hersen, Van Hasselt, McGonigle, and Lubetsky (1988) found that 39% of the 150 child participants exhibited evidence of past and/or current maltreatment. Physical abuse was the most common form, occurring in 69% of the maltreated sample. This was followed by neglect (45%) and sexual abuse (36%). In addition, 52% of the maltreated children experienced more than one form of maltreatment (e.g., physical abuse and neglect).

While research in this field is at the nascent stage, etiological factors implicated in maltreatment of disabled children are: (1) child characteristics, such as chronic and pervasive behavioral disturbances (e.g., aggression, self-injury, screaming), severe disability, and unresponsiveness to parental attention or commands (Friedrich & Boriskin, 1976; Frodi, 1981), and (2) family variables, including inadequate coping and stress management, deficient child management skills, and insufficient social support networks (Ammerman, Van Hasselt, & Hersen, 1988; Kadushin & Martin, 1981; Murphy, 1982). Similar child and family factors also have been found to have causal significance in a family's decision to place their disabled children out of the home (Janicki, 1981; McDowell & Gabel, 1981; Sherman, 1988; Turnbull, Summers, & Brotherson, 1986).

## Prevalence

As indicated in the May, 1984, issue of the *American Psychologist*, there is an increasing number of individuals with some form of developmental or physical disability. Recent surveys indicate that as many as 36 million people, or 14% of the population of the United States, have some form of disability (Bowe, 1980). This is consistent with a previous report by the 1976 United States Census Survey of Income and Education, which revealed a figure of 13.6%. Also, 46% of persons 65 years of age and over report a serious and disabling health impairment (DeJong & Lifchez, 1983). Further, there are indications that as many as 10% of children under the age of 21 are disabled (Gliedman & Roth, 1980). Moreover, as a result of improved prenatal care, better nutrition, decreased infant mortality rates due to advances in surgical and medical care, and more effective treatments for infant diseases, the number of disabled persons is expected to rise sharply over the next decade (Dibedenetto, 1976; Mulliken & Buckley, 1983).

Related to the growing population of persons with a disability are the high economic costs of habilitative and rehabilitative programs (e.g., Goldenson, Dunham, & Dunham, 1978). For example, in 1977, disability-related payments to working-age individuals amounted to almost $63.5 billion. Social Security Insurance and Supplemental Security Income programs alone paid $20.6 billion to more than four million working-age people with disabilities in 1980 (DeJong & Lifchez, 1983).

## Legal and Legislative Initiatives

Sweeping changes in the law and federal funding began with President John F. Kennedy's President's Panel on Mental Retardation, established in 1962. The efforts of the panel resulted in the enactment of Public Laws (P.L.) 88-164 and 88-156, which authorized the funding of research centers for the study of the causes, prevention, and treatment of developmental disabilities. Since that time, a number of funding agencies, especially those under the aegis of the Department of Education (e.g., National Institute on Disabilities and Rehabilitation Research, Office of Special Education Programs, Handicapped Children's Early Education Program) have provided substantial fiscal support for field-initiated research, model demonstration projects, professional training, and research centers directed toward disabled persons.

An action of major consequence was passage of P.L. 94-142, the Education for all Handicapped Children Act of 1975. Under this law, free and appropriate public education was made available to all handicapped children in the "least restrictive setting" possible. Since enactment of P.L. 94-142, many handicapped children residing in institutions or residential settings have been "mainstreamed" into public schools for placement in regular or specialized classrooms (Weicker, 1984). Concurrently, there has been an emphasis on the deinstitutionalization of adults and placement in less restrictive settings (e.g., group homes, community facilities) as well. Such shifts have been instigated largely by the concerted efforts of advocacy and special interest groups, such as the National Association for Retarded Citizens, Association for Children with Learning Disabilities, and the Council for Exceptional Children. These and many other organizations have worked diligently to make possible the "normalization" of life experiences for disabled members of society (Wolfensberger, 1972). By adhering to this concept, advocates are striving to enable disabled persons to lead a normal existence. This includes, for example, schooling, dining, dating, and working in environments that support these and other life activities to the fullest extent possible, given the individual's level of functioning.

## Psychological Assessment and Treatment

Passage of P.L. 94-142 and related initiatives have had significant implications for psychologists. Psychological assessors now have greater involvement in decisions concerning diagnosis, classification, and placement of disabled children and adults. For example, psychological evaluation may involve tests of intellectual functioning to determine possible mental retardation or deficits in skill areas. Or, assessment data may be utilized to specify the nature of a disability and to justify placement decisions (e.g., residential versus public school, institution versus community living arrangement).

Psychological assessment strategies also are being increasingly employed to identify psychological disorders or behavior problems that may coexist with a disability. Evaluative methods derived from the fields of behavior therapy and applied behavior analysis have been particularly valuable in this regard. Indeed, *behavioral assessment* procedures have provided important data on *behavioral excesses* and *deficits* (see Bellack & Hersen, 1977; Kanfer & Saslow, 1969) in persons with disabilities. Behavioral excesses refer to behaviors that occur with too great a frequency, intensity, or duration, or that occur when they are not socially sanctioned (e.g., self-injury, aggression). Behavioral deficits are responses that are emitted with insufficient frequency or intensity, or with inadequate form, or fail to occur at appropriate times (e.g., low activity level, social withdrawal). Behavioral assessment has been most useful in the evaluation of maladaptive response patterns (e.g., self-stimulation, stereotypies, social isolation) in the developmentally disabled. Further, they have been instrumental in the assessment of treatment programs designed to ameliorate these problems (see Van Hasselt & Hersen, 1987).

Psychological interventions with developmentally and physically disabled persons have included numerous and disparate therapeutic modalities and techniques. Most notable over the past decade have been the methods of applied behavior analysis. As mentioned above, these are commonly initiated to remediate behavioral disorders of severely impaired individuals. However, behavioral approaches have been successfully applied with a large number of disabled populations and problems. (See Hersen, Van Hasselt, & Matson, 1983, for a comprehensive review of behavior therapy with disabled persons.) Behavior modification strategies also have proven effective in teaching a number of independent living skills (e.g., dressing, cooking, transportation usage, emergency safety skills) necessary for adaptive functioning in the community (Hersen, Van Hasselt, & Matson, 1983; Matson & Mulick, 1983).

In a related trend, the heuristic value of behavioral medicine (i.e., the application of the knowledge and techniques of the behavioral sciences to physical health problems and illness) has become increasingly recognized in the past few years (see Luiselli, 1989). Behavioral medicine techniques have been used with several difficulties in the disabled, such as feeding disorders, obesity and weight regulation, bladder and bowel incontinence, and compliance with medical and pharmacological regimens. Also under the purview of behavioral medicine is behavioral pharmacology, an area of study that examines how pharmacological agents affect behavior. Some knowledge of behavioral pharmacology is now imperative given current figures for rates of drug administration in severely disabled individuals. For example, a recent survey by Singh and Winton (1989) showed that the prevalence of psychotropic and antiepileptic medication for mentally retarded persons is between 18% and 33% for children and 36% and 48% for adults.

Interventions by rehabilitation psychologies have improved the so-cial, emotional, and vocational adjustment of disabled persons. Further, they have been instrumental in facilitating integration of the disabled person into more normalized and less restrictive environments. The important function of rehabilitation psychologists in ameliorating the problems of the disabled is cogently described by Fraser (1984), who states that these professionals are "concerned with the total re-adapta-tion of the person with a disability into the community from the psy-chological aspects of activities for daily living through issues of social and vocational reintegration" (p. 2). Fraser (1984) further distinguishes the role of rehabilitation psychologists from other fields of study by their emphasis on "orchestrating environment modifications rather than on assisting individuals to modify their personal needs or behavior" (p. 2). Rehabilitation psychologists also are vigorously involved in family interventions by: (1) assisting the family to establish realistic rehabilitation goals following the onset of a disability, (2) providing ongoing family support, (3) restructuring the financial planner-provider role, and (4) serving as a consultant in the sexual adjustment process. Also, to facilitate successful community adjustment of their clients, rehabilitation psychologists have taken a lead role in the formation of self-help groups dealing with stroke, spinal cord injury, cerebral palsy, mental retardation, blindness, and other disabilities. (For a thorough examination of current strategies and issues in rehabilitation psychol-ogy, see Golden, 1984.)

## Scope of this Book

In recent years, a number of texts have appeared that have pre-sented comprehensive overviews of various psychological assessment and treatment strategies with disabled populations (see Golden, 1984; Hersen, Van Hasselt, & Matson, 1983; Lindemann, 1981; Matson & Andrasik, 1983; Van Hasselt, Strain, & Hersen, 1988). These efforts generally have involved extensive and scholarly reviews of relevant literatures on evaluation and intervention methods and outcomes. How-ever, the format and space limitations of such books have precluded inclusion of detailed case descriptions and in-depth discussions of specific evaluation and treatment techniques. Consequently, the clini-cian or practitioner is often unable to: (1) achieve a clear understanding of the nature of the problem(s) in targeted clients, (2) determine the process by which particular evaluation and treatment methods were selected, and (3) obtain enough information regarding procedures utilized, thus making replication difficult, if not impossible.

The purpose of this book is to provide a practitioner with a casebook approach to the direct application of psychological strategies with developmentally and physically disabled individuals. The emphasis is on detailed presentations of individual cases treated by experts who work with the respective populations covered in the book. Following a discussion of medical considerations with the developmentally and physically disabled in Part I, case illustrations with a wide range of disorders are presented in Part II. Each of these chapters includes sufficient detail and is organized in such a manner as to provide the reader with a direct and practical perspective on the entire assessment and intervention process. Specifically, each chapter in Part II includes the following sections: description of the disorder, case identification, presenting complaints, history, assessment, selection of treatment, course of treatment, termination and follow-up, and overall evaluation.

In light of the dramatic increase in clinical and research endeavors with developmentally and physically disabled individuals, it is believed that such a casebook will be of considerable value to professionals working directly with these populations. Significant strides have been made to improve the adjustment and overall quality of life in persons with disabilities. The goal is to present those strategies that have found utility in dealing with the problems and challenges encountered by many disabled individuals. This book is dedicated to the extension and expansion of efficacious approaches that will further promote the normalization process.

# References

Aman, M. G., & Singh, N. N. (1988). Introduction: Drug prevalence and patterns of drug use, programs to reduce medication use, measurement techniques, and future trends. In M. G. Aman & N. N. Singh (Eds.), *Psychopharmacology of the developmental disabilities*. New York: Springer-Verlag.

Ammerman, R. T., Hersen, M., Van Hasselt, V. B., McGonigle, J. J., & Lubetsky, M. (1989). Abuse and neglect in psychiatrically hospitalized multihandicapped children. *Child Abuse and Neglect, 13*, 335-343.

Ammerman, R. T., Lubetsky, M. J., Hersen, M., & Van Hasselt, V. B. (1988). Maltreatment of multihandicapped children and adolescents. *Journal of the Multihandicapped Person, 1*, 129-140.

Asch, A. (1984). The experience of disability: A challenge for psychology. *American Psychologist, 39*, 529-536.

Bauman, M. K. (1964). Group differences disclosed by inventory items. *International Journal for the Education of the Blind, 13*, 101-107.

Bellack, A. S., & Hersen, M. (1977). *Behavior modification: An introductory textbook.* Baltimore, MD: Williams & Wilkins.

Blacher, J. (Ed.). (1984). *Severely handicapped young children and their families: Research in review.* New York: Academic Press.

Bowe, F. (1980). *Rehabilitation America.* New York: Harper & Row.

Catena, J. (1961). Pre-adolescence: The caseworker and the family. *New Outlook for the Blind, 55*, 297-299.

Cohen, P. C. (1964). The impact of the handicapped child on the family. *New Outlook for the Blind, 58*, 11-15.

DeJong, G., & Lifchez, R. (1983). Physical disability and public policy. *Scientific American, 48*, 240-249.

Dibedenetto, T. A. (1976). Problems of the deaf and retarded: A review of the literature. *Education and Training of the Mentally Retarded, 11*, 164-170.

Dion, K. K. (1972). Physical attractiveness and evaluation of children's transgressions. *Journal of Personality and Social Psychology, 24*, 207-213.

Dunn, M., Van Horn, E. & Herman, S. (1981). Social skills and spinal cord injury: A comparison of three training procedures. *Behavior Therapy, 12* 153-164.

Eaglestein, A. S. (1975). The social acceptance of blind high school students in an integrated school. *New Outlook for the Blind, 69*, 447-451.

Farkas, G. M., Sherick, R. B., Matson, J. L., & Loebig, M. (1981). Social skills training of a blind child through differential reinforcement. *The Behavior Therapist, 4*, 24-26.

Fraser, R. T. (1984). An introduction to rehabilitation psychology. In C. J. Golden (Ed.), *Current topics in rehabilitation psychology.* New York: Grune & Stratton.

Friedrich, M. P. H., & Boriskin, J. A. (1976). The role of the child in abuse: A review of the literature. *American Journal of Orthopsychiatry, 46*, 580-590.

Frodi, A. M. (1981). Contribution of infant characteristics to child abuse. *American Journal of Mental Deficiency, 85*, 341-349.

Froyd, H. E. (1973). Counseling families of severely visually handicapped children. *New Outlook for the Blind, 67*, 251-257.

Gentile, A., & McCarthy, B. (1973). *Additional handicapping conditions among hearing impaired students, United States, 1971-72.* Washington, DC: Office of Demographic Studies, Gallaudet College.

Gil, D. G. (1970). *Violence against children: Physical child abuse in the United States.* Cambridge, MA: Harvard University Press.

Glaser, D., & Bentovim, A. (1979). Abuse and risk to handicapped and chronically ill children. *Child Abuse and Neglect, 3*, 565-575.

Gliedman, J., & Roth, W. (1980). *The unexpected minority: Handicapped children in America.* New York: Harcourt Brace Jovanovich.

Golden, C. J. (Ed.). (1984). *Current topics in rehabilitation psychology.* New York: Grune & Stratton.

Goldenson, R. M., Dunham, J. R., & Dunham, C. S. (Eds.). (1978). *Disability and rehabilitation handbook.* New York: McGraw-Hill.

Griffin, J. C., Locke, B. J., & Landers, W. (1975). Manipulation of potential punishment parameters in the treatment of self-injury. *Journal of Applied Behavior Analysis, 8*, 458-464.

Harris, S. L. (1983). *Families of the developmentally disabled: A guide to behavioral intervention.* Elmsford, NY: Pergamon.

Hersen, M., Van Hasselt, V. B., & Matson, J. L. (Eds.). (1983). *Behavior therapy for the developmentally and physically disabled*. New York: Academic Press.

Jackman, M. (1983). Enabling the disabled. *Perspectives: The Civil Rights Quarterly, 15*, 23-36.

Jan, J. E., Freeman, R. D., & Scott, E. P. (Eds.). (1977). *Visual impairment in children and adolescents*. New York: Grune & Stratton.

Janicki, M. P. (1981). *Etiological factors as determinants of institutional or alternative care placements*. New York State Office of Mental Retardation and Developmental Disabilities.

Jensema, C., & Trybus, R. J. (1975). *Reported emotional/behavioral problems among hearing impaired children in special education programs: United States, 1972-73*. Washington, DC: Office of Demographic Studies, Gallaudet College.

Kadushin, A., & Martin, J. A. (1981). *Child abuse: An interactional event*. New York: Columbia University Press.

Kanfer, F. H., & Saslow, G. (1969). Behavioral diagnosis. In C. M. Franks (Ed.), *Behavior therapy: Appraisal and status*. New York: McGraw-Hill.

Kleck, R. E. (1968). Physical stigma and nonverbal cues emitted in face-to-face interaction. *Human Relations, 21*, 19-28.

Kleck, R. E., Richardson, S. A., & Ronald, L. (1974). Physical appearance cues and interpersonal attraction in children. *Child Development, 45*, 305-310.

Kübler-Ross, E. (1969). *On death and dying*. New York: Macmillan.

Lambert, R., & West, M. (1980). Parenting styles and the depressive syndrome in congenitally blind individuals. *Journal of Visual Impairment and Blindness, 74*, 333-337.

Lemanek, K. L., Williamson, D. A., Gresham, F. M., & Jensen, B. J. (1986). Social skills training with hearing-impaired children. *Behavior Modification, 10*, 55-71.

Lindemann, J. E. (Ed.). (1981). *Psychological and behavioral aspects of physical disability*. New York: Plenum.

Lowenfeld, B. (1971). *Our blind children: Growing and learning with them*. Springfield, IL: Charles C Thomas.

Luiselli, J. K. (Ed.). (1989). *Behavioral medicine and developmental disabilities*. New York: Springer-Verlag.

Matson, J. L., & Andrasik, F. (Eds.). (1983). *Treatment issues and innovations in mental retardation*. New York: Plenum.

Matson, J. L., & Helsel, W. H. (1986). Psychopathology of sensory impaired children. In B. B. Lahey & A. E. Kazdin (Eds.), *Advances in clinical child psychology* (Vol 9). New York: Plenum.

Matson, J. L., & Mulick, J. A. (Eds.). (1983). *Handbook of mental retardation*. New York: Pergamon.

Matson, J. L., Senatore, V., Kazdin, A. E., & Helsel, W. J. (1983). Verbal behaviors in depressed and non-depressed mentally retarded persons. *Applied Research in Mental Retardation, 14*, 79-84.

Matson, J. L., Stephens, R. M., & Smith, C. (1978). Treatment of self-injurious behavior with overcorrection. *Journal of Mental Deficiency Research, 22*, 175-178.

Matson, J. L., & Zeiss, R. (1978). Group training of social skills in chronically explosive severely disturbed psychiatric patients. *Behavioral Engineering, 5*, 41-50.

McDowell, J., & Gabel, H. (1981). *Social support among mothers of retarded infants*. Unpublished manuscript, George Peabody College, Nashville, TN.

Mulliken, R. K., & Buckley, J. J. (Eds.). (1983). *Assessment of multihandicapped and developmentally disabled children*. Rockville, MD: Aspen.

Murphy, M. A. (1982). The family with a handicapped child: A review of the literature. *Developmental and Behavioral Pediatrics, 3*, 73-82.

Repp, A. C., & Brulle, A. R. (1981). Reducing aggressive behavior of mentally retarded persons. In J. L. Matson & J. R. McCartney (Eds.), *Handbook of behavior modification with the mentally retarded*. New York: Plenum.

Richardson, S. A. 91976). Attitudes and behavior toward the physically handicapped. *Birth Defects: Original Article Series, 12*, 15-34.

Richardson, S. A., Goodman, N., Hastorf, A. H., & Dornbusch, S. M. (1961). Cultural uniformity in reaction to physical disabilities. *American Sociological Review, 26*, 241-247.

Sherman, B. R. (1988). Predictors of the decision to place developmentally disabled family members in residential care. *American Journal of Mental Retardation, 92*, 344-351.

Siller, J. A., Chipman, A., Ferguson, L., & Vann, D. H. (1967). *Studies in reaction to disability: Vol. II. Attitudes of the nondisabled toward the physically disabled*. New York: New York University School of Education.

Singh, N. N., & Winton, A. S. W. (1989). Behavioral Pharmacology. In J. K. Luiselli (Ed.), *Behavioral medicine and developmental disabilities*. New York: Springer-Verlag.

Sisson, L. A., Van Hasselt, V. B., Hersen, M., & Strain, P. S. (1985). Peer interventions: Increasing social behaviors in multihandicapped children. *Behavior Modification, 9*, 293-321.

Strain, P. S. (1983). Generalization of autistic children's social behavior change: Effects of developmentally integrated and segregated settings. *Analysis and Intervention in Developmental Disabilities, 3*, 23-34.

Turnbull, A. P., Simmers, J. A., & Brotherson, M. J. (1986). Family life cycle: Theoretical and empirical implications and future directions for families with mentally retarded members. In J. J. Gallagher & P. H. Vietze (Eds.), *Families of handicapped persons: Research, programs, and policy issues*. Baltimore, MD: Brookes.

Turner, S. M., Hersen, M., & Bellack, A. S. (1978). Social skills training to teach prosocial behaviors in an organically impaired and retarded patient. *Journal of Behavior Therapy and Experimental Psychiatry, 9*, 253-258.

United States Bureau of the Census. (1976). *Survey of income and education*. Washington, DC: Author.

Van Hasselt, V. B. (1983). Social adaptation in the blind. *Clinical Psychology Review, 3*, 87-102.

Van Hasselt, V. B., & Hersen, M. (Eds.). (1987). *Psychological evaluation of the developmentally and physically disabled*. New York: Plenum.

Van Hasselt, V. B., Hersen, M., Kazdin, A. E., Simon, J., & Mastantuono, A. K. (1983). Training blind adolescents in social skills. *Journal of Visual Impairment and Blindness, 77*, 199-203.

Van Hasselt, V. B., Kazdin, A. E., & Hersen, M. (1986). Assessment of problem behavior in visually handicapped adolescents. *Journal of Clinical Child Psychology, 15*, 134-141.

Van Hasselt, V. B., Strain, P. S., & Hersen, M. (Eds.). (1988). *Handbook of developmental and physical disabilities*. New York: Pergamon.

Vernon, M. (1972). Psychodynamics surrounding the diagnosis of a child's deafness. *Rehabilitation Psychology, 19*, 127-134.

Weicker, L. (1984). Defining liberty for handicapped Americans. *American Psychologist, 39*, 518-523.

Weller, D. J., & Miller, P. M. (1977). Emotional reactions of patient, family, and staff in acute-care period of spinal cord injury: I. *Social Work in Health Care, 2,* 369-377.

Wolfensberger, W. (1972). *The principle of normalization in human services.* Toronto, Canada: National Institute of Mental Retardation.

# Chapter 2

---

# Diagnostic and Medical Considerations

## Martin J. Lubetsky

## Introduction

The word *disability* can be defined as "the consequence of an impairment" and the word *handicap* defined as "the social disadvantage of a disability" (Liptak, 1987). A disability may be cognitive, physical, sensory, or behavioral in nature. According to the National Center for Health Statistics' 1976 National Survey of Children, up to 20% of all children in the United States have some form of disability (Myers, 1987a). A *developmental disability* is defined by the Federal Developmental Disability Title V Rehabilitation Act of 1978 as follows: "A severe chronic disability that is attributable to a mental or physical impairment or combination of mental or physical impairments, is manifested before the person attains the age of 22 years; is likely to continue indefinitely; results in substantial functional limitations in three or more areas of major life activity, specified as self-care, language, learning, mobility, self-direction, capacity for independent living, and economic self-sufficiency; and that reflects the person's need for life long and individually planned services" (Chess & Hassibi, 1982, p. 60).

Among children with chronic illnesses including developmental and physical disabilities, Rutter and Graham found in their Isle of Wright

Study that there is an increased risk for behavioral and emotional problems (Chess & Hassibi, 1982; Myers, 1987b; Rutter, Graham, & Yule, 1970). In this study, 6.6% of normal 10- to 11-year-old children had behavioral and emotional problems. However, 11.5% of those children with chronic illnesses (not central nervous system) and 36% of those with central nervous system disorders had behavioral and emotional problems. This increased risk may be further altered by parental response to the disability as well as child adaptation. Parents need the physician's early support in developing a relatively guilt-free understanding of the disease, treatment approaches, chronicity, and prognosis. When parents are informed about their child's birth defect (a structural, functional, or metabolic abnormality present at birth), they can begin to work through their own emotional reaction or grief response to the diagnosis. Irving, Kennel, and Klaus (1982) have described parental response to their child's disability in five stages, from shock, denial and disbelief, sadness and anger, to equilibrium, and recognition. In more instances equilibrium and reorganization do not eventuate and the parental response is maladaptive. A product of such a maladaptive response is the vulnerable child syndrome (Green & Solnit, 1984). In this syndrome a parent perceives that the child might die for any number of reasons. The parent than develops a variety of maladaptive caretaking behaviors, and the child may respond with a variety of maladaptive coping behaviors.

It has been reported that 10% to 20% of all pregnancies are identified during the first obstetric appointment as at increased risk of death or disability (Creasy & Parer, 1982). The maternal risk factors are numerous and may include the history of a previous problem birth or disabled child, mother's own disability, health risks, maternal age less than 18, drug use, or malnutrition during pregnancy. The list of prevention for maternal risk factors is also numerous and includes quality of maternal upbringing and training, adequate maternal health care prior to and during pregnancy, reduction of health hazards in maternal environment, and reasonable maternal support system. Prevention may include adequate prepartum health care and diagnostic testing such as ultrasound and amniocentesis when appropriate. These tests are conducted prior to birth and may aid in diagnosing many disabilities, including Down's syndrome, structural anomalies, and growth retardation. At the time of birth many congenital anomalies may be noted. For instance, hypothyroidism or phenylketonuria can be diagnosed and treated at birth. Other disabilities may not be found until screening at later ages of development. For example, vision and hearing testing may reveal sensory impairments; screening of developmental milestones may reflect mental retardation; and examination of communication or social-relatedness may reveal characteristics of autism. Interventions during childhood can prevent some disabilities through immunizations, treatment of recurrent ear infections, early diagnosis and treatment of seizures, and psychological/psychiatric therapies.

The diagnosis of a developmental or physical disability begins with parental, family, school, or physician suspicion. Complete medical, pediatric, developmental, neurologic, psychiatric, and psychologic assessments may identify the disability. In this initial assessment process and subsequent treatment and continued care, a multidisciplinary team approach is vital for parental education, clarification of developmental expectations, treatment, facilitation of services, and lifelong future planning.

In this introductory chapter, the diagnostic and medical considerations will be briefly reviewed for each of the disorders discussed in this casebook.

## Asthma

The word *asthma* was derived from the Greek word for panting or breathlessness, and can be defined as a recurrent disease causing intermittent wheezing, breathlessness, and cough (Kaliner, Eggleston, & Mathews, 1987). It is a multifactorial respiratory illness involving immunologic, infectious, biochemical, environmental, autonomic nervous system, and psychological factors. This condition is a reversible episodic obstructive lung disease caused by genetically influenced hyperactive airways. Wheezing is caused by obstruction or narrowing in small airways during expiration, onset of asthma usually is under the age of 5. Five to 10% of children have asthma at some time during their lives, with 10% needing medical emergency room visits and another 10% requiring hospitalizations. Among chronic illnesses of childhood, it is the most frequent cause of school absenteeism (Kaliner, Eggleston, & Mathews, 1987). The childhood ratio of boys to girls is 3 to 1 (Fireman, 1987). One-third of asthmatic patients' first degree relatives have some form of airway hyperreactivity.

The causes and classifications of asthma have undergone much revision over the years. Asthma can be classified according to its causes: allergy; infection; industrial, occupational, or environmental exposure; chemical or drug ingestion; exercise; vasculitis; and idio-pathic (intrinsic). Allergic asthma is one of the most common types. About 90% of asthmatics younger than 30 years old have allergies as compared to 50% of asthmatics over the age of 40. There is a better prognosis when the onset of asthma is between the ages of 2 years and puberty as compared to a more severe asthma appearing before the age of 2 (Kaliner, Eggleston, & Mathews, 1987). Allergic asthma should be suspected when there is a personal history of allergy and seasonal exacerbations in addition to a family history of asthma.

Infections may be the precipitant for the onset of asthma. The history of bronchiolitis or croup is a risk factor for the development of asthma. Some patients may experience a worsening of their asthma symptoms during times of concurrent infections. Others have no clinical asthma except during infections. About 50% of children with bronchiolitis develop recurrent wheezing (Kaliner, Eggleston, & Mathews, 1987).

Environmental elements may precipitate the onset of asthma or exacerbate asthmatic symptoms. Chemicals in the air may irritate the respiratory tract or may be allergens for the allergic individual. Some of these irritants include cold air, tobacco smoke, aerosolized chemi-cals, and strong aromas. Approximately 2% to 15% of all cases of adult onset asthma in men are of occupational origin (Kaliner, Eggleston, & Mathews, 1987).

Other causes of asthma include chemical or drug ingestion, such as aspirin or other nonsteroidal anti-inflammatory drugs, causing 5% of asthmatics to worsen. Beta-adrenergic blocking agents such as propran-olol (Inderal) and sulfiting agents (food additives, bleaching agents, processed foods, wine, or beer) have been known to precipitate asth-matic symptoms. Exercise-induced asthma is a known cause that inter-feres with school and recreational activities for at least 67% of adoles-cents with asthma.

As it has been taught in medical school classes, "not all that wheezes is asthma and all asthma does not wheeze." It is important to differen-tiate other causes of wheezing prior to diagnosing and treating asthma. It is also important to diagnose and treat asthma when there is respira-tory distress or coughing without wheezing symptoms. In addition, other conditions that may exacerbate asthma include sinusitis, preg-nancy, heightened emotional responses, gastroesophageal reflex, and hyperthyroidism.

Treatment of asthma involves proper diagnosis and identification of causes if possible. The key to treatment is to reverse symptoms as quickly as possible and to prevent recurrence. Prevention includes avoidance of known allergens, education about decreasing exposure to allergens, immediate treatment of infections with antibiotics when bacterial in nature, and reduction of stress when possible. Medications can be classified into adrenergic agonists such as isoetharine (Bronkosol) or albuterol (Ventolin); methylxanthines include theophylline preparations (Aminophylline, Slobid, and the like); steroids (Prednisone) are the most potent and also have the most serious side effects; and cromolyn is an example of a medication used for prevention. There are many side effects to each of the medications as well as side effects to combined medication use. For example, the adrenergic agonists cause cardiac side effects, such as palpitations, increased heart rate, arrhythmias, and tremor. The methylxanthines may cause nervousness, nausea, vomiting, anorexia, personality changes, hyperactivity, abdominal discomfort, and headache. Steroid therapy may cause weight gain, easy bruisability, osteoporosis, emotional changes, edema, hypertension, and growth retardation in children with long-term daily administration.

## Autism

Leo Kanner first described the syndrome that he called *infantile autism* in 1943. Kanner identified features of autism to include inability to develop relationships with people, delay in speech acquisition, noncommunicative use of speech, delayed echolalia, repetitive and stereotyped play, and insistence on sameness (Kanner, 1943). The classification of autism has undergone revision from the American Psychiatric Association (APA, 1980) *Diagnostic and Statistical Manual III* to the Revised Version, *DSM-III-R* (APA, 1987). The *DSM-III* criteria include pervasive development disorder, with a subclassification of infantile autism occurring prior to 30 months of age (with deviant social and language development, stereotypic behaviors and routines, and the absence of delusions, hallucinations, and schizophrenic-type thought disorder). The second subclassification in *DSM-III* is childhood onset pervasive developmental disorder, with the onset after 30 months of age but before 12 years of age. The criteria also include excessive anxiety manifested by catastrophic reactions, inappropriate affect, and resistance to change in environment. *DSM-III-R* shifted pervasive developmental disorders (PDD), autistic disorder, and PDD not otherwise specified, from Axis I to Axis II, removed age of onset as a major criterion, and emphasized the impairment in social interaction and communication.

The key qualitative impairment according to *DSM-III-R* is in reciprocal social interaction. This is reported to be failure to develop interpersonal relationships and lack of responsiveness or interest in other people. In infancy there may be a failure to cuddle, lack of eye contact, and indifference or aversion to physical contact. This has been described as using people as objects in order to obtain a goal, rather than for the human quality of interpersonal relating. The impairment in communication may be total absence of language or oddities in speech, such as delayed or immediate echolalia, pronoun reversal such as using "you" when "I" is intended, idiosyncratic utterances or abnormal speech tone, melody, or intonation. The content of speech may revolve around an isolated area of expertise or excellent rote memory. Impairment in imaginative play includes a lack of symbolic or representational play. There is commonly a resistance to even minor changes in the environment with a catastrophic response in the child. There may be attachments to common objects, such as a string with no obvious symbolic meaning. Stereotypic movements may include twirling, spinning, hand flapping, or rocking.

Approximately two to four children in every 10,000 show the syndrome of autism and the sex ratio is approximately three boys to one girl. If severe mental retardation with some autistic features is included, the prevalence rates may rise to as high as 20 per 10,000 (Rutter, 1985). Utilizing the *DSM-III-R* (APA, 1987) diagnoses of autistic disorder and PDD not otherwise specified, prevalence rates have been estimated at 10 to 15 children in every 10,000. Autistic disorder has been reported in association with maternal rubella, untreated phenylketonuria, tuberous sclerosis, anoxia during birth, encephalitis, infantile spasms, and fragile-X syndrome (APA, 1987). Autism is more common in siblings of children with the disorder than in the general population. About 2% of the siblings of autistic children have autism and this rate is 50 times that in the general population. A family history of speech delay is much more common, being present in about 25% of cases (Rutter, 1985). A major complication is the development of epilepsy. Most of those who develop seizures have an IQ below 50 and about 25% or more of autistics have had one or more seizures by adulthood (APA, 1987). Also puberty has been a time when the autistic's behaviors may worsen or depressive symptoms may develop in response to poor social adjustment and the realization of being different.

Autism is frequently associated with mental retardation. Approximately 70% of autistic children are mentally retarded. About 40% have an IQ below 50 and 30% have an IQ in the 50 to 69 range, leaving 30% having an IQ of 70 or more. The higher intellectually functioning autistic usually has a better prognosis and outcome (Rutter, 1985).

Much research is being done in the area of etiologies of the autistic disorder. These are too numerous to elaborate in this review and range from gross neuroanatomic structural abnormalities, to microscopic cellular changes, to neurochemical abnormalities. There have also been attempts to link many associated biologic, neurologic, and genetic phenomena (Ornitz & Ritvo, 1976).

Treatment approaches are quite varied and, once again, too numerous to elaborate in this review. Rutter (1985) has listed five main goals in designing an appropriate plan of treatment: fostering of normal development, promotion of learning, reduction of stereotypies and rigidity, elimination of maladaptive behaviors, and alleviation of family distress. A well-controlled structured classroom, use of behavioral principles, and communications aimed at the developmental level of each child have proven helpful. A multidisciplinary team approach to complete medical, pediatric, neurologic, psychiatric, psychological, and speech and language assessment and treatment is helpful. It is important that the family be educated about the child's global impairments as well as assisted in alleviation of guilt, facilitation of services, and future planning.

## Cerebral Palsy

*Cerebral palsy* can be defined as a nonprogressive, static disturbance in motor function present from birth or early life caused by a discrete insult to the central nervous system during gestation, birth, or infancy (DeLong & Adams, 1987). Frequently, the motor disability is of a mixed type as a result of diffuse cortical damage. Cerebral palsy may be classified by patterns of motor disturbance: spastic, athetoid, rigid, ataxic, atonic, or mixed (Taft & Matthews, 1983). The causes of cerebral palsy are diverse and may include: hypoxic-ischemic incidents, infection, cerebral hemorrhage, and cranial trauma. Premature infants are especially susceptible to those types of cerebral disease. The spastic diplegic type constitutes 50% of cerebral palsy and appears to be the mildest form. Only 8% of spastic diplegic are mentally retarded and most are ambulatory. The spastic quadriplegic type constitute 30% of cerebral palsy and have more likelihood of mental retardation and being nonambulatory. The spastic hemiplegic group represent 10% of cerebral palsy with 75% of those having normal intellectual function and another 33% having epilepsy. Those having seizures are more likely to be mentally retarded. The last 10% of cerebral palsy is made up of all the other categories and mixed types (DeLong & Adams, 1987).

Cerebral palsy in infancy usually presents with a delay in motor milestones, variation in muscle tone, asymmetry, poor sucking response, drooling, and hyperreflexia. Involuntary movements of the athetoid, choreic, and ataxic types are rarely manifested prior to 1 year of age. Early handedness may reflect a hemiparesis of the other hand or disarthria may be present when speech begins. The associated handicaps that are frequently found in infants with cerebral palsy are strabismus, near-sightedness, and hearing deficits (Taft & Mathews, 1983).

As in all the other disorders discussed in this book, a multidisciplinary team approach helps maintain optimal assessment and treatment. The team can help parents deal with their distress and help to provide appropriate education for medical care, schooling, and potential complications. Parents need to learn how to use occupational and physical therapy techniques at home in order to maintain gains and to be part of the treatment process. The child will need help in psychosocial adjustment regarding motor disability, dependency issues, communication difficulties, potential for independent functioning, stigma attached by peers, and the growing recognition of the chronicity of the disability. In adolescence, issues of identity, self-esteem, and sexuality arise. It is important to help guide the parents' and child's expectations but not to overestimate limitations or dispel hopes.

## Chronic Pain

*Chronic pain* can be defined as a pain that persists beyond the usual course of an acute disease, longer than a reasonable time for an injury to heal, or recurs at intervals for months or years. In contrast to acute pain, chronic "pain never has a biological function, but is a malevolent force that often imposes severe emotional, physical, economic, and social stresses on the patient and the family; chronic pain is one of the most costly health problems in society" (Aronoff, 1985, p. xxxiv). In 1983, 75 to 80 million Americans were estimated to be suffering from chronic pain, and the cost to the United States was estimated to be 65 to 70 billion dollars (Aronoff, 1985).

A complete medical evaluation is necessary to evaluate all components of the chronic pain by a multidisciplinary team approach. A full medical, employment, and psychosocial history provided by the patient and family, a complete medication and surgical history, a review of all old medical records and reports, and a complete physical examination should be carried out prior to any invasive and expensive diagnostic testing. It is important not to fall into the "organic trap," in which all symptoms are attributed to one disease entity, overlooking the psychosocial aspects. Also, one should avoid the "psychophysiological trap," in which all new complaints are attributed to the old process, resulting in overlooking potential organic pathology (Aronoff, 1985).

Somatic pain of skin, muscles, and joints is easier to localize than visceral pain, which is poorly localized and may be referred to various areas of the body. Neuropathic pain is poorly localized and may be described as either a neuralgia, in which there is irritation to a peripheral nerve, nerve dysfunction, sensory loss, weakness, or dysesthesia (background burning or aching sensation), or a causalgia in which there may be a dull, continuous burning pain from a nerve injury. There may be joint pain described as either arthralgia with discomfort in the joint, or arthritis with inflammation of the joint, frequently leading to a loss of motion and pain. Extremity pain may be caused by a variety of etiologies, including: infection (osteomyelitis), post-infectious diseases (rheumatic fever), allergy, primary connective tissue disorder (juvenile arthritis, systemic lupus erythematosus), inflammatory bowel disease (polyarthritis of ulcerative colitis or Crohn's disease), hematologic disease (sickle cell anemia, hemophilia), metabolic disorders, immunodeficiency, tumors, trauma, or orthopedic abnormalities—congenital or acquired (Wall & Melzack, 1985).

In people with chronic pain syndromes there may be little correlation between severity of active disease and the amount of pain behavior. It is always important to rule out new organic causes. Chronic pain may lead to social withdrawal in which an individual focuses on the pain almost all of the time, has no other social interests, and becomes bored. Pain may lead to insomnia, with altered sleep habits, fatigue, and medication abuse in attempts to regain a more normal sleep pattern. Depression has been associated with 30% of people with chronic pain syndromes. These people may not show or report a full range of depressive symptomatology (Maciewicz & Martin, 1987).

Engel (1959) has described the pain-prone person as having hypochondriacal preoccupation with pain, insomnia, fatigue, despair, history of stress, unmet dependency needs, past denial of conflicts, idealized view of self and family, and history of being a compulsive worker. Hackett (1988) developed a rating scale to quantify psychogenicity of pain. It is called the MADISON Scale, an acronym composed of the first initial of seven characteristics. These include *M*ultiplicity of more than one location or variety of pain; *A*uthenticity that the pain is genuine and accepted by the physician; *D*enial of the presence of emotional problems; *I*nterpersonal relationships being problematic but denied or ignored; *S*ingularity that this pain is unlike anyone else's and is very unusual; *O*nly you can help me, doctor; *N*othing helps, or, no change in the pain.

Psychogenic pain disorder was described in the American Psychiatric Association's (1980) *Diagnostic and Statistical Manual-III* as severe and prolonged pain inconsistent with the anatomic distribution of the nervous system, with no organic pathology found to account for the pain, or when the pain complaint is grossly in excess of what would be expected from physical findings. Psychological factors are judged to be etiologic, as evidenced by a temporal relationship between an environmental stimulus and the pain complaint, pain enabling the individual to avoid or to get support from the environment. Somatoform pain disorder is described in *DSM-III-R* (APA, 1987) as a preoccupation with pain for at least 6 months in the absence of physical findings.

Treatment of chronic pain involves a multidisciplinary team. Medications are a very common treatment and can be categorized as non-narcotic analgesics, such as aspirin, nonsteroidal anti-inflammatory such as Motrin or Naprosyn, narcotic analgesics such as Demerol or codeine usually for acute severe pain, and occasionally anticonvulsants such as Tegretol for neuropathic pain or tricyclic antidepressants for peripheral nerve injuries. Anesthetic nerve blocks have been used for trigger points. Other interventions have included surgery; occupational/physical therapies; biofeedback; relaxation techniques; hypnosis; individual, family, and group therapies; transcutaneous electrical stimulator (TENS); and acupuncture (Wall & Melzack, 1985). The multidisciplinary team approach is vital for a number of reasons, including simplifying and minimizing medications; decreasing side effects from multiple medications; developing better understanding of the pain, factors that exacerbate it, and any psychological significance of the pain; educating the patient in ways to improve functional mobility; and helping the patient gain a sense of control over the pain.

## Epilepsy

The word *epilepsy* refers to the condition of having recurrent seizures. *Seizures* can be defined as a "disturbance of movement, sensation, perception, behavior, mood, or consciousness, due to excessive disorderly neuronal discharge" (Hughes, 1980). Seizures have also been called ictal phenomena, fits, and convulsions. There are many causes of seizures, and frequently no specific etiology is identified. Seizures have been classified by the Commission on Classification and Terminology of the International League Against Epilepsy (Dreifuss, 1981; Dreifuss, Martinez-Lage, Roger, Seino, Wolf, & Dam, 1985). The first major category is partial (focal, local) seizures in which the first clinical and electroencephalographic (EEG) changes are limited to one cerebral hemisphere. There are two types of partial seizures, simple and complex. Simple partial seizures are those in which consciousness is not impaired. These may have motor signs, somatosensory symptoms, autonomic nervous system symptoms (sweating, flushing, pallor), or psychic symptoms (illusions). Complex partial seizures have impairment of consciousness and may follow simple partial seizures. Complex partial seizures have also been called psychomotor epilepsy or temporal lobe epilepsy.

The second major category is the generalized seizure characterized by the first clinical and electroencephalographic changes, indicating involvement in both cerebral hemispheres. Consciousness may be impaired and motor manifestations are bilateral. One type of generalized seizure, absence seizures (petit mal), usually occurs between 4 years of age and puberty and is easily diagnosable on EEG findings. Girls are more commonly affected than boys, and there is a positive family history of this type in some instances. Absence seizures usually consist of cessation of activity, staring vacantly from 5 to 10 seconds, and no postictal phase. Another type of generalized seizure, the tonic-clonic seizure (grand mal), usually begins between the ages of 5 and 15 years. There is a tonic phase in which the whole body stiffens, there may be a cry, and the child may fall to the ground. There may be interference with respiration, cyanosis, and tongue biting. Upon relaxation, clonic jerking of all four limbs usually begins and there may be incontinence of urine or feces. Other generalized seizures include neonatal seizures with onset at birth to 1 month; simple febrile seizures with onset at 6 months to 5 years; myoclonic seizures; atonic seizures; and infantile spasms with onset at 3 to 24 months, and concomitant cessation or regression of intellectual development (Bresnan & Koukol, 1987).

In determining the diagnosis of epilepsy the clinical presentation is vital. One must know the patient's normal level of functioning and be able to observe abrupt interruptions that alter this level of functioning. One must assess the level of alertness and responsiveness through awareness of the environment, verbal communication, gross motor dexterity and balance, fine motor dexterity, muscle tone, mood, and behavior. It is important to obtain an accurate history from the child, parent, other family members, and teachers. A full medical and neurologic evaluation is necessary including an electroencephalogram. It is very helpful to correlate the clinically observable symptoms with the electrical patterns on EEG. It is important to rule out nonepileptic paroxysmal disorders such as breath-holding spells, sleep disorders, syncope, benign paroxysmal vertigo and migraine headaches. It is also important to consider pseudoseizures when clinical symptoms do not correlate even when a true seizure disorder already exists.

The diagnosis of seizures in an infant has a strong emotional impact on the parents. Because epilepsy does not present an obvious physical abnormality, it is harder to understand and yet has a strong social stigma. Epilepsy has a profound effect throughout life. It may cause apprehension that at any time a seizure may occur. It may cause embarrassment and a sense of vulnerability. It may complicate getting a driver's license, participating in sports, getting and keeping a job, acquiring life insurance, and even getting married.

The treatment of epilepsy involves using the fewest anticonvulsant medications in order to maintain optimal seizure control at the least cost for the patient in terms of side effects such as cognitive blunting and drug toxicity (Holmes, 1987). It is important to monitor anticonvulsant medication blood levels to prevent toxicity as well as to maintain a therapeutic dose. Once an accurate diagnosis of the type of seizure is made, then the anticonvulsant best known to treat that seizure can be utilized. A partial list of anticonvulsants includes: phenobarbital, phenytoin (Dilantin), carbamazepine (Tegretol), valproate (Depakene), ethosuximide (Zarontin), and clonazepam (Klonopin). In the treatment of seizures, anticonvulsants are not contraindicated in pregnancy or breast feeding but must be used carefully, because of potential side effects (Hughes, 1980). Epilepsy surgery is now well established, but used very cautiously, in well-known epilepsy centers.

## Hearing Impairment

The hearing impaired population is a heterogeneous one, running a spectrum from a mild hearing loss that may go unnoticed to a profound hearing loss that might be life long. It is common that mild hearing loss is not diagnosed until routine hearing/screening programs in schools, referral for inattentiveness at school, or speech difficulties occur. Three categories of hearing impairment include acquired deafness or known etiology such as congenital rubella or meningitis; genetic deafness or inherited factors; and idiopathic or no clear etiology (Ziring, 1983). One in 2,000 infants is found to have severe congenital hearing loss at birth and one in 25 by the age of 2 years is found to have a mild to moderate loss, estimated at 20 to 50 decibels (Cunningham, 1987).

There are various types of hearing loss. For instance, a conductive hearing loss is the failure of sound waves to be transmitted to the inner ear because of some mechanical interference in the external auditory canal, ear drum, small bones in the ear, middle ear cavity, or its components. This type of hearing loss can be surgically corrected at times. Potential causes of conductive hearing loss include a defect at birth or acquired in childhood, such as middle ear effusion, tympanic membrane perforation, eustachian tube dysfunction, or other ear canal abnormalities. Sensorineural hearing loss involves the sensory component (cochlear) or neural auditory pathway. This loss may be irreversible. Some causes of sensorineural hearing loss include congenital rubella, cytomegalovirus, hyperbilirubinemia, newborn anoxia, or familial (inherited). Other causes occurring in childhood include meningitis, brain tumor, head trauma, viral, or noise (decibel) induced. There are also mixed conditions, central nervous system involvement, and functional/emotional components (Conner, 1987).

There are two dichotomous approaches to educating the hearing impaired. The first is the oral communication method, which encourages the need to talk in a speaking and hearing world. Second is the manual communication method designed to allow the hearing impaired to communicate with each other utilizing a broad range of sign language. The "total communication" approach relies on both oral speech and manual sign language (Downs, 1987).

## Hyperactivity and Attention Deficit Disorders

Children with hyperactivity, inattention, impulsivity, and distractibility have been given many labels including attention deficit disorder (ADD) with or without hyperactivity, hyperkinesis, minimal brain damage/dysfunction, and now according to the American Psychiatric Association's (1987) *Diagnostic and Statistical Manual III-R*, attention deficit hyperactivity disorder (ADHD). This disorder may occur in as many as 3% of children; is from three to nine times more common in males than in females; and is believed to be more common in first degree biologic relatives than in the general population. The features of ADHD according to *DSM III-R* (APA, 1987) include fidgeting, restlessness, difficulty remaining in seat, distractibility, difficulty waiting turn, impulsivity, failure to complete tasks, difficulty sustaining attention, talking excessively, interrupting or intruding, appearing not to listen, disorganization, and difficulty considering consequences to actions. Approximately half of these children are diagnosed before the age of 4.

Levine (1983) considers five subtypes of attention deficits. The first is primary attention deficit, which is often evident in the preschool years and manifests in multiple settings. The second subtype is secondary to information processing deficits and may not appear until school age. The third subtype is secondary to psychosocial stressors and has onset linked to a critical life event or may be part of an identifiable psychiatric disorder. The fourth is situational inattention and manifests only during certain situations or settings. The fifth subtype is mixed forms in any combination of the other four. It is important to differentiate other primary diagnoses such as: oppositional-defiant or conduct disorders, learning disabilities, language disorders, pervasive developmental disorders, mental retardation, and mood disorders.

Many predisposing factors or etiologic events have been postulated for ADHD (Gottlieb, 1987a). Some specific exogenous etiologic agents have included infectious and metabolic factors, toxic agents such as lead, and head trauma; endogenous influences such as genetic factors; prenatal factors like minor congenital anomalies; and central nervous system abnormalities such as epilepsy. A variety of chemical causes have also been suggested, including altered catecholamine neurotransmitters like dopamine and norepinephrine, a low central nervous system arousal state, and poor inhibitory feedback mechanism.

Rutter (1983) has defined overactivity to mean an excessive quantity of movement and not necessarily evidence for any abnormality of development. He defined hyperactivity to reflect the approximate behavioral style of restlessness, impulsivity, inattention, and overactivity. Hyperactivity may change as the child progresses in development. The infant may display poor and irregular sleep, irritability, or feeding problems. The toddler may display excessive running and jumping, climbing out of the crib, impulsivity, no fear of danger, always on the go and acting as if "driven by a motor." The preschooler appears demanding, not listening, not goal directed, and "always getting into everything." The elementary school age child begins to have school difficulties, low frustration tolerance, displaying fidgetiness, and peer-relationship problems. The adolescent has school failure, antisocial and impulsive behavior, truancy, and restlessness (Gottlieb, 1987a).

Hechtman and Weiss (1983) and Hechtman, Weiss, and Perlman (1984) have suggested that the clinical outcome for hyperactive young adults can be divided into 30% to 40% of hyperactive young adults functioning normally; 40% to 50% of hyperactive young adults displaying significant difficulty in concentration, impulse control, work relationships, self-esteem and mood; and approximately 10% of hyperactive young adults exhibiting significant psychiatric or antisocial problems. Some conclusions from studies of Hechtman, Weiss, and Perlman (1984) include the following: stimulant treatment in childhood may not eliminate educational, psychosocial, and life difficulties; treatment may result in less social isolation and better self-concept; treatment does not influence the outcome of antisocial behaviors; and approximately 50% of hyperactive children seem to outgrow the symptoms before adulthood.

Assessment should include pediatric evaluation to rule out treatable organic or neurologic causes, psychiatric evaluation to rule out other treatable psychiatric disorders, and psychological testing to evaluate for low intellectual functioning or learning disabilities. Family history and the psychosocial situations should be explored. Also, parent-teacher behavior ratings such as the Conners (1969) should be completed.

Treatment should begin after complete evaluation, assessment, and involvement of parents and teachers. Teacher counseling may be recommended for behavior management and structuring of academic tasks in the classroom, parent counseling for behavior management at home (Barkley, 1981), and self-control training or cognitive therapy for the child (Kendall & Braswell, 1985; Meichenbaum, 1978). Many times these treatments in combination with stimulant medication show marked improvement in symptomatology (Gittelman, 1983). The most common stimulants are methylphenidate (Ritalin), dextroamphetamine (Dexedrine), and pemoline (Cylert). Approximately 67% to 75% of children with inattentive and hyperactive symptoms appear to show a positive response to stimulant medications (Gottlieb, 1987a). It is important to monitor the effects (decreased hyperactivity, decreased impulsivity, prolonged attention span) and side effects (anorexia, tremor, insomnia, irritability). In addition, tricyclic antidepressants, such as imipramine (Tofranil) have been tried in the treatment of ADD with hyperactivity (Rapoport, 1983). The pharmacological effects, length of medication trials, dosages, and prediction of drug response will not be discussed in this review (Rapoport, 1983).

## Learning Disabilities

A learning disability is defined as a disorder in language usage that is manifested by imperfect listening, thinking, speaking, reading, writing, spelling, or mathematics ability (Yule & Rutter, 1985). The learning disabilities are developmentally determined delays in children's acquisition of certain mental skills (Wodrich, 1986). Samuel Kirk (1962, 1983) first used the term *learning disabilities* to describe the problems of intellectually and functionally capable children who failed to learn in school because of intrinsic deficiencies. One approach to the study of learning disabilities is the "individual difference model." This model takes into consideration the problem of brain variability of intellect. Other models look at disabilities with respect to the deficit in learning ability. For example, the continuity-discontinuity approach suggests that there are a spectrum of disorders. There is also the neurologic deficit theory that suggests an organic etiology (Kinsbourne, 1987). Whatever the model, the learning disabled child has a selective difficulty in a certain kind of learning usually with intact intellectual functioning. Different approaches to the diagnosis of learning disability have included the following: the child's achievement performance being approximately 2 years behind; relating how many grade levels behind the child falls; and looking at the child's mental age rather than chronological age. These formulations do not consider a variety of influences to the child. For instance, there is environmental deprivation, emotional disorder, inadequate schooling, inadequate school attendance, incomplete command of English as a second language, hearing and vision impairments, and neurologic disorders such as seizures (Kinsbourne, 1987).

Silver and Brunstetter (1987) have looked at learning with regard to four processes: input, integration, memory, and output. Input can occur through visual perception with specific problems in letter reversal, inability to separate figure-ground (part from the whole), and depth perception misjudgment. Input also occurs through auditory perception with problems in separating figure-ground (words from background noise), depth perception (direction of sound), and auditory lag (inability to process fast enough). Integration or organization problems can occur in the ability to make sense from the input utilizing sequencing, abstractions, or meanings, and then putting it all together. Memory or storage deficits can occur from short-term retention (as long as one is paying attention) to long-term storage. Output or retrieval difficulties may present in the spoken language or motor skills both gross and fine motor. Silver has also described how learning disabilities have been "lumped together" by some or "split" into specific impairments by others.

The American Psychiatric Association's (1987) *Diagnostic and Statistical Manual III-R* categorized learning disabilities under specific developmental disorders on Axis II. They are separated into subtypes of developmental disorders in arithmetic, expressive writing, and reading. Developmental language disorders—expressive/receptive and motor skills disorder (coordination deficits) have also been specified in *DSM-III-R*.

Treatment modalities are quite numerous and controversial. Basic clinical interventions include school-based programs utilizing educational and behavioral techniques; education for child, family and teachers; family counseling; individual psychotherapy to build on strengths, improve self-esteem, and learn coping skills; behavioral interventions; and medications when appropriate for inattention, hyperactivity, anxiety, or depression. Some of the controversial treatments reported include neurophysiological retaining or "patterning" sensory motor integration; optometric training; medication for vestibular-cerebellar dysfunction; megavitamins; trace-elements; restriction of refined sugars, food additives, and preservatives (Feingold, 1975); allergy medication; and negative ion therapy (Kinsbourne, 1987; Silver & Brunstetter, 1987).

## Mental Retardation

Mental retardation is defined as significantly subaverage intellectual functioning, accompanied by significant deficits or impairments in adaptive functioning, with the onset before the age of 18 or during the developmental period (APA, 1987; Grossman, 1983). Subaverage intellectual functioning refers to an intelligence quotient below 70: that is, performance greater than 2 or more standard deviations below the population mean (Gottlieb, 1987b). The mentally retarded, who constitute approximately 1% of the general population, are categorized by degree of intellectual impairment (APA, 1987). The mild mentally retarded have an IQ range of 50-55 to 69 and constitute about 85% of that population. They are usually not diagnosed until school age and may acquire academic skills up to approximately the 6th grade level. The moderately retarded have an IQ range of 35-40 to 49-54 and constitute approximately 10% of the mentally retarded. They are usually diagnosed during the preschool years and may progress up to the 2nd grade level in academic skills. The severely retarded have an IQ range of 20-25 to 34-39 and constitute 3% to 4% of the mentally retarded. The profoundly retarded have an IQ range below 20-25 and constitute 1% to 2% of the mentally retarded.

Etiologies of mental retardation are frequently unknown. Some are diagnosable and preventable or treatable. A multidisciplinary team should evaluate fully and consist of medical, pediatric, neurologic, and genetic assessors. Gottlieb's (1987b) classification for high risk factors categorize prenatal, perinatal, and postnatal factors. Prenatal or congenital factors include familial retardation; neurocutaneous syndromes such as tuberous sclerosis, neurofibromatosis; cranio-facial anomalies such as microcephaly; central nervous system degenerative diseases; metabolic disorders such as Tay-Sachs disease; lipid disorders such as Gaucher's disease; amino acid disorders such as phenylketonuria (PKU); mucopolysaccharidosis such as Hurler's syndrome; endocrine disorders such as hypothyroidism (cretinism); and skeletal anomalies. Specific chromosomal anomalies include: autosomal disorders such as Down's syndrome (trisomy 21); and sex chromosome disorders such as Klinefelter's syndrome (XXY) and Fragile-X syndrome. Other prenatal factors include maternal and fetal infections during pregnancy, such as rubella, chicken pox, syphilis; maternal anoxia during pregnancy, toxemia of pregnancy; maternal alcohol or drug abuse; maternal metabolic/endocrine disorders, such as hypothyroidism or diabetes mellitus. Some prenatal factors include breech presentation; prolonged labor; prolapsed cord; placenta problems; prematurity (less than 34 weeks); newborn birth injuries; infections; anoxia, or seizures. Postnatal factors include infections such as encephalitis or menigitis; encephalopathies like lead contamination or post immunization; head injuries or aneurysms; cerebral anoxia from chemicals, infections or seizures; and nutritional disorders (DeLong & Adams, 1987; Gottlieb, 1987b; Kirman, 1985). This list is far from complete and is only one form of categorizing causes of mental retardation. Other disorders in this book that are associated with mental retardation include autism, cerebral palsy, epilepsy, and multiple disabilities. Approximately 75% of mental retardation has no known causative factor (Grossman, 1983).

Prenatal diagnosis has become a special field in which certain diagnostic tests can provide selective information for the parents. Two of these tests are amniocentesis and ultrasound and provide data on selected gross anatomical defects (e.g., hydrocephalus) or chromosomal anomalies (e.g., Down's syndrome). Neonatal diagnostic testing has included the detection of phenylketonuria and hypothyroidism leading to early treatment. Prenatal diagnosis has led to prevention and the neonatal diagnosis has led to early identification and sometimes intervention.

The diagnosis of mental retardation can be devastating to the parents and family. Parents go through a grieving process, mourning the loss of their expected normal child; responding with anger toward caregivers, family, and each other; attempting to deny the severity of the problem; and, it is hoped, slowly accepting the diagnosis and its ramifications. The medical and mental health professionals help to provide diagnosis, education, support, treatment, and facilitation of services (Gottlieb, 1987b). Coordination of health needs involves interfacing with multiple professionals and agencies, including the school system, community advocacy, and long-range planning.

Mentally retarded individuals have a higher rate of psychiatric disorders than the general population (Corbett, 1985). In the severely retarded group, for instance, psychiatric disorder was present in 50% as compared to 7% in the general population (Rutter, Graham, & Yule, 1970). Autism, hyperactivity, stereotyped behaviors, self-injurious behavior, and pica are a few disorders that commonly accompany the diagnoses of mental retardation. A variety of psychiatric disorders can be found in this population. The treatment of psychiatric disorders in the mentally retarded includes the full range of therapies, including behavioral, psychotherapeutic, psychoeducational, supportive, and pharmacologic.

## Multiply Disabled Children

Approximately 67% of handicapped children present with more than one handicap, 33% have one handicap, 33% have two handicaps, and 33% have three or more handicaps (Gottlieb, 1987b). Accardo and Capute (1979) state that "the more severe the retardation the greater the probability of an associated disability." Prevalence of other disabilities associated with mental retardation includes hearing loss 3%, visual loss 1%, cerebral palsy 10%, epilepsy 4%, and psychiatric disorders 40%. In addition, mental retardation is associated with disabilities such as 15% of deafness, 23% of blindness, 50% of cerebral palsy, 15% of epileptics, and 12% with psychiatric disorders (Accardo & Capute, 1979; Kirman, 1985).

The combination of mild forms of disabilities can result in a severely impaired child with multiple handicaps. It is important to evaluate each handicap specifically and provide the most optimal care in order to allow for greater progress in the least restrictive setting. Several syndromes include multiple impairments under one diagnosable disorder. Some of these syndromes include Down's syndrome (congenital anomalies like heart malformation 40%, hypothyroidism 20%, cataracts 50%, myopia–nearsightedness 35%, hearing loss 40% to 80%, moderate mental retardation 40%, and a 6 to 10 times increase in likelihood of a presenile dementia of the Alzheimer's type); congenital rubella syndrome (mental retardation, microcephaly, sensory neural hearing loss, cataracts, and heart malformation); Prader-Willi syndrome (hypotonia, mental retardation, obesity, hyperphagia, aggression, stubbornness, and oppositionality) (Nelson & Crocker, 1983). In addition, the dual diagnosed child has another form of multiple disability in which mental retardation and mental illness are combined (Corbett, 1985).

These chronic multiply disabled children share common characteristics including disruption of the family, stress in the educational system necessitating special services, superimposed behavioral or emotional complications, and difficulties in long-term future planning for adulthood (Szymanski, 1983).

## Spina Bifida

Myelodysplasia encompasses the group of major malformations (including spina bifida) in which there are disturbances of the development of the neural tube, occurring in 1 to 2 per 1,000 births (Liptak, 1987).

Children born with spina bifida occulta have a normal spinal cord and surrounding soft tissue with incomplete vertebral arches. Those born with meningocele have a normal spinal cord with meninges protruding through the abnormal vertebral arches and soft tissue. Meningomyelocele consists of a malformed spinal cord and nerve routes protruding through the abnormal vertebral arches and soft tissue. These occur more commonly in females, have an unknown cause other than faulty fetal development, and an increased risk of 2 to 3 per 100 in the second affected child and 10 per 100 in the third affected child born to the same parents. An adult born with this malformation and able to procreate has a 2% to 3% chance of having a child with a neural tube defect. In addition, the majority are born with normal intellectual functioning (Crocker & Nelson, 1983).

A majority of these children have physical handicaps, neurologic difficulties, and medical complications (Liptak, 1987). A combination of spastic and flaccid paralysis is present in 10% to 40%. Those with lesions at the lumbar or sacral spinal levels may become ambulatory through surgical and orthotic management. Children with lesions above the lumbar region are usually nonambulatory and require a wheelchair. In addition to the motor impairment, sensation loss may prevent the child from feeling skin ulcers, burns, or abrasions. Depending on the level of the lesion, there may be varying degrees of bowel and bladder incontinence, kidney infections, and kidney failure. There is altered sexual functioning, with males having a loss of erection and fertility, and females having a loss of sensation but normal fertility.

Management involves the surgical repair of the spinal malformation and shunting of hydrocephalus if present. Medical, neurologic, and urologic care need to be ongoing. Physical therapy, training in adaptive functioning and self-care skills, independent ambulation, and bowel and bladder management are vital for appropriate habilitation.

## Spinal Cord Injuries

Approximately 3 to 5 people per 100,000 in the general population or 10,000 per year incur spinal cord injuries (Abroms, 1983; Ropper, 1987). Males outnumber females as high as 3.5 to 1 (Kraus, 1980). Car accidents are the most frequent single cause of spinal cord injury. Spinal cord injury can also be the result of birth trauma, most commonly involving the cervical and upper thoracic cord areas, and frequently follow breech birth presentations (Healey, Hein, & Rubin, 1983).

The spinal cord is organized in a stereotyped fashion segmentally through 31 pairs of spinal nerves. This allows for localization of spinal cord injury based on horizontal level of sensory and motor impairment as well as reflex changes (Ropper & Martin, 1987). Lesions may occur within the cord or outside the cord as well as by compression. Causes of spinal cord trauma include tumor, which may be primary within the cord; metastic or extrinsic cord compression; abscess from osteomyelitis; hemorrhage of a spinal blood vessel; disc herniation; arthritic disease affecting the spine; infarction or ischemia of spinal cord artery; and vertebral dislocation or fraction. Damage secondary to spinal cord injury may vary in the hours following the trauma. Edema or swelling, hemorrhage, and further movement of the patient may cause more damage. Complications of spinal cord injuries may include problems with bowel and bladder incontinence, muscle weakness or paralysis, and sensory loss (Abroms, 1983).

Rehabilitation following spinal cord injuries is best provided by a multidisciplinary program (Ropper, 1987). Preventative and maintenance treatment involves bladder or bowel training including self-catheterization, prevention of bladder infection, prevention of bed sores, respiratory assistance, prevention of pulmonary embolism, and treatment of hypertension or hypotension as a result of autonomic system dysfunction. Rehabilitation should involve physical and occupational therapy, bladder training, psychological counseling for the individual and family, teaching of self-help skills, and plans for future training of functional adaptive and academic skills.

## Stroke

Stroke is the third leading cause of death after heart disease and cancer (Kistler, Ropper, & Martin, 1987). It is one of the most lethal and disabling diseases in adults. There is a 20% to 30% initial mortality rate, 30% have a residual disability, and 16% remain in an institutional setting. Only 25% are without impairment of work ability (Marshall & Thomas, 1986). Five percent of the population over the age of 65 have had a stroke. A stroke or cerebrovascular accident can be defined as an abrupt onset of focal neurologic symptoms especially when they correspond to specific cerebrovascular areas.

In general strokes can be divided into 80% cerebral infarction and 20% cerebral hemorrhage (Marshall & Thomas, 1986). Cerebral infarction may be caused by blood vessels of the brain developing atherosclerosis or plaque formation inside the blood vessel. An embolus may develop and travel from a distant site such as the heart or blood vessel and lodge in a much smaller vessel such as one in the brain resulting in a stroke. This blockage in a blood vessel in the brain may result in ischemia, defined as the inadequate blood flow to the brain tissues or infarction resulting from complete blockage of blood flow. The following events may result from a cerebral infarction: possible hemorrhage, cerebral edema surrounding the infarcted tissues, compression on the cerebral tissues as a result of the edema, possible long-term brain tissue scar formation, or death. If the blood vessel only becomes partially blocked periodically, a transient ischemic attack (TIA) may result in sudden focal neurologic deficits that clear in less than 24 hours. Repeated TIAs may be a warning sign for future stroke. Cerebral hemorrhage may result from an aneurysm, which is a developmental or congenital malformation that causes a ballooning out of the blood vessel with the potential for future rupture.

In order to understand the extent and diverse nature of cerebrovascular accidents, a few stroke syndromes will be mentioned (Marshall & Thomas, 1986). The middle cerebral artery syndrome presents with weakness of the body on the side opposite from the cerebrovascular accident in the brain, and weakness greater in the face and arm than leg; sensory loss on the same side of the body; dominant hemisphere findings of aphasia, word deafness, anomia or jargon speech; or nondominant hemisphere signs of agnosia (inability to recognize familiar items), or apraxia (inability to perform familiar tasks). The anterior cerebral artery syndrome presents with paralysis of the foot and leg opposite from the side of the cerebrovascular accident, and weakness of the opposite arm; sensory loss in the toes, foot, and leg of the same side; urinary incontinence; and slowness in mentation with perseveration. The posterior cerebral artery syndrome presents with visual loss for the half of the visual field opposite from the side of the cerebrovascular accident; little or no paralysis; alexia without agraphia (writing but not reading); and recent memory loss.

In order to diagnose a stroke, the medical investigation begins with a complete physical examination, especially for focal neurological signs. A Computerized Assisted Tomography (CAT) scan may aid in distinguishing a fresh cerebral hemorrhage from an infarction. It may also show shifting of intracranial contents, hematomas outside of the brain (subarachnoid or subdural), or brain tumors. A lumbar puncture (LP) may show blood in the cerebral spinal fluid (CSF) or infection.

The electroencephalogram (EEG) may help to localize deficits and seizure activity. Also, arteriography helps to visualize specific arteries and may show aneurysms, blood vessel blockage, or narrowing.

One approach to treatment is prevention (Kistler, Ropper, & Martin, 1987). Risk factors that may be decreased include cardiovascular disease such as hypertension, peripheral vascular disease, thrombophlebitis, and embolus formation from heart arrhythmias or heart attacks. Other risk factors include age, smoking, heredity, diabetes mellitus, and hyperlipidemia. Seeking treatment following transient ischemic attacks may prevent future strokes. Treatment approaches are diverse, controversial, and will not be discussed in detail. Some of these include anticoagulation to prevent further embolization; platelet suppressing drugs such as aspirin; lowering hypertensive blood pressure; surgery for stenosis of one carotid artery (endarterectomy); and new techniques including microsurgical intracranial bypass. A comprehensive multidisciplinary rehabilitation program clearly benefits most stroke patients in regaining functional and adaptive skills to return to independent living and reduce future morbidity.

## Visual Impairment

Blindness and serious visual impairment are estimated at approximately 64 children per 100,000 with another 100 children per 100,000 having less serious visual impairment. Only about 10% of all expected cases of blindness in the total population occur in children and adolescents. Goldstein (1980) reported prevalence rates for blindness per 100,000 population in the United States with 64 under the age of 20, 206 between the ages of 20 to 64, and 996 for age 65 and over. The leading causes of childhood blindness include congenital cataract, prenatal retinopathy, and optic nerve disease (Kahn & Moorhead, 1973). In the adult population the leading causes of blindness include diabetic retinopathy, senile cataracts, and glaucoma.

Visual acuity can be tested in the preschool age child. Common visual disorders found (Davidson, 1983) may include amblyopia, referring to "lazy eye"; amaurosis referring to a "dimming" or partial loss of vision; obscurations or "blurring"; photopsias referring to abnormal visual phenomena; disturbances of vision appearing smaller (micropsia) or larger (macropsia) than their actual size; color blindness; diplopia or double vision. Amblyopia is commonly caused by a difference in refraction between the eyes (anisometropia); or the turning in or out of one eye (strabismus). Eye patching commonly corrects amblyopia. Refractive errors are the most common visual anomalies. Types of refractive error include far-sightedness (hyperopia), nearsightedness (myopia), and astigmatism. Wearing corrective lenses commonly treats refractive errors.

The more serious visual impairments (Hiatt, 1987) due to congenital defects may be a result of genetic and chromosomal defects such as in Down's syndrome, embryological disorders such as congenital cataracts or retinitis pigmentosa, and albinism. Other visual disorders may be secondary to neurologic deficits such as in cerebral palsy, nystagmus, and optic atrophy. Visual loss may be secondary to CNS inflammation and infection such as congenital rubella, syphilis, and other viral and bacterial corneal ulcers, and systemic diseases. Accidents and trauma have caused retinal detachments, corneal burns, and permanent loss of the eyeball.

There are significant delays found in the development of the blind child (Fraiberg, 1977). The development of attachment, gross motor behavior patterns, locomotion, and language can be affected by blindness. Separation anxiety seems to be delayed and "tactile-seeking" behaviors become a main form of communication. Fraiberg (1977) reported that 90% of blind infants were substantially delayed in the onset of walking and did not appear independent until after 20 months. She also reported a delay in hand grasping and coordinated hand movements. Social, cognitive, and perceptual development in a blind child may parallel normal sighted children in regard to auditory based functions (Warren, 1976). Visual perception for the blind is replaced by haptic and auditory perception. Haptic refers to the process of actively exploring with one's hands. This utilizes the sense of touch as well as perception in space. Auditory cues are used to facilitate localization and distance perception (Davidson, 1983).

Educational issues for the visually impaired involve reading ability, mobility, school placement, vocational, and occupational training (Hiatt, 1987). Reading has expanded through the use of large print for those who are partially sighted, braille, the OPTACON Scanner (optical to tactile converter), audio tapes (talking books), and the Kurzweil Print to Speech Converter (Davidson, 1983). Independence can be achieved through mobility training, use of a guide dog, cane, and new technical advances to replace the cane. Future employment opportunities are based on the availability and quality of academic, vocational, and occupational training.

## Conclusion

The diagnostic and medical considerations of each of the disorders discussed in this book have been briefly reviewed. There are several common issues that apply to all of these disorders. First, diagnosis of all of these disorders involves a thorough medical and family history, physical examination, and possibly other laboratory and radiologic procedures. Second, all of these disorders result in a grief or loss response to normal functioning in the impaired person and family. Education, support, and guidance by professionals aid the impaired individual and family in the acute period following diagnosis and in the future. Third, long-term medical care is needed for prevention of relapse or recurrence (e.g., stroke), maintenance of gains (e.g., chronic pain), rehabilitation (e.g., spinal cord injury), physical or sensory aids (e.g., visual impairment), or concomitant medical problems (e.g., spina bifida). Fourth, psychological or psychiatric care is often needed for support and acceptance of the diagnosis, treatment for emotional sequelae of impaired functioning, and treatment for behavioral disturbances.

In conclusion, a multidisciplinary diagnostic and treatment team approach maximizes the quality of care for the developmentally and physically disabled. In addition, medical, psychological, and psychiatric care may aid in minimizing the consequences of the impairment, and the social disadvantages of the disability.

## References

Abroms, I. F. (1983). Central nervous system trauma. In M. D. Levine, W. B. Carey, A. C. Crocker, & R. T. Gross (Eds.), *Developmental-behavioral pediatrics* (pp. 444-446). Philadelphia: W. B. Saunders.

Accardo, P. J., & Capute, A. J. (Eds.). (1979). *The pediatrician and the developmentally disabled child.* Baltimore, MD: University Park Press.

American Psychiatric Association. (1980). *Diagnostic and statistical manual of mental disorders* (3rd Ed.) Washington, DC: Author.

American Psychiatric Association. (1987). *Diagnostic and statistical manual of mental disorders* (3rd Ed.-Rev.), Washington, DC: Author.

Aronoff, G. M. (1985). *Evaluation and treatment of chronic pain.* Baltimore: Urban & Schwarzenberg.

Barkley, R. A. (1981). *Hyperactive children: A handbook for diagnosis and treatment.* Chichester: John Wiley.

Bresnan, M. J., & Koukol, R. J. (1987). Seizure disorders. In R. A. Hoekelman, S. Blatman, S. B. Friedman, N. M. Nelson, & H. M. Seidel (Eds.), *Primary pediatric care* (pp. 1467-1477). St. Louis: C. V. Mosby.

Chess, S., & Hassibi, M. (1982). Normal and abnormal psychological development—Developmental disabilities. In A. M. Rudolph & J. I. Hoffman (Eds.), *Pediatrics* (pp. 60-67). Norwalk: Appleton-Century-Crofts.

Cohen, H. J. (1987). Developmental disabilities: A pediatrician's perspective. In M. I. Gottlieb & J. E. Williams (Eds.), *Textbook of developmental pediatrics* (pp. 3-10). New York: Plenum.

Conner, G. H. (1987). Hearing loss. In R. A. Hoekelman, S. Blatman, S. B. Friedman, N. M. Nelson, & H. M. Seidel (Eds.), *Primary pediatric care* (pp. 985-989). St. Louis: C. V. Mosby.

Conners, C. K. (1969). A teacher rating scale for use in drug studies with children. *American Journal of Psychiatry, 126*, 884-888.

Corbett, J. A. (1985). Mental retardation: Psychiatric aspects. In M. Rutter & L. Hersov (Eds.), *Child and adolescent psychiatry modern approaches*, (pp. 661-678). Boston: Blackwell/Year Book Medical.

Cotton, E. K. (1987). Wheezing. In R. A. Hoekelman, S. Blatman, S. B. Friedman, N. M. Nelson, & H. M. Seidel (Eds.), *Primary pediatric care* (pp. 1125-1129). St. Louis: C. V. Mosby.

Creasy, R. K., & Parer, J. T. (1982). Pediatric care and diagnosis. In A. M. Rudolph & J. I. Hoffman (Eds.), *Pediatrics* (pp. 105-117). Norwalk: Appleton-Century-Crofts.

Crocker, A. C., & Nelson, R. P. (1983). Major handicapping conditions. In M. D. Levine, W. B. Carey, A. C. Crocker, & R. T. Gross (Eds.), *Developmental-behavioral pediatrics* (pp. 756-769). Philadelphia: W. B. Saunders.

Cunningham, D. R. (1987). Auditory screening. In R. A. Hoekelman, S. Blatman, S. B. Friedman, N. M. Nelson, & H. M. Seidel (Eds.), *Primary pediatric care* (pp. 211-217). St. Louis: C. V. Mosby.

Davidson, P. W. (1983). Visual impairment and blindness. In M. D. Levine, W. B. Carey, A. C. Crocker, & R. T. Gross (Eds.), *Developmental-behavioral pediatrics* (pp. 778-788). Philadelphia: W. B. Saunders.

DeLong, G. R., & Adams, R. D. (1987). Developmental and congenital abnormalities of the nervous system. In E. Braunwald, K. J. Isselbacher, R. G. Petersdorf, J. D. Wilson, J. B. Martin, & A. S. Fauci (Eds.), *Harrison's principles of internal medicine* (pp. 2027-2034). New York: McGraw-Hill.

Douglas, V. I. (1983). Attentional and cognitive problems. In M. Rutter (Ed.), *Developmental neuropsychiatry* (pp. 280-329). New York: Guilford.

Downs, M. P. (1987). Hearing problems in childhood. In M. I. Gottlieb & J. E. Williams (Eds.) *Textbook of developmental pediatrics* (pp. 349-356). New York: Plenum.

Dreifuss, F. E. (1981). International league against epilepsy—Proposal for revised clinical and electroencephalographic classification of epileptic seizures. *Epilepsia, 20*, 489-501.

Dreifuss, F. E., Martinez-Lage, M., Roger, J., Seino, M., Wolf, P., & Dam, M. (1985). International league against epilepsy—Proposal for classification of epilepsies and epileptic syndromes. *Epilepsia, 26*, 268-278.

Engel, G. L. (1959). Psychogenic pain and the pain prone patient. *American Journal of Medicine, 26*, 899-918.

Feingold, B. F. (1975). Hyperkinesis and learning disabilities linked to artificial food flavors and colors. *American Journal of Nursing, 75*, 797-803.

Fireman, P. (1987). Asthma. In R. A. Hoekelman, S. Blatman, S. B. Friedman, N. M. Nelson, & H. M. Seidel (Eds.), *Primary pediatric care* (pp. 1145-1149). St. Louis: C. V. Mosby.

Fraiberg, S. (1977). *Insights from the blind: Comparative studies of blind and sighted infants*. New York: Basic Books.

Gittelman, R. (1983). Hyperkinetic syndrome: Treatment issues and principles. In M. Rutter (Ed.), *Developmental neuropsychiatry* (pp. 437-449). New York: Guilford.

Goldstein, H. (1980). The reported demography and causes of blindness throughout the world. *Advances in Ophthalmology, 40*, 1-99.

Gottlieb, M. I. (1987a). The hyperactive child. In M. I. Gottlieb & J. E. Williams (Eds.), *Textbook of developmental pediatrics* (pp. 303-329). New York: Plenum.

Gottleib, M. I. (1987b). Major variations in intelligence. In M. I. Gottlieb & J. E. Williams, (Eds.), *Textbook of developmental pediatrics* (pp. 127-150). New York: Plenum.

Green, M., & Solnit, A. J. (1964). Reactions to the threatened loss of a child: A vulnerable child syndrome. *Pediatrics, 34*, 58-66.

Grossman, H. J. (Ed.) (1983). *Classification in mental retardation*. Washington, DC: American Association on Mental Deficiency.

Hackett, T. P. (1978). The pain patient: Evaluation and treatment. In T. P. Hackett & N. H. Cassem (Eds.), *Massachusetts General Hospital handbook of general hospital psychiatry* (pp. 41-63). St. Louis: C. V. Mosby.

Healy, A., Hein, H. A., & Rubin, I. L. (1983). Perinatal stresses. In M. D. Levine, W. B. Carey, A. C. Crocker, & R. T. Gross (Eds.), *Developmental-behavioral pediatrics* (pp. 399-400). Philadelphia: W. B. Saunders.

Hechtman, L., & Weiss, G. (1983). Long-term outcomes of hyperactive children. *American Journal of Orthopsychiatry, 53*, 532-541.

Hechtman, L., Weiss, G., & Perlman, T. (1984). Young adult outcome of hyperactive children who received long-term stimulant treatment. *Journal of the American Academy of Child Psychiatry, 23*, 261-269.

Hiatt, R. L., (1987). Visual problems in childhood. In M. I. Gottlieb & J. E. Williams (Ed.), *Textbook of developmental pediatrics* (pp. 335-348). New York: Plenum.

Holmes, G. L. (1987). *Diagnosis and management of seizures in children*. Philadelphia: W. B. Saunders.

Hughes, J. R. (1980). Epilepsy: A medical overview. In B. P. Hermann (Ed.), *A multidisciplinary handbook of epilepsy* (pp. 3-35). Springfield, IL: Charles C Thomas.

Irving, N. A., Kennel, J. H., & Klaus, M. H. (1982). Caring for parents of an infant with a congenital malformation. In M. H. Klaus & J. H. Kennel (Eds.), *Parent infant bonding* (p. 231). St. Louis: C. V. Mosby.

Kahn, H., & Moorhead, W. (1973). *Statistics on blindness in the model reporting area*. DHEW Publication (NIH). Washington, DC: National Eye Institute.

Kaliner, M., Eggleston, P. A., & Mathews, K. P. (1987). Rhinitis and asthma. *Journal of the American Medical Association, 258*(20), 2851-2873.

Kanner, L. (1943), Autistic disturbances of affective contact. *Nervous Child, 2*, 217-250.

Kendall, P. C., & Braswell, L. (1985). *Cognitive-behavioral treatment for impulsive children*. New York: Guilford.

Kinsbourne, M. (1987). Specific learning disabilities and attention deficit disorder with hyperactivity. In M. I. Gottlieb & J. E. Williams (Eds.), *Textbook of developmental pediatrics* (pp. 53-83). New York: Plenum.

Kirk, S. A. (1962). *Educational exceptional children*. Boston: Houghton Mifflin.

Kirk, S. A. & Kirk, W. D. (1983). On defining learning disabilities. *Journal of Learning Disabilities, 16*, 20-21.

Kirman, B. H. (1985). Mental retardation: Medical aspects. In M. Rutter & L. Hersov (Eds.), *Child and adolescent psychiatry modern approaches* (pp. 650-660). Boston: Blackwell/Year Book Medical.

Kistler, J. B., Ropper, A. H., & Martin, J. B. (1987). Cerebrovascular diseases. In E. Braunwald, K. J. Isselbacher, R. G. Petersdorf, J. D. Wilson, J. B. Martin, & A. S. Fauci (Eds.), *Harrison's principles of internal medicine* (pp. 1930-1959). New York: McGraw-Hill.

Kraus, J. F. (1980). A comparison of recent studies on the extent of the head and spinal cord injuries problems in the United States. *Journal of Neurosurgery, 53,* 335-343.

Levine, M. D. (1983). Developmental variations and dysfunctions in the school child. In M. D. Levine, W. B. Carey, A. C. Crocker, & R. T. Gross (Eds.), *Developmental-behavioral pediatrics* (pp. 709-742). Philadelphia: W. B. Saunders.

Liptak, G. S. (1987). Spina bifida. In R. A. Hoekelman, S. Blatman, S. B. Friedman, N. M. Nelson, & H. M. Seidel (Eds.), *Primary pediatric care* (pp. 1487-1492). St. Louis: C. V. Mosby.

Maciewicz, R., & Martin, J. B. (1987). Pain: Pathophysiology and management. In E. Braunwald, K. J. Isselbacher, R. G. Petersdorf, J. D. Wilson, J. B. Martin, & A. S. Fauci (Eds.), *Harrison's principles of internal medicine* (pp. 13-16). New York: McGraw-Hill.

Marshall, J., & Thomas, D. J. (1986). Vascular disease. In A. K. Asbury, G. M. McKhann, & W. I. McDonald (Eds.), *Diseases of the nervous system clinical neurobiology* (pp. 1101-1135). Philadelphia: Ardmore.

Meichenbaum, D. (1978). Teaching children self-control. In B. Lahey & A. Kazdin (Eds.), *Advances in child clinical psychology Volume 2.* New York: Plenum.

Myers, B. A. (1987a). Chronically disabled children in school. In R. A. Hoekelman, S. Blatman, S. B. Friedman, N. M. Nelson, & H. M. Seidel (Eds.), *Primary pediatric care* (pp. 683-687). St. Louis: C. V. Mosby.

Myers, B. A. (1987b). Physical handicaps. In R. A. Hoekelman, S. Blatman, S. B. Friedman, N. M. Nelson, & H. M. Seidel (Eds.), *Primary pediatric care* (pp. 754-756). St. Louis: C. V. Mosby.

Nelson, R. P., & Crocker, A. C. (1983). The child with multiple handicaps. In M. D. Levine, W. B. Carey, A. C. Crocker, & R. T. Gross (Eds.), *Developmental-behavioral pediatrics* (pp. 828-839). Philadelphia: W. B. Saunders.

Ornitz, E. M., & Ritvo, E. R. (1976). The syndrome of autism: A critical review. *American Journal of Psychiatry, 133*(6), 609-619.

Rapoport, J. L. (1983). The use of drugs: Trends in research: Hyperkinetic/Attentional deficit syndrome. In M. Rutter (Ed.), *Developmental neuropsychiatry* (pp. 385-403). New York: Guilford.

Ropper, A. H. (1987). Trauma of the head and spinal cord. In E. Braunwald, K. J. Isselbacher, R. G. Petersdorf, J. D. Wilson, J. B. Martin, & A. S. Fauci (Eds.), *Harrison's principles of internal medicine* (pp. 1960-1967). New York: McGraw-Hill.

Ropper, A. H. & Martin J. B. (1987). Diseases of the spinal cord. In E. Braunwald, K. J. Isselbacher, R. G. Petersdorf, J. D. Wilson, J. B. Martin, & A. S. Fauci (Eds.), *Harrison's principles of internal medicine* (pp. 2040-2046). New York: McGraw-Hill.

Rutter, M. (1983). Behavioral studies: Questions and findings on the concept of a distinctive syndrome: Hyperkinetic/Attentional deficit syndrome. In M. Rutter (Ed.), *Developmental neuropsychiatry* (pp. 259-279). New York: Guilford.

Rutter, M. (1985). Infantile autism and other pervasive developmental disorders. In M. Rutter & L. Hersov (Eds.), *Child and adolescent psychiatry modern approaches* (pp. 545-566). Boston: Blackwell/Year Book Medical.

Rutter, M., Graham, P., & Yule, W. (1970). *A neurospychiatric study in childhood.* London: Spastics International.

Shaprio, B. K., Palmer, F. B., & Capute, A. J. (1987). Cerebral palsy. In M. I. Gottleib & J. E. Williams (Eds.), *Textbook of developmental pediatrics* (pp. 11-25). New York: Plenum.

Silver, L. B., & Brunstetter, R. W. (1987). Learning disabilities: Recent advances. In J. D. Noshpitz, J. D. Call, R. L. Cohen, S. I. Harrison, I. N. Berlin, & L. A. Stone (Eds.), *Basic handbook of child psychiatry Volume 5: Advances and new directions* (pp. 354-360). New York: Basic Books.

Szymanski, L. S. (1983). Emotional problems in a child with serious developmental handicaps. In M. D. Levine, W. B. Carey, A. C. Crocker, & R. T. Gross (Eds.), *Developmental-behavioral pediatrics* (pp. 839-846). Philadelphia: W. B. Saunders.

Taft, L. T. (1987). Cerebral palsy. In R. A. Hoekelman, S. Blatman, S. B. Friedman, N. M. Nelson, & H. M. Seidel (Eds.), *Primary pediatric care* (pp. 1183-1186). St. Louis: C. V. Mosby.

Taft, L. T., & Matthews, W. S. (1983). Cerebral palsy. In M. D. Levine, W. B. Carey, A. C. Crocker, & R. T. Gross (Eds.), *Developmental-behavioral pediatrics* (pp. 789-800). Philadelphia: W. B. Saunders.

Taylor, E. (1985). Syndromes of overactivity and attention deficit. In M. Rutter & L. Hersov (Eds.), *Child and adolescent psychiatry modern approaches* (pp. 424-443). Boston: Blackwell/Year Book Medical Publishers.

Wall, P. D., & Melzack, R. (1985). *Textbook of pain.* New York: Churchill Livingstone.

Warren, D. H. (1976). *Blindness and early childhood development.* New York: American Foundation for the Blind.

Wodrich, D. L. (1986). The terminology and purposes of assessment. In D. L. Wodrich & J. E. Joy (Eds.), *Multidisciplinary assessment of children with learning disabilities and mental retardation* (pp. 1-29). Baltimore, MD: Brookes.

Yule, W., & Rutter, M. (1985). Reading and other learning difficulties. In M. Rutter & L. Hersov (Eds.), *Child and adolescent psychiatry modern approaches* (pp. 444-464). Boston: Blackwell/Year Book Medical Publishers.

Ziring, P. R. (1983). The child with hearing impairment. In M. D. Levine, W. B. Carey, A. C. Crocker, & R. T. Gross (Eds.), *Developmental-behavioral pediatrics* (pp. 770-777). Philadelphia: W. B. Saunders.

# PART II

SPECIFIC DISORDERS

# Chapter 3

# Asthma

Thomas L. Creer
Russ V. Reynolds

## Description of the Disorder

There is no generally accepted definition of asthma. This is due to the fact that any definition would include approximately one-fourth of the patients diagnosed as suffering chronic bronchitis. Nevertheless, despite the lack of a precise definition, since antiquity there has been considerable agreement among written descriptions of asthma. These descriptions highlight certain features of the disorder, which are characterized by increased hyperreactivity of the airways to various stimuli. The stimuli include: (a) allergens that react with antibodies on the surface of mast cells, in a classic allergic reaction, and release chemical mediators; (b) nonspecific irritants, such as exercise and cold air, that stimulate nerve receptors in the respiratory tract; and (c) infections in the airways that produce inflammation and swelling of the mucosa. These stimuli may produce a combination of several responses: (a) constriction of the smooth muscle in the bronchial wall; (b) swelling of

AUTHOR'S NOTE: Preparation of this chapter was supported, in part, by Grant No. 32538 from the National Heart, Lung, and Blood Institute.

the bronchial walls; (c) increased mucus secretion; or (d) infiltration of the inflammatory cells. The consequence of these responses is commonly referred to as an asthma attack, flare-up, or episode. Asthma attacks occur on an intermittent basis, are variable in severity, and may reverse either spontaneously or as a result of therapy.

This definition emphasizes four major characteristics of asthmatic patients and their condition: the hyperreactivity of the airways, the intermittent nature of attacks, the variable severity of asthma, and the reversibility of attacks. Each of these characteristics merits amplification.

## Hyperreactivity of the Airways

Hyperreactivity of the airways refers to the fact that stimuli that have no effect when inhaled in normal individuals can cause bronchoconstriction in those afflicted by asthma. A large number of stimuli have been identified as leading to attacks, although the stimuli that trigger flare-ups vary from patient to patient or attack to attack. There are patients, predominantly children, who suffer seasonal episodes. Patients who experience seasonal or allergic asthma are often asthma-free during the remainder of the year. A second class of patients, including most adults with late-onset asthma, experience attacks the year around or on a perennial basis. A gamut of stimuli may trigger their attacks, including allergens, nonspecific irritants, and infections.

## Intermittency of Attacks

The frequency of attacks varies from patient to patient and, for any given individual, from time to time. The frequency of attacks is due, in part, to the number of diversified stimuli that trigger attacks in an individual patient. The precipitating stimuli in some patients are relatively easy to detect in that they only suffer attacks during months when certain stimuli, usually airborne, abound in the environment. For other patients, however, it is impossible to determine the specific trigger for given attacks due to the great number of external or internal stimuli that can potentially induce an attack. These patients are quite likely to suffer perennial asthma.

*Variability*

Variability refers to fluctuations in the severity both of discrete attacks and the overall course of a given patient's asthma (Reynolds, Creer, & Kotses, 1988). This characteristic is credited by Williams (1980) as the major reason asthma has eluded a precise definition. Asthma severity presents two major concerns to practitioners and investigators. First, despite the pervasive use of the term *severity* throughout the asthma literature, there is no standard way of classifying either a given flare-up or a patient's disease as mild, moderate, or severe asthma. What one observer may describe as mild asthma is perceived by another observer as moderate asthma. Second, the lack of operational definitions concerning the severity of asthma attacks complicates the already intricate matter of assessing a condition that is likely to vary across evaluations.

*Reversibility of Asthma*

Reversibility is the *sine qua non* of asthma (McFadden, 1980). It distinguishes the condition from other types of respiratory conditions, particularly emphysema, where there is no reversibility. The characteristic presents two major concerns to clinicians and researchers. First, it is a relative condition; while many patients show complete reversibility of airway obstruction, others do not. Loren, Leung, Cooley, Chai, Bell, and Buck (1978), in fact, reported that there were patients who exhibited reduced airflow that was irreversible even with intensive therapy. Second, the ability of attacks to remit spontaneously makes it difficult to establish, with certainty, that a therapeutic agent produced the change (Creer, 1982).

# Case Identification

Matt Jones is a 14-year-old boy with chronic bronchial asthma. He lives in a large city with his parents and two younger sisters. Despite a record of frequent school absenteeism, Matt is an excellent student and hopes to become an immunologist when he completes school. He is also a member of the varsity swim team at his school. While there is considerable air pollution in his community, Matt's home has been carefully prepared to remove possible precipitants or aggravants of his asthma. The house is always dusted, the temperature is maintained at

65 to 70 degrees Fahrenheit with a relative humidity of 30% to 50%, and washable throw rugs are scattered about the polished wood and tile floor. No smoking is permitted in the house, and an exhaust fan is used during cooking. There is no family pet, although Matt does have a collection of tropical fish. Because he spends approximately one-third of his time in his bedroom, Matt's parents have provided him with a waterbed covered with pillows and blankets made from synthetic materials. Mrs. Jones cleans Matt's room each week while Matt is at school, thus making it unlikely that he would be affected by dust that is stirred up.

Mr. Jones is a manager of a local department store. His firm has excellent health insurance that covers any hospital expenditures, as well as most medication costs. Mr. and Mrs. Jones have been married for almost 20 years; they appear to have a stable marriage. Neither of their daughters has asthma, although the youngest child, Jennifer, experiences hay fever in the spring and summer.

## History

Matt appeared as a normal infant until the age of 3. At that time, he developed eczema that covered his arms and legs. This cleared up with medical treatment, although occasional eczema continued to occur. Matt also seemed to experience more than his share of colds. This was accompanied by persistent coughing that was diagnosed as croup by his pediatrician.

When Matt was 6 years of age, he suffered a particularly severe viral infection. This not only produced coughing, but for the first time wheezing was noticed. These symptoms appeared worse during the night and in the early morning and improved throughout the day. His pediatrician had Matt inhale a beta-adrenergic bronchodilating medication during an office visit when the boy appeared to experience a pronounced episode of coughing and wheezing. This produced greater than 20% improvement in the youngster's pulmonary function test. On this basis, Matt was tentatively diagnosed as having childhood asthma (American Thoracic Society, 1987).

Following the above episode, Matt was referred to a pediatric allergist for a more extensive evaluation. The allergist subjected Matt to a complete medical examination to investigate potential precipitants and characteristics of Matt's asthma. This involved obtaining a detailed family history of usual pediatric information, such as Matt's birth weight and any complications his mother may have experienced during pregnancy, and data regarding potential allergic factors that could be related to asthma. In addition, the allergist conducted a thorough physical examination that focused on the areas of overall growth and development, respiratory mechanics and chest checkup, and the presence of other atopic conditions (e.g., eczema) that frequently coexist with asthma. On the basis of this detailed examination, she decided to conduct three types of tests frequently performed with children thought to experience asthma (Shapiro & Bierman, 1987): skin tests, bronchoprovocation challenges, and pulmonary function (spirometry) tests. These common types of tests yielded the information presented in the sections below.

## Skin Testing

Based on the patient's history, the allergist challenged Matt with allergens thought to be potential precipitants of his asthma. While several types of skin tests are available, Matt was challenged with prick tests. With this procedure, skin test sites are cleansed and marked. Single drops of the solutions to be tested are then applied to the sites from plastic containers. A disposable sterile needle is passed through the drop and inserted into the skin. With a slight lifting of the skin, the needle is withdrawn and the remaining solution wiped away (Norman, 1983). When fully developed, the sites are inspected and read with a millimeter ruler. On this basis, it was found that Matt was allergic to animal dander, mold, pollens from certain grasses and trees, house dust, and house dust mites. A treatment plan was formulated to manage these precipitants.

## Bronchoprovocation Testing

Bronchoprovocation refers to having a patient inhale a substance, such as histamine, which is known to produce bronchoconstriction in patients with asthma. This test was used with Matt for two reasons. First, it confirmed the etiological importance of the stimuli found through skin testing to induce a reaction. When he inhaled a minute amount of a dust extract, for example, his allergist found that Matt experienced bronchoconstriction and tightness of his chest. Slight wheezing was also induced by this challenge. Second, Matt exercised on a treadmill to determine if he experienced any exercise-induced asthma.

As occurs with approximately 70% to 90% of children with the disorder, Matt showed a decline on pulmonary function testing, particularly a drop in forced expiratory volume in one second (FEV-1), an indication of the amount of air he could maximally exhale in 1 second. Thus, it was determined that Matt experienced exercise-induced bronchospasm (EIB). On this basis, he later took up swimming, an activity he could perform and not induce EIB.

*Spirometry Testing*

Spirometry testing is a simple, inexpensive procedure that permits physicians to determine large and small airway flow, the amount of air that can be maximally exhaled by the patient, and the degree of respiratory impairment he or she experiences in comparison to normal individuals of the same age, sex, and height. For example, a normal child will expire in excess of 80% of his or her vital capacity within 1 second. When an individual exhales less than this value, a respiratory disorder is suspected; this test further confirmed the diagnosis of asthma in Matt.

Following testing, Matt was placed on medications. Initially, he took medications on an as-needed basis. However, since he experienced one or more attacks per month that required the use of sundry medications for several days, he was placed on continuous therapy (Naspitz & Tinkelman, 1987). Currently, Matt takes a sustained-release theophylline medication twice a day and uses an inhaled theophylline medication during asthmatic episodes. He also inhales doses of the latter medication prior to exercising to prevent EIB. His allergist occasionally performs theophylline assays to ensure that there is the proper amount of theophylline in Matt's bloodstream.

# Presenting Complaints

The medical management of Matt's asthma has, for the most part, been successful. However, Matt recently suffered a severe attack where he experienced steadily worsening asthma referred to as status asthmaticus. Without the competent care he received in the emergency room of a local hospital, he might have died. Normally, asthma is rarely fatal. However, recent evidence of increased mortality from asthma (Sheffer & Bruist, 1987), as well as the intensity of his last attack, raised concerns with Matt's treatment team. In addition, his physician reported that Matt and his parents appeared to panic during the life-threatening episode. This response both aggravated the flare-up and interfered with medical attempts to manage the episode. Considering the situation, Matt's allergist requested behavioral assistance with her patient.

Specific questions generated in a conference of medical and behavioral scientists were as follows:

1. Are Matt and his parents knowledgeable about asthma and recent trends in managing the disorder?
2. Was Matt compliant with medication and medical instructions prior to his near-fatal attack?
3. Did Matt recognize the onset of his asthma and initiate treatment in an appropriate period of time while the attack was still mild?
4. Did Matt and his parents wait too long before seeking the medical attention the boy required?
5. Are there behavioral procedures that can be applied to reduce the panic displayed by Matt and his parents in future attacks?
6. Can a method be developed to provide more information to Matt, his parents, and his physician to predict the likelihood that the boy is about to suffer an impending asthma flare-up?

By pooling medical and behavioral expertise, it was thought that answers could be provided to solve these problems.

## Assessment

The initial question was whether Matt and his parents had a basic understanding of asthma. This was answered by administering the Basic Information Quiz found in *Living with Asthma* (Creer, Backial, Ullman, & Leung, 1986). This self-management program includes separate written tests for children and their parents, which were developed to assess knowledge relevant to the management of asthma. Results indicated that Matt and his parents were generally knowledgeable about the physiology of respiration and medications used to treat asthma. However, they appeared less informed about how self-management skills could be applied to help control asthma.

Concerns were expressed about whether Matt was compliant with medical and medication instructions. The lack of compliance is frequently noted in asthma; it is especially common in adolescents with the disorder (Creer, 1979; Falliers, 1987). His allergist reported that

Matt always appeared compliant according to the blood theophylline checks she regularly performed during office visits. However, she noted that, Matt and his parents always knew beforehand when samples of his blood would be drawn and a blood assay performed. Therefore, the expectation that this would occur may have contributed to what appeared as excellent compliance; thus, his allergist suggested that random testing might offer more accurate information as to how compliant Matt was to medication instructions on a day-to-day basis. In addition, a major component of self-management entails that patients monitor their medication compliance on a daily basis (Creer, 1987). In this case, Matt was asked to record daily information concerning four areas: (a) the occurrence of flare-ups, as well as the severity of each episode; (b) the highest of three peak expiratory flow rates obtained both in the morning and evening with a peak flow meter; (c) medication compliance; and (d) morbidity costs associated with attacks (e.g., school absenteeism). Matt's role was to monitor his behavior and record this information in a weekly asthma diary (Creer et al., 1986); his parents served as a reliability check on the information entered by their son in the diary. A copy of the diary is depicted in Figure 3.1.

Most asthmatic patients encounter few problems in discriminating symptoms of asthma. The wheezing and chest tightness they experience warns them of the onset of an asthma episode and they initiate action to manage the flare-up. Symptom discrimination can, however, be poor. As Creer (1983) noted, it requires the recognition by patients of physical, cognitive, physiological and behavioral events. If there is a flaw in any of these components, symptoms of asthma are not immediately detected and attacks can intensify. Poor symptom awareness can occur due to a lack of hypoxic drive or a failure to consciously be aware of the episode, leading to a failure to perform treatment steps.

To assess Matt's ability to detect and initiate early treatment of asthma episodes, he was asked to complete a report of attack/episode form each time he experienced asthma. A copy of this form is depicted in Figure 3.2; it is an adaptation of the report used by Creer et al. (1986) in *Living with Asthma*. The form is designed to identify significant events that surround the onset of an attack and the exact sequence of steps taken to bring an episode under control. Completed forms were reviewed by Matt and his allergist during office visits to determine: (a) if there was any pattern that signaled the onset of an attack; and (b) how Matt reacted to any signs of an impending attack. By requesting Matt to indicate exactly how much time expired between discriminating

## ASTHMA DIARY

Patient: _____ I.D.#_____ Date Dispensed: _____

Please review the instructions for the Asthma Diary before completing the Diary.

### DATES:

| | | | | | | | | | | | | | |
|---|---|---|---|---|---|---|---|---|---|---|---|---|---|

**SYMPTOMS :**

| | | | | | | | | | | | | | |
|---|---|---|---|---|---|---|---|---|---|---|---|---|---|
| Chest Wheezing | | | | | | | | | | | | | |
| Breathlessness | | | | | | | | | | | | | |
| Chest tightness | | | | | | | | | | | | | |
| Cough | | | | | | | | | | | | | |

**NUMBER OF ATTACKS:**

| | | | | | | | | | | | | | |
|---|---|---|---|---|---|---|---|---|---|---|---|---|---|
| # of daytime asthma attacks | | | | | | | | | | | | | |
| # of times awakened by asthma last night | | | | | | | | | | | | | |

**PEFR:**

| | | | | | | | | | | | | | |
|---|---|---|---|---|---|---|---|---|---|---|---|---|---|
| Morning (AM) | | | | | | | | | | | | | |
| Evening (4:00 PM) | | | | | | | | | | | | | |

**ASTHMA MEDS:**

| | | | | | | | | | | | | | |
|---|---|---|---|---|---|---|---|---|---|---|---|---|---|
| 1. | | | | | | | | | | | | | |
| 2. | | | | | | | | | | | | | |
| 3. | | | | | | | | | | | | | |
| 4. | | | | | | | | | | | | | |
| 5. | | | | | | | | | | | | | |

**Figure 3.1.** Asthma diary.

## Report of Episode/Attack of Asthma

NAME: _____ DATE: _____ Time of Episode: _____(am or pm)

1.  Check degree of severity according to instructions on the Diary:

    _____ Mild _____ Moderate _____ Severe

2.  Note peak flow reading during attack: _____

3.  Did you take all medication on time over last 24 hours? _____ Yes _____ No

4.  Where did the episode occur? _____ Home _____ Work _____ Outside

    _____ In Bed _____ Other (describe)

5.  Did you notice any Early Warning Signs? _____ Yes _____ No

6.  What factors do you think caused this episode?

    | Allergy (specify) | _____ | Dust | _____ |
    |---|---|---|---|
    | Cold or infection | _____ | Excitement | _____ |
    | Cold weather | _____ | Laughing | _____ |
    | Crying | _____ | Overexertion | _____ |
    | Damp or high humidity | _____ | Pollution | _____ |
    | Not taking medication | _____ | Wind | _____ |
    | Sudden weather change | _____ | Coughing | _____ |
    | Becoming overtired | _____ | No idea | _____ |
    | Other (describe) | _____ | Getting upset | _____ |

7.  Check what you were doing before the episode:

    _____ A quiet activity _____ Sleeping _____ Working

    _____ Running or exercising _____ Don't know _____ Other

8.  How long did you wait between between discriminating the attack and initiating treatment?

    _____ hours _____ minutes

9.  Number in rank order what you did during the episode:

    _____ Measured lung functions
    _____ Called doctor
    _____ Went to the doctor or emergency room
    _____ Did breathing exercises
    _____ Drank cold liquids
    _____ Tried to get away from the cause
    _____ Used steam (vaporizer, shower)
    _____ Drank warm or hot liquid
    _____ Got upset
    _____ Rested or did quiet activity
    _____ Took medication
    _____ Waited to see if symptoms would go away
    _____ Other (describe) _____

10. (a) Were you upset by the episode?                      _____ Yes _____ No

    (b) Were other family members upset by the
        episode?                                            _____ Yes _____ No

**LIST ALL MEDICATIONS TAKEN DURING THE ATTACK ON THE BACK OF THIS FORM.**

**Figure 3.2.** Report of episode/Attack of asthma.

- a flare-up and initiating treatment, his allergist was able to determine whether too much time elapsed before appropriate management steps were initiated.

Many patients only experience one life-threatening asthma episode (Williams, 1982). Nevertheless, how children and their parents respond to a severe attack can establish patterns that continue to be exhibited on subsequent flare-ups (Creer, 1979). An illustration of this is the panic that is displayed by some youngsters and their parents following a severe attack. Panic can be manifested by the demand for more and more medication to the frozen silence of someone struggling to breathe (Creer, 1974, 1979). Discussions with Matt and his parents revealed that the entire family displayed signs of panic during Matt's flare-ups since the life-threatening episode he experienced several months earlier. Matt reported he would freeze and think about the trip to the hospital. This would immobilize him, diverting his attention away from the management of any episode he was currently experiencing. In addition, the panic resulted in rapid and shallow breathing, accompanied by sustained muscle tension in the face and neck. This further exacerbated the asthma episode. Other family members appeared to be extremely frightened by the severe episode. Further, Mr. and Mrs. Jones could describe no series of distinct steps or general approach they were following in helping their son manage a flare-up. Instead, they tended to overmedicate Matt with the hope that the attack would "just go away."

## Selection and Course of Treatment

Matt and his parents were enrolled in the next course of *Living with Asthma* presented by the allergist and members of her staff. Paper-and-pencil tests, as well as the comments of Matt and his parents during the eight sessions, indicated that they significantly enhanced their knowledge of asthma and its management by the end of the program. Random theophylline testing conducted by his physician showed, for the most part, that Matt was compliant with medication instructions. This finding was corroborated with information provided on the weekly asthma diary and the report of attack/episode form. It was anticipated that participation in *Living with Asthma* would further improve Matt's compliance with his medication regime. Meanwhile, his allergist increased the daily dosage of medications taken by Matt. The safe range for theophylline in the blood is between 10 and 20 microgr/ml. Below this level, theophylline may not control the patient's asthma; above the level the patient can experience toxic side effects. Matt had been receiving 12-hour medications that produced a serum level of 10 to 12 microgr/ml; his medications were increased to show a serum level of 14 to 15 microgr/ml. This was found to improve control of Matt's asthma without inducing major side effects.

Learning to observe and monitor his behavior taught Matt to better recognize the onset of most of his attacks and to take prompt action to alleviate the flare-ups. This was reflected in the data he submitted on the report of attack/episode forms. It appears that Matt learned to carefully observe smaller changes in his breathing and was initiating treatment more quickly.

Unfortunately, two vexing problems remained. First, while Matt panicked only during one later attack, his behavior had exacerbated his asthma and frightened attending medical personnel. Since it was thought that this pattern could be modified without further baseline data, an attempt to change the behavior was undertaken. Second, medical personnel speculated that if Matt had more warning of an impending attack, he could avoid the occasional severe episodes he experienced. Thus, they developed a procedure where, based on his peak flow rates and the probability he would experience asthma, Matt could initiate appropriate action to keep the flare-up mild and to prevent a severe episode.

*Panic*

Systematic desensitization, a procedure developed by Wolpe (1958), was introduced to treat the panic. First, Matt was taught progressive muscle relaxation. This skill is an important part of all self-management programs for asthma; if a patient can relax during an attack, he or she can concentrate on performing steps required to bring asthma under control (Creer & Winder, 1986). Matt learned progressive relaxation exercises in three hour-long sessions. Second, he was asked to describe the events that occurred during the two attacks when he had panicked. These descriptions were then ordered according to the degree of panic Matt experienced when thinking of each detail. Finally, he learned to relax while thinking of the events associated with panic. The juxtaposition of relaxation and the vivid imagination of panic-inducing events reduced the fears he had about asthma flare-ups.

Asthmatic patients are likely to obtain other benefits from systematic desensitization training. First, relaxation training, in addition to extinguishing the panic associated with past events, can be used as an active coping strategy to manage emotional reactions during future attacks or in other stressful situations (Creer, 1974). Second, the use of relaxation training has been shown to produce significant improvements in pulmonary function measures for some children with asthma (Miklich, Renne, Creer, Alexander, Chai, Davis, Hoffman, & Danker-Brown, 1977).

*Predicting Attacks and Initiating Treatment*

From the beginning, the treatment team had been concerned that Matt did not discriminate attacks and take immediate action to bring them under control. To improve his ability to detect respiratory changes and to start treatment, the following procedure was used:

First, the peak flow data Matt gathered were reviewed to determine if flow values dropped in the 12-hour period prior to an attack. In many cases, it appears as if this was the case. Based on the peak flow data, it was possible to take the values and predict the likelihood that Matt would experience an attack within the succeeding 12-hour period. This involved treating the data with a conditional probability procedure described by Harm, Kotses, and Creer (1985). The resultant probability table showed a five-fold improvement in the ability of peak flow values to predict attacks over base rates.

Second, a treatment decision aid was constructed showing the probability of an asthma attack on the $x$ axis and the percent deviation from his predicted peak expiratory flow rate (PEFR) on the $y$ axis. As depicted in Figure 3.3, this permitted Matt to read a single peak flow value and determine the likelihood that he would suffer an attack within the coming 12 hours.

Finally, Matt's allergist developed a particular treatment for each of the six zones shown in Figure 3.3 (marked with Roman numerals). If Matt's PEFR value fell within Zone I, he was told to carefully monitor his condition and to be certain to take all prescribed medications. If his PEFR was in Zone II, he was instructed to rest, drink warm liquids, and to take a dose of prescribed nebulized medications; the approach was similar in Zone III with the exception that Matt was told that he could take more than one dose of a nebulized medication if necessary. If Matt's peak flow values fell into the ranges of Zones IV and V, he was instructed to notify his physician immediately. She could provide any instruction, in addition to the sequential steps he had been taught to

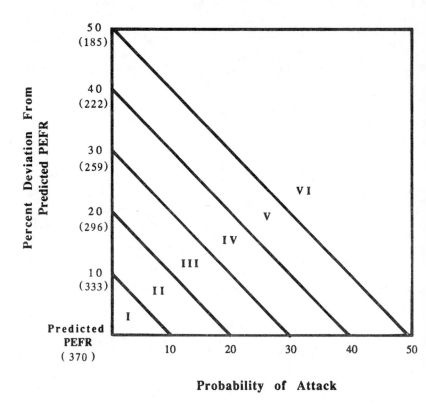

**Figure 3.3.** Treatment decision aid.

follow to manage attacks in *Living with Asthma*, to bring the attack
under control. If Matt blew a flow value that was 50% or lower than his
predicted flow value (Zone VI), he was told to report to an emergency
room at once. Thus, the ability to predict attacks served as the basis for
any treatment initiated by Matt and his parents.

## Termination and Follow-Up

The procedures instituted by the medical and behavioral treatment
team improved the management of Matt's asthma. He not only learned
to better monitor his asthma and to take corrective steps to treat flare-
ups, but he ceased to exhibit panic during subsequent attacks. Matt has

continued to be followed by the same treatment team for the past year. He still is regarded as having potentially severe asthma; thus, he continues to take maintenance medications on a twice-daily basis. His physician has contemplated reducing Matt's medications, but since his asthma has been well controlled, she has postponed any action. Matt has missed little school this year; both he and his parents appear more confident about managing any future asthma attacks.

## Overall Evaluation

There is no known cure for asthma. The best that can be anticipated is that, over time, the symptoms of the disorder become less severe and incapacitating. There is evidence that some children appear to "outgrow" asthma as they grow older, but no one can predict exactly who will be the fortunate youngsters. With Matt, there is the likelihood that he could always experience asthma. The fact that he suffered his initial attack at an early age, coupled with his need for maintenance medications to maintain his health, indicate that he will continue to suffer asthma flare-ups. His allergist is aware of this possibility, and will continue to treat Matt according to the philosophy of permitting him to live as normal a life as possible while his health is maintained by minimal medications. The medical and behavioral treatment team, too, are aware that they may have helped Matt resolve but one crisis in his life. As he continues to grow and develop, he and his asthma may present even more serious problems that will require the cooperative skills and expertise of the entire team.

## References

American Thoracic Society (1987). Standards for the diagnosis and care of patients with chronic obstructive pulmonary disease (COPD) and asthma. *American Review of Respiratory Disease, 136*, 225-244.

Creer, T. L. (1974). Biofeedback and asthma. *Advances in Asthma and Allergy, 1*, 6-11.

Creer, T. L. (1979). *Asthma therapy: A behavioral health care system for respiratory disorders*. New York: Springer-Verlag.

Creer, T. L. (1982). Asthma. *Journal of Consulting & Clinical Psychology, 50*, 912-921.

Creer, T. L. (1983). Self-management psychology and treatment of childhood asthma. *Journal of Allergy & Clinical Immunology, 72*, 607-610.

Creer, T. L. (1987). Psychological and neurophysiological aspects of childhood asthma. In D. G. Tinkelman, C. J. Falliers, & C. K. Naspitz (Eds.), *Childhood asthma: Pathophysiology and treatment* (pp. 341-371). New York: Marcel Dekker.

Creer, T. L., Backial, M., Ullman, S., & Leung, P. (1986). *Living with asthma. Part 1. Manual for teaching parents the self-management of childhood asthma. Part 2. Manual for teaching children the self-management of asthma* (NIH Publication No. 86-2364). Washington, DC: U.S. Government Printing Office.

Creer, T. L., & Winder, J. A. (1986). Asthma. In K. A. Holroyd & T. L. Creer (Eds.), *Self-management of chronic disease: Handbook of clinical interventions and research* (pp. 269-303). Orlando, FL: Academic Press.

Falliers, C. J. (1987). Characteristic patterns and management of asthma in adolescence. In D. G. Tinkelman, C. J. Falliers, & C. K. Naspitz (Eds.), *Childhood asthma: Pathophysiology and treatment* (pp. 327-339). New York: Marcel Dekker.

Harm, D. L., Kotses, H., and Creer, T. L. (1985). Improving the ability of peak expiratory flow rates to predict asthma. *Journal of Allergy and Clinical Immunology, 75,* 688-694.

Loren, M. L., Leung, P. K., Cooley, R. L., Chai, H., Bell, T. D., & Buck, V. M. (1978). Irreversibility of obstructive changes in severe asthma in children. *Chest, 74,* 126-129.

McFadden, E. R., Jr. (1980). Asthma: Pathophysiology. *Seminars in Respiratory Medicine, 1,* 297-303.

Miklich, D. R., Renne, C. M., Creer, T. L., Alexander, A. B., Chai, H., Davis, M. H., Hoffman, A., & Danker-Brown, P. (1977). The clinical utility of behavior therapy as an adjunctive treatment for asthma. *Journal of Allergy & Clinical Immunology, 60,* 285-294.

Naspitz, C. K., & Tinkelman, D. G. (1987). Therapeutic approaches to the treatment of chronic asthma. In D. G. Tinkelman, C. J. Falliers, & C. K. Naspitz (Eds.), *Childhood asthma: Pathophysiology and treatment* (pp. 249-280). New York: Marcel Dekker.

Norman, P. S. (1983). In vivo methods of study of allergy: Skin and mucosal tests, techniques, and interpretation. In E. Middleton, Jr., C. E. Reed, & E. F. Ellis (Eds.), *Allergy: Principles and practice* (pp. 295-302). St. Louis: C. V. Mosby.

Reynolds, R. V., Creer, T. L., & Kotses, H. (1988). *Asthma severity: A synthesis of perspectives.* Manuscript submitted for publication.

Shapiro, G. G., & Bierman, C. W. (1987). Presentation of asthma in children: Differential diagnosis. In D. G. Tinkelman, C. J. Falliers, & C. K. Naspitz (Eds.), *Childhood asthma: Pathophysiology and treatment* (pp. 203-229). New York: Marcel Dekker.

Sheffer, A. L., & Bruist, A. S. (1987). Proceedings of the asthma mortality task force. *Journal of Allergy & Clinical Immunology, 80,* 361-514.

Williams, M. H., Jr. (1980). Clinical features. *Seminars in Respiratory Medicine, 1,* 304-314.

Williams, M. H., Jr. (1982). *Essentials of pulmonary medicine.* Philadelphia: W. B. Saunders.

Wolpe, J. (1958). *Psychotherapy by reciprocal inhibition.* Stanford, CA: Stanford University Press.

# Chapter 4

# Autism

## Phillip S. Strain

## Description of the Disorder

Autism has been and remains today one of the more elusive of childhood disorders. Even after decades of intensive research and refinement of diagnostic procedures, autism exists as a syndrome in name only. Consider, for example, that autistic children represent an enormously heterogeneous population, that there are no clear treatments of choice specific to the condition, and that its etiology is essentially unknown. This seeming lack of precision may well reflect the fact that the behavioral manifestations of autism arise via multiple etiological paths that occur in isolation and in combination.

Amid the confusion surrounding autism, Johnson and Koegel (1982, p. 2) have offered a particularly comprehensive yet concise sketch of the relevant behavioral dimensions of the disorder. These "symptoms" include the following:

AUTHOR'S NOTE: Support for this chapter was provided by grant numbers MH 37110-05 from the National Institute of Mental Health and G008630247 from the U.S. Department of Education to the University of Pittsburgh.

73

1. Autistic children exhibit a profound failure to relate to other people, which is often apparent from birth. They may show an absent or delayed social smile, and may not reach upwards in anticipation of being picked up. Some children fail to form emotional attachments to significant people in their environment, for example, not showing distress when their mother leaves the room. Similarly, a child might play in the vicinity of other children without interacting or participating with them.

2. Autistic children commonly show various levels of impaired or delayed language acquisition and comprehension. Many autistic children are mute and others may show echolalia. For example, a child may repeat numerous phrases or conversations previously heard without indication that the words convey meaning. Immature grammar, pronoun reversals, and/or the inability to use abstract terms may also be apparent.

3. Many children show apparent sensory dysfunction, as if they do not see or hear some environmental events. They may exhibit under- or over-responsiveness to touch, light, sound, or pain. For instance, the child may not exhibit a startle response to a loud disturbance, but may respond to the sound of a candy wrapper, or may tantrum excessively every time a siren goes by.

4. Many autistic children show inappropriate and/or flat affect. They may not display appropriate facial expressions and may not exhibit fear in dangerous situations, such as crossing the street. They may respond to even simple requests with severe, prolonged tantrums. They may also laugh and giggle uncontrollably in the absence of any apparent eliciting stimuli, or cry inconsolably for hours.

5. Typically, autistic children will occupy themselves for hours in stereo-typed, repetitive self-stimulatory behaviors, which serve no apparent purpose other than providing them with sensory input. Commonly, self-stimulatory behaviors take the form of manipulation of hands or fingers in front of the eyes, eye crossing, repetitive, meaningless vocalizations (e.g., "aeh, aeh, aeh, . . . "), suspending or spinning objects in front of the eyes, mouthing objects, hand tapping, body rocking, and other stereotyped behavior. Such behaviors have been found to significantly impair learning in autistic children (Koegel & Covert, 1972).

6. Autistic children often fail to develop normal, appropriate play. They may forsake toys altogether, preferring instead to spin a lampshade or flick a light switch on and off. If they do interact with toys, they may do so in an abnormal manner. For instance, the child may arrange, stack, or sort stimuli repetitively in the same pattern, and may show extreme disruption if the pattern is altered. Or they may turn a truck over and spin the wheels rather than roll it on the ground. Social play with peers may develop spontaneously, but usually does not.

7. Finally, autistic children commonly show obsessive, ritualistic behaviors that have been characterized as a profound resistance to change in the environment or normal routines. Familiar bedtime routines, insistence on one type of food, one type of furniture arrangement, and particular routes to familiar places are examples of routines that, when altered even in minor fashion, can create extreme disruptions in a child's behavior.

## Case Identification

The following sections of this chapter describe the history, course of treatment, and outcomes for the Henderson family and their son, Mark.

The Hendersons first became concerned with Mark's development when he was 18 months old. At that time he made no attempts to communicate, he seemed to avoid seeking out or responding positively to physical affection from his parents, and he often tantrumed in an unprovoked fashion. The Hendersons took their complaints to their pediatrician, who referred them to a developmental assessment service affiliated with a major children's hospital. After a thorough neurological, pediatric, and developmental workup, the Hendersons were told that Mark had "autistic tendencies" and that he should be enrolled in an early intervention program.

Subsequent to this initial diagnosis, the Hendersons took Mark to a psychologist in private practice for a second opinion. After meeting with the Hendersons and observing Mark at home and in the office, the autism diagnosis was confirmed.

The Hendersons reported that they were "devastated" psychologically by their son's diagnosis. It was not until Mark was 30 months old that they finally sought intervention help.

## Presenting Complaints

The Hendersons contacted the early intervention program known as LEAP (Learning Experiences . . . an Alternative Program for Preschools) by phone, and an interview was arranged with the family. During the course of this 1½ hour interview with staff, the Hendersons expressed the following concerns:

### Social Skills

Mark was reported to spend most of his day lying on the floor and rolling objects back and forth. When someone approached he would often whimper or simply isolate himself in an corner. Moreover, Mark seldom looked at his parents when they spoke to him.

*Language Skills*

At 30 months of age Mark spoke no words. He would gesture, grunt, and point to obtain food. Receptively, his skills were difficult to determine, as he was often noncompliant to simple commands.

*Adaptive Skills*

Mark was not toilet trained, he did not assist in his dressing, he ate only with his fingers, and he did not appear to have any fear of heights or heat.

*Deviant Behavior*

The Hendersons had, by and large, become homebound as a consequence of Mark's deviant behaviors. He would have a tantrum for up to 1 hour at a time, he engaged in multiple stereotypies, and he would scream in a high-pitched voice for several minutes when upset.

## History

The Hendersons were married at 23 years of age. They both completed college at a large midwestern university and began parallel careers in marketing and sales. Mrs. Henderson became pregnant with Mark when she was 27 years old. She had an uneventful, full-term pregnancy. Labor was protracted, however, and a caesarean procedure was performed in the 22nd hour of labor. Mark's Apgar scores were all 9 plus, and mother and baby were discharged from the hospital after 72 hours.

During Mark's first year of life his pediatric history was unremarkable with the exception of a 4-day fever that reached 102° Fahrenheit. Over this same time span Mark was reported to have displayed problems with feeding and developing a predictable sleep cycle. He had many bouts of colic and seldom slept more than 4 hours without waking. Mrs. Henderson was most concerned about his seeming unresponsiveness to her as an infant. Mark seldom smiled, seemed not to enjoy being tickled, and he seemed equally comfortable with any adult. The Hendersons reported these problems to their pediatrician, who suggested that these "problems" were routine and well within normal limits.

Mark's motor milestones emerged on schedule; however, he would often crawl about many months after he learned to walk. Unlike his motor skills, Mark's communicative behaviors were always delayed. The Hendersons reported that his only words were "Mommy" and "ball". He did, however, string together many sounds in a repetitive, flat tone of voice (e.g., "Goo, Goo, Goo, Goo"). They estimated that he had 20 to 30 words in his receptive vocabulary.

At about 24 months the Hendersons reported that Mark began to engage in a wide variety of bizarre behaviors. For example, he would open and shut certain doors in their house for 20 to 30 minutes at a time. He gazed outdoors and would shriek periodically, although they could not identify any stimulus for his vocalizations. Mark also had episodes of body-rocking and hand-flapping, and these increased in duration, amplitude, and frequency of occurrence over time.

Beginning at about 18 months of age, Mark's behavior was of such concern that his family began to curtail their involvement outside the home. At the point the family came for intervention both husband and wife were distraught about their son. They reported that they felt embarrassed to go out in public. Mrs. Henderson had refused any baby-sitting services for the prior 15 months, and she had assumed all child-care functions, quit her job, and reported feelings of exhaustion and hopelessness.

## Assessment

The assessment process focused upon three primary concerns: (a) was Mark's diagnosis accurate; (b) where should intervention begin across developmental domains; and (c) what parental concerns, needs, and competencies should be addressed?

### Diagnostic Confirmation

Because of the notorious unreliability of the autism diagnosis from one assessor to the next, the original diagnosis needed to be confirmed. Two procedures were used. First, the Hendersons were asked to see two board-certified child psychiatrists who would use a common diagnostic tool, *DSM-III* in this case, to render an opinion. After each psychiatrist conducted a 1½ hour interview and observation, they independently

arrived at an autism diagnosis. Second, it was asked that Mark participate in a 1-week observational assessment period at the early intervention program. In this context, free-field observations are made over
several days in order to pinpoint a level of behavioral severity. Across
five school days, Mark was never observed to interact with peers, he
used no functional speech, he had a tantrum whenever any request was
made of him, and when left alone he engaged in stereotypic activity for
over 80% of the time. Over time then, Mark clearly displayed the skill
deficits and behavioral excesses associated with the autism diagnosis.

*Instruction-based Assessment*

Several standardized instruments were used in order to fix a beginning point of instruction for Mark. First, the Sequenced Inventory of
Communication Development (SICD) was used to assess his receptive
and expressive language skills. The SICD is particularly useful with this
population as it demands social or communicative behavior (not merely
a pointing response) on the part of children. As expressed in months,
Mark's receptive skills were found to be at the 15-month level and his
expressive skills at the 12-month level. On the SICD, Mark produced
more words than the original parent interview had indicated. Throughout this and other testing, Mark was highly distractible, and the examiner conducted the full test over six 10-minute blocks. After every 1 or
2 minutes, the examiner gave Mark a favorite toy to play with as he
wished.

In order to determine his general cognitive skills, the Learning
Accomplishment Profile (LAP) was administered. The LAP provides a
range of scores in developmental months across eight performance
domains. For Mark, the following developmental levels were achieved:
fine-motor writing: did not score; fine-motor manipulation: 18 to 24
months; language comprehension: 18 to 30 months; language naming:
did not score; cognitive matching: 24 to 30 months; cognitive counting:
did not score; gross motor body movement: 24 to 30 months; gross
motor object movement: 18 to 24 months. Mark's failure to score on
various subtests was difficult to interpret accurately, as he was very
oppositional during testing. As a continuing measure of developmental
process, the LAP was repeated at 3-month intervals throughout Mark's
stay in the intervention program. The SICD was readministered at
6-month intervals for the same purpose.

*Family-focused Assessment*

Four separate assessment procedures were used with the family. Three of the measures were designed to give the program staff some indication of family functioning and whether any ancillary services were appropriate. These measures included the Beck Depression Inventory, the Questionnaire on Resources and Stress (Holyroyd, 1974), and the Community Interaction Checklist (Wahler, 1980). On the Beck, neither of the Hendersons reported a clinically relevant level of depression. On the Questionnaire on Resources and Stress (QRS), which measures the parents' attitude toward, and impact of, the child on the family, some problem areas emerged. Both parties were concerned about the financial impact that Mark might pose, and both parents saw him as damaging to their careers and long-term happiness. On the Community Interaction Checklist (CIC), which measures the self-imposed insularity of the family from supportive, extrafamilial community contact, the Hendersons were prototypically insular. They seldom, if ever, ventured from their home; when they did they were embarrassed by Mark. The Hendersons, it appeared, had spent considerable energy "hiding" Mark's severe handicap.

The final family-focused measure included three direct observational assessments of parent-child interaction in an analogue situation. Here, the parents are asked to switch toys and play themes with their child every 5 minutes for a total of 20 minutes. The situation is designed to examine parents' skill in managing their child's behavior. Across the three play sessions, Mark's behavior was scored as noncompliant or inappropriate 87% of the time. His parents' use of clear commands and appropriate consequences was scored on 13% of the available opportunities.

The family picture, then, highlighted the psychological toll to the Hendersons as well as their limited skills in handling their son's difficult behaviors.

## Selection and Course of Treatment

The Hendersons elected to enroll their son in the LEAP preschool program, an experimental intervention model for autistic and normally developing preschool children. Following is a description of the intervention program. Prior evaluations of the LEAP model are available in

Hoyson, Jamieson, and Strain (1984) and Strain, Jamieson, and Hoyson (1985).

## Overview of LEAP

This experimental intervention program is designed to meet the educational needs of both normally developing and autistic preschool children within an integrated classroom setting. LEAP offers parents a cost-free program operating 5 days a week in a local community public school. This program is jointly sponsored by the Department of Psychiatry, University of Pittsburgh, and the Pittsburgh Public Schools.

Two post-master's level developmental specialists provide individualized educational programming to six normally developing and six autistic preschoolers. Parents of handicapped children participate in a parent-training program designed to teach more effective skills for working with their preschoolers in school, home, and community environments. LEAP also offers consultation services to parents from physicians, child development specialists, and mental health personnel.

LEAP is comprised of four major program components: (a) referral and screening; (b) classroom instruction; (c) parent involvement and training; and (d) future educational placement planning. Each of these components will be briefly described below.

## Referral and Screening

Referrals for the preschool originate from a variety of different sources. Referrals for normally developing preschoolers originate primarily from families and friends whose children attend the community public school. Referrals for autistic children originate from: (a) local preschools serving handicapped children; (b) residential treatment programs; (c) local medical and mental health specialists; and (d) direct parent contact.

During the initial contact with the family, information is obtained concerning any existing handicapping condition, general parental concerns, provisions for transportation, and availability for parent involvement. An initial screening interview is then scheduled for interested parents. During this interview, parents are provided with a detailed description of the program and admission criteria. Specific information relating to the child's current level of functioning and parental concerns are reviewed and discussed.

For families of autistic children, a 1-week diagnostic evaluation is scheduled. The child participates in the classroom each day and the parent in one additional interview. Data are collected from preschool assessments, behavioral observations, family histories, and parent reports, as described previously.

A team meeting is then scheduled among the staff to review the assessment data. Children who are considered to be appropriate candidates for LEAP are those autistic children who typically display three of the following behavior criteria: (a) significantly delayed social skills; (b) significantly delayed language skills; (c) excessive levels of disruptive or stereotypic behaviors; and (d) minimal level of academic competencies. With families for whom it is determined that the LEAP preschool is not the most appropriate program, assistance is provided in the selection of an alternative program.

## Classroom Instruction·

*Assessment.* The first four weeks of each child's placement within the LEAP classroom is devoted to assessment of the child's current level of functioning. Three standardized preschool assessment instruments are included in the assessment process. These are: (a) the Learning Accomplishment Profile (Diagnostic Edition); (b) the McCarthy Scales of Children's Abilities; and (c) the Developmental Profile II. In addition to these standardized preschool assessments, behavioral observational data are collected on: (a) prerequisite learning skills (i.e., appropriate sitting, on-task behavior, and appropriate verbalizations); (b) independent work skills; and (c) social interaction skills. A speech and language consultant evaluates each child who is suspected of, or who demonstrates, significant delays in language development.

At the end of this assessment period, an individual program planning meeting is scheduled with the family. Short-term objectives for each child are selected from a "multiple curriculum" and from target behavior checklists completed by parents. Individualized goal plans are then developed for each child and reviewed weekly.

*Curriculum and instructional strategies.* Individualized group instruction and a multiple curriculum are two unique aspects of the LEAP classroom program. Individualized group instruction is accomplished through a continual process of assessing each child's current skill level and the selection of appropriate learning objectives. After each child's current learning objectives have been identified, they are matched to an instructional lesson contained within the LEAP multiple curriculum. The curriculum represents the incorporation of objectives from a variety of different curricular instruments. Each lesson within the curriculum is coded to identify the skill area and developmental age of the objectives that are included. Instructional lessons within the curriculum have been carefully designed by the LEAP teaching staff to include objectives from several different skill areas and to cover a broad range of developmental levels. If a lesson cannot be retrieved that contains the required objectives, a new lesson is designed and added to the curriculum file. This unique technology permits the teachers to work with children within a group instructional format while meeting the individual needs of all students, regardless of developmental level.

A staggered placement of autistic children and an instructional format hierarchy are employed within the classroom program. The rationale for these procedures is to allow for any intensive individualization that may be needed with the autistic child prior to placement in less-supervised instructional settings. Initial training in minimal competencies occurs simultaneously in a variety of different settings with a 1-to-1 adult/child ratio. During group instruction, one adult may be initially assigned to directly intervene in the handicapped child's behavior. As the child meets criterion levels of performance, the teacher/child ratio is gradually increased. This hierarchy is employed to ensure that the child achieves a minimal level of competency in particular skill domains that have been identified to be necessary for successful performance in multiple-child instructional formats.

*Social interaction training.* Social interaction training is another important component of the LEAP classroom. Systematic intervention is believed to be a necessary catalyst for the development of positive social interaction between normally developing and autistic preschoolers within the integrated classroom. The LEAP program, therefore, utilizes a variety of different intervention strategies to encourage social interaction. These include: (a) teacher prompting and reinforcement; (b) structuring the environment to facilitate interaction; (c) selection of materials to promote interaction; and, most importantly, (d) peer-mediated social interaction training.

*Evaluation.* Student progress on both academic and social skill objectives are monitored daily. For autistic preschoolers, child progress demonstrated in the classroom environment is compared with skill competencies demonstrated in the home and community. Multiple baseline designs across settings are utilized to evaluate long-term maintenance and generalization of treatment gains. Parents of all children meet with the LEAP staff every 3 months to review and plan their child's individualized program.

*Parent Involvement and Training*

Parent involvement and parent training are considered to be essential to the LEAP program. All families participate in the program in some capacity. In the classroom, parents participate in a variety of activities, which include: (a) construction of instructional materials; (b) preparation of activity centers; and, (c) provision of direct instruction. Parents of autistic children participate in a parent-training program three mornings a week. In addition, training is provided to parents in home and community environments.

Training begins with an assessment of parent and child entry level skills. Specific parent and child target behaviors are assessed through several initial play observation sessions. Child target behaviors are also determined by having parents select specific child behaviors that they would like to see either increased or decreased. All parents begin instruction by targeting for change their child's behavior that is most difficult for them.

While parents may necessarily be taught different skills to meet the educational needs of their children, all parents are provided with a core curriculum that addresses such skills as providing clear instructions, prompting and shaping successive approximations, and providing consistent consequences. Initially, parents are trained to replicate instructional procedures that project teachers have demonstrated to be most effective with their child. In addition to training on skills originally taught in the program, there are a number of specific behaviors that are most logically and effectively taught in the home or community. Examples of such skills include mealtime behaviors, grooming, and leisure-time skills.

Along with individualized training in the home, school, and community, parents are also trained to apply these skills in the classroom setting. The skill performance of parents in both individual and group instructional formats is closely monitored.

Evaluation of project participation is conducted by assessing the effects of parent training on both parent and child target behaviors. In addition, the generalization of these skills to other settings is also assessed. Nonprogrammed changes in the social functioning of the family are assessed through preintervention and follow-up assessment of stress variables within the family, extrafamily social contacts, and self-perception.

*Future Education Placement Planning*

The LEAP staff and parents work together on planning the future educational placement for LEAP's autistic preschoolers. During a program planning meeting, educational placement options are outlined for each family, and staff recommendations are reviewed. Possible future placement sites are visited by the staff as well as by the parents. It is the goal of the LEAP project to work cooperatively with the professionals who will be serving the child once he or she leaves the program. Future teachers of LEAP preschoolers are invited into the classroom to observe the child in the present classroom environment. Training is offered to future teachers on the intervention strategies that have been identified by the LEAP staff to be most effective for working with a particular child. Follow-up visits are scheduled with future teachers to monitor maintenance and generalization of child treatment gains. Parents are provided with several informational sessions that review such topics as Public Law 94-142, individualized educational plans, and the utilization of community resources.

In addition to this individual planning, the goals and objectives selected for all handicapped preschoolers while enrolled at LEAP reflect a preparation for the next environment. School "survival" skills, that is, those skills that teachers have identified to be essential for successful placement, are considered to be an integral part of the classroom curriculum. The autistic child's level of performance on these skills is closely monitored and compared to normative data on age-matched peers. Intervention strategies are designed to target specific survival skills.

*Other Treatment Issues*

Like most of the younger children seen at the LEAP program, Mark's deviant repertoire initially was not the direct focus of intervention. That is, it was not the object to reduce these behaviors with a deceleration program. Rather, it was hoped to build skills that were incompatible and more directly reinforcing to him. The vast majority of his deviant behaviors were treated in this fashion. A directly focused intervention was necessary for his shrieking behavior. In this instance, non-exclusionary time-out was employed for 30 seconds when he engaged in shrieking. This intervention was in effect for 6 weeks.

## Termination

Mark and his parents made exceptional progress at LEAP. After 2 years of intervention, Mark was performing at age-level on the LAP and SICD. His tantrums had been eliminated and he and his family now enjoyed routine experiences such as going for a ride, shopping, and visiting friends. The Hendersons were also quite skillful in their management of Mark. The only active "programming" in the home after 2 years involved a "star chart" on Mark's bedroom door that designated his chore completion and an activity reward if he completed all his chores for 1 week.

In order to prepare Mark for a regular kindergarten class, his experience at LEAP was designed to replicate many of the demands he would face in this new setting. For example, he learned to work for longer periods of time without direction and feedback, he got and replaced his own materials, and he worked in larger groups of children. Two months prior to his departure from LEAP, he spent 1 to 2 hours each day in an adjoining kindergarten classroom with an accompanying staff member.

## Follow-Up

A series of routine follow-up measures was used, as with all LEAP clients. Every 6 months, the SICD and Stanford-Binet were administered. Also, on a 6-month schedule, Mark and his parents were observed at home to test treatment maintenance for all parties.

The Hendersons are now 18 months away from active involvement at LEAP. Mark is now in 1st grade and he is progressing satisfactorily. There have been no problem behaviors noted by his teachers. His scores on the SICD and Stanford-Binet are within normal limits for his age.

The Hendersons report that Mark is doing fine at home, and the observational data confirm their judgment. The Hendersons now have a second child, a four-month-old girl. Occasionally, Mark will whine and behave in a pouty fashion when his sister is the focus of attention. The Hendersons see this behavior as normal and they have tried to engage Mark in some minor child-care responsibilities. Mrs. Henderson has not returned to work, although she has plans of doing so when her daughter is 2 years old.

## Overall Evaluation

The case of Mark and is his family was uniquely positive in outcome, and the outcome was not one that would have been predicted typically. There are several key factors in the treatment received at LEAP that likely are responsible for this level of success. The first is *intensity of intervention*. When home-programming hours are considered, Mark received approximately 1,500 hours of intervention each year for 2 years.

Mark was also *enrolled in intervention at an early age*. Although Mark certainly displayed all of the indicators of autism on entry into treatment, his timely enrollment seems important for the following reasons: (a) his deviant behaviors were successfully treated largely with incompatible behavior programming, not a common occurrence with this class of behavior; and (b) his parents were still willing to commit a large amount of time and effort to Mark's treatment, though they were quickly becoming exhausted and frustrated with him.

Finally, this program offered *daily opportunities to program for generalized behavior change* by conducting therapeutic sessions on the same behavioral targets at school, at home, and in the community.

## References

Holyroyd, J. (1974). The questionnaire on resources and stress: An instrument to measure family response to a handicapped family member. *Journal of Community Psychology, 2,* 92-94.

Hoyson, M., Jamieson, B., & Strain, P. S. (1984). Individualized group instruction for normally developing and autistic-like children: The LEAP curriculum model. *Journal of the Division for Early Childhood, 8,* 157-172.

Johnson, J., & Koegel, R. L. (1982). Behavioral assessment and curriculum development. In R. L. Koegel, A. Rincover, & A. L. Egel (Eds.), *Educating and understanding autistic children.* Boston: Little, Brown.

Koegel, R. L., & Covert, A. (1972). The relationship of self-stimulation to learning in autistic children. *Journal of Applied Behavior Analysis, 5,* 381-387.

Strain, P. S., Jamieson, B., & Hoyson, M. (1985). Class deportment and social outcomes for normally developing and autistic-like children in integrated preschool. *Journal of the Division for Early Childhood, 10,* 105-115.

Wahler, R. G. (1980). The insular mother: Her problems in parent-child treatment. *Journal of Applied Behavior Analysis, 13,* 207-219.

# Chapter 5

# Cerebral Palsy

## Michael A. Alexander

## Description of the Disorder

Cerebral palsy (CP) represents a constellation of disorders that have several common features (Molnar, 1985). The first is an insult to the nervous system that affects motor control. In general, CP refers to any lesion to the brain that occurs above the level of the brain stem. The second feature is that it occurs in utero, at birth, or within the first 5 years of life. The third and most important feature is that it is nonprogressive. However, it is often the case that a lesion that would affect motor control in the child also would have an impact on other areas, such as cognitive function, sensory disorders (deafness, blindness), motor control problems, and sensory disturbances. Finally, there are psychological problems observed in these children that have varying causes—from behavioral reaction to the disability, to dysfunctional child-rearing practice, to hyperkinetic syndromes.

The motor patterns in children with cerebral palsy fall into several discrete areas. Most systems of classification refer to either the motor pattern or the pattern of the extremity involved. The most common type of motor involvement seen in cerebral palsy is the *spastic* variety. Children with CP have some degree of injury to the cortical spinal tract that (1) affects their ability to use muscles selectively and to extinguish abnormal tone in groups they do not wish to involve directly, and (2) diminishes the rapidity with which they can turn muscles on and off. These children are characterized by brisk to hyperactive stretch reflexes, the presence of clonus, and the presence of certain primitive reflexes, such as the asymmetrical tonic neck, tonic neck, labyrinthine, or Moro reflexes.

The second type of patient pattern is the *athetoid*. These children show a pattern of movement that is characterized by the overflow and recruitment of synergistic muscles at a time when it is not appropriate. The child typically presents with grimacing and distortion of movement. These children often will exhibit the interaction of asymmetric tonic neck reflexes or tonic neck reflexes, which can inhibit directly their ability to accomplish the voluntary activity they wish to perform.

The third type of motor pattern involvement is *ataxic*. These children have deficiencies of cerebellar function, balance, and coordination of muscle groups. Many children will present with some components of the deficiencies mentioned above, but tend to fall into one category more than the others. These children are also characterized by the pattern of their involvement.

The hemiplegic child would demonstrate involvement of the arm and leg on the same side. These children are more often full term and have sustained some type of cerebrovascular accident. Children who present with the diplegic pattern have involvement of the lower extremities and to some extent may have some involvement of the upper extremities. However, as a rule, such children can be ambulatory with the aid of crutches and braces. Characteristically, these children are premature infants and at autopsy would show a periventricular leukomalacia. The quadriplegic child usually has severe involvement of both upper and lower extremities and is more often mentally affected and developmentally delayed. These children are often full-term infants and are often victims of perinatal infections or anoxic or hypoxic events.

As a child with cerebral palsy grows toward adulthood, he or she encounters myriad problems that are both physical/medical and developmental/psychological. A child with abnormal muscle tone and asymmetric strength is predisposed toward the development of musculoskeletal abnormalities. These children have a higher incidence of scoliosis, contractures in the lower extremities, and dislocated hips. Scoliosis and dislocation problems contribute to the early onset of degenerative arthritis, with resultant pain problems in the 20s and 30s. Scoliosis has a primary effect on respiratory function and, if left untreated, can progrss to right heart failure, congestive heart failure, and death. The distortion of the rib cage leads to incompetence of the gastroesophageal junction, and these children can develop gastroesophageal reflux and inhalation pneumonitis from recurrent aspiration of material from the stomach. These children and adults also are prone to epileptic disorders as a result of abnormal foci in the brain and in many cases will require long-term anticonvulsant therapy. Some of these anticonvulsants, such as phenytoin (Dilantin), contribute to a coarseness of facial features and hirsutism, which then complicate their appearance to the general public.

The physical abnormalities, decreased mobility, and distorted physical appearance contribute to isolation and difficulty in attainment of normal milestones.

## Case Identification

John is a child who first presented at 14 months of age. At that time, he could sit if propped, but was not pulling to stand. He had no language. The family's concern for the previous 5 or 6 months was that he could not use his legs normally. They have been to see a number of physicians and had not received a definitive diagnosis. He had been born at 32 weeks' gestation and had a birth weight of 1,000 gm. He was kept in the hospital for approximately 3 weeks after his birth. During that time, he was on a respirator, developed a collapsed lung, and had to have ligation of a patent ductus arteriosus. On being brought home, he was a poor feeder and did tolerate breast milk; his mother had to give up breast feeding and go to bottle feedings.

## Assessment

John had had a series of insignificant respiratory tract infections, colds, and pneumonia before his presentation at 14 months of age. At this time, he was noted to be alert, apprehensive of the strange examiner, and would follow objects about the room. He had no spontaneous speech, was attentive to his father and mother, and would attempt to make eye contact with them and flirt. He had no sitting ability and would show poor neck and upper-trunk control if stabilized at the pelvis. When shifted from side to side, he was unable to place his hands out in a protective response to catch himself. When suspended in a vertical position, under the axilla his legs would cross in the midline or scissor and his toes would point down toward the floor. His back was not scoliotic, his hips did not fully abduct, with the right hip being slightly tighter than the left. Assessment at this stage was difficult on Baley testing. He did not have the motor agility to score well. However, given the fact he seemed to be attuned to verbal input and was bright and interacting with his parents, it was felt that his cognitive ability was ahead of the gross motor deficit. Because of the asymmetry in the hips, he underwent radiographic examination, which revealed early subluxation of the hip.

## Selection of Treatment

The assessment at this point was a child who was grossly motor delayed, more so than cognitive, and who had no speech; however, he was 14 months old and had received no therapy interventions to date. Initial management was to send him for the x-ray, and then he was positioned and braced to maintain hips and abduction. He was referred to an infant neurodevelopmental therapy program where he received physical, occupational, and speech therapies. In addition, social work support was provided to the family.

Neurodevelopmental therapy involved application of management and therapy techniques to minimize the effect of primitive reflexes and to favor more normal neurodevelopmental patterns in children. This usually is administered by therapists who are certified in neurodevelopmental therapy, a position that involves participation in a postgraduate didactic and hands-on experience.

## Course of Treatment

John was reassessed at 20 months of age. At that time, he had developed some rudimentary sitting ability by using his arms for support. If tipped from side to side, he was able to extend his arms to protect himself and catch himself on forward, sideways, and, to a lesser extent, being tipped backward. He still stood in a scissored position with his feet somewhat in equinous. His hip had stabilized, there was no change in the radiographic pattern, and he was beginning to develop some tightness in his heel cords. It was decided that he would wear short leg braces to hold his ankles at 90 degrees. He continued in the physical therapy program.

The next formal assessment took place at 26 months of age. At this time, he was pulling to stand and was cruising in his short leg braces. He continued to scissor, and there was some further progression in the subluxation of his hip. Cognitively, he now was speaking in simple sentences and following simple commands without difficulty. Upper-extremity hand function had improved to the point where he could feed himself and handle his own cup. Because of the progression of the tightness in his hips and the subluxation, he was taken to the operating room and underwent obdurator nerve blocks, using 45% ethanol. He continued in the physical and occupational therapy programs. However, it was felt that given his language development and progression, he was not a candidate for speech therapy services.

At 4 years of age, he was ambulatory for short distances with the assistance of upper-extremity crutches. He was attending a preschool situation 3 half-days a week and was progressing verbally. At 6 years of age, John was enrolled in first grade and appeared to be doing well. Yet, at the end of the year, a recommendation was made that he be held back. This decision was based on the fact that he had not done as well in first grade curriculum as had been anticipated. Careful analysis revealed that John was showing some learning difficulties and, rather than holding him back and repeating the first grade, he was placed in a special classroom for the second grade and moved along.

John completed his high school curriculum and graduated in the middle of his class. He was ambulatory with the short leg braces and crutches for reasonable distances. He had come to grips with the issue of using a wheelchair for going longer distances and used one when he went to the mall or on day outings. He did not develop scoliosis over the years, and his hip remained well seated.

John's situation represents a typical course for a diplegic child with cerebral palsy. These children often have some problems with learning. However, they may show some degree of academic accomplishment by the time they graduate. Since he had demonstrated protective responses on being tipped to the side, it was clear that, ultimately, John would do well as an independent ambulator. Results of a number of investigations have indicated that if children show an absence of significant primitive reflexes and, more importantly, the presence of protective responses, they will be able to move or progress to ambulating with crutches with no difficulty (see Alexander, 1984).

From the standpoint of this child's psychological development, the salient issues that needed to be addressed over his lifetime were those of transition and enhancing his sense of self-efficacy. One of the leading causes of failure in the rehabilitation of children with CP is that they are not encouraged to become self-initiating. Nor are they expected to be responsible for their own care as they mature. Instead, they tend to be infantalized. And the health care providers interact with the parents rather than with the child. This is most problematic when the child reaches adolescence and when he or she should be treated more like an adult. Often, as adolescents, they are still dealt with as if they are in a much earlier developmental stage.

Over the course of John's development, the family encouraged him to develop friends outside of the special school situation. He was active in Cub Scouts and Boy Scouts and had opportunities to be away from his home with other children. By the time he reached his teens, he was able to realistically plan for a future career and had decided to attend trade school on graduation from high school.

## Follow-Up

Children such as John present a constellation of orthopedic problems, which are a consequence of their abnormal tone. Further, they are at risk for developmental and educational problems that result from injuries to other areas of the brain. Children with more severe motor involvement have greater difficulty with issues of transition and establishment of independence in the adult word. Many of the children with lesser problems are of the hemiplegic type. If they have normal intelligence and they demonstrate an adequate behavioral repertoire, they are much more quickly assimilated and mainstreamed. Interestingly enough, many of the children with hemiplegia have more pronounced problems with body image and fears of acceptance than the diplegic children.

## Overall Evaluation

Every child presenting with the diagnosis of cerebral palsy represents a patient who needs to be moved from childhood to adulthood and transitioned into an independent and autonomous adult. Children with cerebral palsy require careful screening and observation for associated orthopedic problems. One must anticipate possible educational or behavioral issues, intervene early, and provide appropriate treatment and training. If such efforts are made, the maturation, overall development, and adjustment of the child with cerebral palsy will be maximized.

# References

Alexander, M. A. Rehabilitation of children. (1984). In J. V. Basmajian & R. L. Kirby (Eds.), *Medical rehabilitation* (pp. 282-287). Baltimore, MD: Williams & Wilkins.

Alexander, M. A. Orthotics, adapted seating, and assistive devices. In G. E. Molnar (Ed.), *Pediatric rehabilitation* (pp. 158-175). Baltimore, MD: Williams & Wilkins.

Bleck, E. E. (1987). *Orthopaedic management in cerebral palsy.* Philadelphia: J. B. Lippincott.

Molnar, G. E. (1985). Cerebral palsy. In G. E. Molnar (Ed.), *Pediatric rehabilitation* (pp. 420-467). Baltimore, MD: Williams & Wilkins.

# Chapter 6

# Chronic Pain

Francisco X. Barrios
Dennis C. Turk
Thomas E. Rudy

## Description of the Disorder

Chronic pain is a major health problem in American society affecting millions of persons and causing great physical and emotional suffering (Holzman & Turk, 1986). One particularly frustrating aspect of chronic pain, to patient and practitioner alike, is its highly refractory nature to conventional medical treatment. To a large degree, this problem has been created by the conceptualization of chronic pain within an acute disease model, leading to unrealistic expectations on the part of the patient and inappropriate treatments on the part of the health provider (Turk, Holzman, & Kerns, 1986).

Recently, however, there is increasing evidence that chronic pain may be successfully treated by a comprehensive approach to rehabili-

AUTHOR'S NOTE: Support for the completion of this chapter was provided in part by a National Institute of Dental Research Grant DEO7514-02 and a National Institute of Arthritis Musculoskeletal and Skin Diseases Grant ARNS38698-01 awarded to the second author.

tation that considers both the medical-psychological and the socio-psychological aspects of chronic pain (Mayer, Gatchel, Mayer, Kishino, Keeley, & Mooney, 1987; Meilman, Skultety, Guck, & Sullivan, 1985). Such treatment appears to be effective in improving mood disturbance, reducing medication use and overutilization of the health care system, and enhancing the likelihood of returning patients to employment.

This chapter describes the treatment of a chronic pain sufferer who manifested many of the social, emotional, cognitive, and psychological disruptions that characterize many chronic pain patients. The treatment was conducted at the Pain Evaluation and Treatment Institute of the University of Pittsburgh School of Medicine and Presbyterian-University Hospital, a major comprehensive pain center.

## Case Identification

Ron C. is a 35-year-old, white, married male who was initially evaluated at the Pain Evaluation and Treatment Institute (PETI) in March, 1987. Ron was born and grew up in rural Pennsylvania and dropped out of school when he was in the 10th grade. While still in school, he began his employment history as a part-time stockboy, a position that entailed unloading trucks and stocking shelves. On dropping out of high school, Ron joined the U.S. Army and was stationed in Vietnam. During his time in the army, Ron attended Supply Clerk School and drove a truck. After completing his military service, Ron returned to his hometown and began a 12-year career as a laborer, with a particular interest in bricklaying. Eventually, he devoted most of his time to bricklaying and had a steady work history, spending 10 years with one employer. In October, 1984, Ron went to work for another employer, also as a bricklayer, where he was employed for approximately 2 months before he was injured. Subsequent to his injury, which will be described below, he was unable to return to work, although he attempted to do so on several occasions.

Ron married for the first time on his return to Pennsylvania from military service and he remained married for approximately 12 years. His wife left him and their 10-year-old son approximately 2 months after the date of his injury, at least in part due to pain-related adjustment problems. At the time that he was seen at PETI, he had been remarried for approximately 1½ years, and he and his second wife had an infant son.

## Presenting Complaints

Ron's chronic pain problem began with an on-the-job injury that occurred in December, 1984. He and his co-workers were carrying a sign while walking on a broken concrete driveway. Ron fell backward, landed on his back, and a piece of concrete struck him directly on the lower back. The sign that he was carrying then fell on top of him. The onset of pain was immediate after the accident, and the pain involved primarily his lower back, although there was also pain radiating down his right leg. He, in addition, experienced intermittent neck and interscapular pain, with occasional headaches. By the time he was evaluated at PETI, Ron spent up to 18 hours a day either lying down or sitting.

Immediately after the accident, Ron's injury was treated conservatively, with analgesic medication, heat packs, and chiropractic manipulations, all of which were unsuccessful in relieving his symptoms. As the problem remained unsuccessfully treated, Ron began to visit a series of physicians (12 to 15) in a search for a cure. In addition to multiple physician visits, he also underwent numerous diagnostic tests, including a CT scan and an MRI scan. These tests failed to show any evidence of disc rupture or other physiological basis for the pain, with the exception of slight disc degenerative disease of the lumbar spine (generally acknowledged by his physicians as insufficient to account for his symptoms). He attended a back clinic that focused exclusively on progressive exercises using machines; however, this regimen aggravated his pain. He was eventually referred to a neurosurgeon who concluded that there was no surgical remediation for his problem (i.e., there was no requirement for surgery). Therefore, he was referred to the PETI for rehabilitation.

## History

Due to his limited educational background and his interests overwhelmingly oriented toward manual labor and physical activity, Ron found that his life was severely disrupted as a result of his injury and subsequent chronic pain problem. As part of his Workmen's Compensation case, Ron was referred to a psychologist for a vocational assessment when it became apparent that return to his previous occupation might not be feasible. The results of this assessment indicated that Ron's Full-Scale Wechsler Adult Intelligence Scale (WAIS) IQ score was 94, with a verbal IQ score of 88 and a performance IQ score of 108. However, his performance on the Wide Range Achievement Test (WRAT) demonstrated his educational deficits, suggesting that his reading achievement was at the fourth grade level, and his spelling and arithmetic achievement were at the fifth grade levels. His occupational interests, as might well be expected, focused on pursuits such as building, redecorating, and other physical activities. Not unexpectedly, as the pain made it impossible for Ron to pursue these vocational or recreational activities, he experienced a corresponding increase in dysphoric mood and a decrease in his self-perceptions of competence and self-esteem. To compound the problem, when a copy of this vocational assessment became available to Ron, he misunderstood the content and interpreted it to mean that he possessed limited intellectual ability, thus further increasing his depression.

Another factor that exacerbated Ron's depression and sense of helplessness was the reaction of the insurance carrier responsible for his Workmen's Compensation claim. On referral to PETI by his neurosurgeon, center staff contacted the insurance carrier to notify them of his impending evaluation. After Ron was evaluated and found to be an appropriate candidate for treatment, efforts were directed to obtain preauthorized approval for treatment from this carrier. After initial contact with the adjuster, this approval was initially given and within 1 or 2 days rescinded by the supervisor, who felt that this treatment was unnecessary and excessively expensive.

Subsequent telephone contacts and correspondence from the medical director of PETI to the insurance company were unsuccessful in securing approval for treatment or in persuading the insurance company personnel that Ron was, in fact, experiencing pain and emotional distress secondary to the pain and that he was not malingering, exaggerating his symptoms, or simply attempting to evade work and go on permanent and total disability. The insurance company's position made treatment of Ron's pain problem extremely difficult, in that he lived a considerable distance from the center and he was financially unable to afford either the hotel lodging or transportation expenses required to make the daily commute.

These events contributed significantly to Ron's deteriorating emotional state and, approximately 6 weeks after his initial evaluation, Ron was brought to the center by his wife, as he was manifesting symptoms of a major depressive episode and admitted that he was contemplating suicide. Ron was evaluated at Western Psychiatric Institute and Clinic. His diagnosis of major depression, single episode, was confirmed. He was prescribed a trial of antidepressants (amitryptiline) and was referred to his local mental health center for outpatient treatment. It was at this point that PETI staff made the decision to admit Ron for immediate treatment without authorization, with help from Ron's attorney who devised a way to help him defray his expenses.

## Assessment

Evaluation at PETI consisted of a half-day assessment procedure that included examinations by a physician, a physical therapist, and a psychologist. In addition to this, Ron, like all other patients evaluated at PETI, completed the Multiaxial Assessment of Pain Taxonomy System (MAP) developed at PETI specifically for the assessment of chronic pain (Turk & Rudy, 1987, 1988), as well as the Center for Epidemiological Studies Depression Scale (CES-D) (Radloff, 1977) and the Locke-Wallace Marital Adjustment Scale (Locke & Wallace, 1959).

### Physical Examination

Neurological examination was found to be entirely within normal limits. No sensory abnormalities or reflex changes were observed in either Ron's arms or legs. No evidence of focal muscle weakness, atrophy, or fasciculations was found. The only noteworthy physical finding based on his examination was tenderness over the right buttock.

The physical therapy examination found that Ron was experiencing significant postural and gait abnormalities that were judged to be mechanical in nature and secondary to the original soft tissue injury suffered at the time of his accident. His musculoskeletal examination revealed that he had a flat lumbar spine and a tendency to hold his shoulders back and splint his upper back. Extreme tenderness was found over the right sacroiliac joint involving the right pyriformis muscle. Limitations in range of motion were observed by the therapist when Ron was asked to perform forward bends, back bends, or side bends, accompanied by increases in pain. When lying down, he was observed to manifest tightness in all muscle groups in his legs and he was unable to do sit-ups, as this resulted in increased pain. Tightness and restricted range of motion was also observed when Ron was asked to stand on all four extremities.

## Psychological Examination

Psychological evaluation indicated that Ron was displaying a considerable amount of verbal and nonverbal pain behavior at the time of the interview and administration of the Pain Behavior Checklist (Turk, Wack, & Kerns, 1985). Included were an antalgic gait, poor posture, moaning, and grimacing. Nevertheless, he was judged by the examiner to be cooperative and a reliable reporter. He demonstrated normal levels of social skill, and his interactions with his wife and the examiner were appropriate. Ron reported at that time that his normal level of physical activity had been significantly impaired by the pain. He described his efforts to remain active, which usually lasted no longer than an hour and were followed by a considerable amount of down time, often lasting the remainder of the day. Recreational activity was almost nonexistent. Ron initially maintained that his mood was "okay" and denied any changes in his functioning. His wife, however, disagreed with this and reported that she had noticed increases in dysphoric mood, irritability, and some social withdrawal. Ron agreed when faced with this information and added that he was also experiencing some sleep disturbance and appetite changes. These, however, were not deemed to be indicative of any major depressive disorder by the examiner.

Ron and his wife both acknowledged that there had been a degree of marital discord in their relationship dating back almost to the time of their marriage. They reported a two-week separation, apparently precipitated by the wife's father and his insistence that Ron was "faking" his pain, urging the wife to leave him. Ron's wife indicated that she ultimately came to the conclusion that Ron was indeed suffering pain and she returned to the relationship, severing her contact with her father as well.

The examining psychologist felt that the limitations on Ron's functioning in his vocational, social, and recreational activities were having a significant impact on Ron, leading him to view himself as inadequate in these areas. Moreover, the lack of alternative job skills was felt to be a major concern for Ron, insofar as he had been told by other physicians he had consulted that return to his activities as a bricklayer was unlikely. He did manifest some initiative prior to the evaluation date, in that he had already made contact with the Department of Vocational Rehabili-

tation and had started to make plans to obtain his high school equivalency certificate. Despite these problems and his marital difficulties
described above, Ron was not judged to be suffering from a major
depressive episode at the time of initial evaluation and he was given a
diagnosis of adjustment disorder with mixed emotional features.

In addition to the interviews and examinations, the assessment of
Ron's chronic pain was also dependent on his scores on the Multidimensional Pain Inventory (MPI), which is used in the MAP taxomet-
ric classification system (Turk & Rudy, 1988). As has been described
elsewhere (Kerns, Turk, & Rudy, 1985), the MPI is an assessment
instrument that has been developed exclusively for use with chronic
pain patients and has demonstrated good psychometric properties when
used with this population. This pain inventory consists of 13 separate
scales, divided into two main categories: the psychosocial axis and the
behavioral axis. The former includes the following scales: (a) pain
severity; (b) pain interference with life satisfaction; (c) life control;
(d) affective distress; and (e) social support. The behavioral axis includes the following scales: (a) punishing responses from significant
other; (b) solicitous responses from significant other; (c) distracting
responses from significant other; (d) household chores; (e) outdoor
work around home; (f) activities away from home; (g) social activities;
and (h) general activity level.

Ron's MPI scale scores, plotted as T scores ($M = 50$, $SD = 10$) in
Figure 6.1, indicated that he fell into the cluster of patients that had
been empirically derived and classified as dysfunctional (Turk & Rudy,
1988). Compared to other chronic pain patients (the normative population for the MAP and used to derive the T scores displayed in Figure
6.1), Ron's life control and affective distress scores were all close to
the mean. His pain severity score was approximately one-half a standard deviation above the mean, while his interference and social support
scores were approximately one standard deviation above the mean. On
the behavioral axis, Ron reported that his interactions with his spouse
were predominantly characterized by distracting responses (that is,
responses that encourage coping responses when in pain). His score on
this scale was about one and one-half standard deviations above the
mean, while his scores on punishing responses and solicitous responses
were about one-half a standard deviation below the mean and one-half
a standard deviation above the mean, respectively.

Ron's level of activity was deemed to be low, even for a chronic pain
patient population. His overall activity level was approximately one and

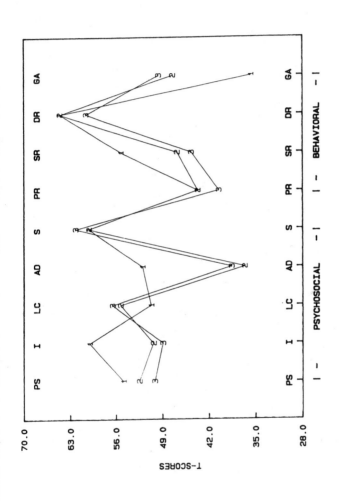

**Figure 6.1.** Ron C.'s T scores on the MPI.

NOTE: 1 = Pretreatment assessment, 2 = Posttreatment assessment, 3 = 6-month follow-up, assessment. MPI scale abbreviations are as follows: PS = pain severity, I = interference, LC = life control, AD = affective distress, S = support, PR, = punishing responses, SR = solicitous responses, DR = distracting responses, GA = general activity.

one-half standard deviations below the mean (see Figure 6.1), as were his scores on household chores and activities away from home. His social activities score was about one standard deviation below the mean; his outdoor work score was below, but within one-half a standard deviation from, the mean. Ron reported that his emotional reactions to pain, as measured by the Pain Experience Scale (Turk & Rudy, 1985), were low (about one standard deviation below the mean), while his worry reactions were almost one standard deviation above the mean. His CES-D score was about one-half a standard deviation below the mean for chronic pain patients and was not judged to be at a clinically significant level. His marital adjustment, as measured by the Locke-Wallace scale, indicated that he was at about the mean for chronic pain patients and above the cutoff that distinguishes between distressed and nondistressed relationships.

## Selection of Treatment

Based on the results of his evaluation, Ron was assessed to be an appropriate candidate for an intensive rehabilation program at PETI. This conclusion was based on several factors, including the failure of conventional medical treatment to alleviate his pain complaint, absence of organic pathology amenable to surgical intervention, and determination that his pain was predominantly muscular in origin and aggravated by postural and gait abnormalities. In addition, it was felt that, although he was not suffering from a severe affective disorder at the time of evaluation, Ron was at risk for developing such a disorder, given his limited vocational skills and the low likelihood of returning to premorbid levels of physical activity. It was therefore determined that he could benefit from a program designed to increase his level of activity and provide him with self-management coping skills gradually and simultaneously.

The PETI clinical team decided to offer Ron participation in an intensive pain rehabilitation program that would meet every day for a 3 week period for 7 hours a day. This treatment program consists of individual and group physical therapy, occupational therapy, psychological stress management and coping skills training, and medication management. It was felt that this would provide Ron with a comprehensive, interdisciplinary approach to his chronic pain complaint that would enable him to become more skilled at managing his pain.

## Course of Treatment

The intensive pain rehabilitation program in which Ron participated was a highly structured 3-week program conducted primarily in a group format. Groups of up to 12 patients are periodically admitted for treatment at PETI as a cohort that begins treatment together, develops group cohesiveness, and is discharged after a 3-week program. The treatment sessions are conducted by team members that include a physician, psychologists, physical therapist, occupational therapist, and nurse practitioner. Each discipline is responsible for developing a curriculum that is presented to patients during the group sessions. These sessions are supplemented with individual contact as the need arises for each patient.

The physical therapy curriculum includes not only daily exercise sessions that are individualized for each group member, but also a series of lectures designed to increase patients' understanding of the anatomical and physiological bases for their pain and of physical activities they can utilize in order to better self-manage and alleviate their pain. Patients are taught the reasons they continue to have pain despite previous treatment interventions, and these (primarily passive) modalities are contrasted with the active regimen they will follow in treatment. The contributions of poor posture and distorted gait to chronic pain is discussed, as are effects of deconditioning caused by prolonged physical inactivity. Reasons for previous failures with physical therapy (boredom, poor technique, worry) are discussed. Patients are also introduced to progressive exercise regimens and are taught how to use various self-management modalities at home, such as heat and ice massage, when pain flares up after discharge.

The occupational therapy curriculum covers such topics as body mechanics and energy conservation. These principles are discussed as they apply to activities of daily living, housekeeping, and leisure activities. Demonstrations and structured simulations of lifting, carrying, pushing, and pulling are conducted.

The physician component of the curriculum includes discussions of the role of physicians in society and the health care system, the concepts of impairment and disability, the functioning of the compensation and insurance systems, and information concerning recent developments in the area of pain research, with an emphasis on corrected popular misconceptions.

The nurse practitioner's curriculum includes sessions devoted to information concerning the most common analgesic medications, their side effects, mode of operation, and possible interactions with one another. Patients are also educated concerning other medications commonly prescribed for chronic pain, such as anti-inflammatory drugs, antidepressants, and hypnotics. Other sessions cover life-style issues that are likely to be affected by chronic pain, such as diet and weight loss, blood pressure, smoking, and human sexuality.

The psychological component of the treatment program is actually composed of two distinct curriculae. The first of these focuses on providing group members with skills in the areas of progressive muscle relaxation, problem solving, and general stress management. Group members are introduced to the concept of coping and its application to pain management. They are also exposed to a definition of stress that emphasizes its inevitability in everyday life and encourages patients to conceptualize stress as a natural event, rather than as a catastrophe. The importance of perceived stress, rather than actual stress, is noted. Once they have begun to reconceptualize stress and coping in these ways, patients are introduced to progressive muscle relaxation and cognitive problem solving as strategies designed to combat the psychological, cognitive, and behavioral components of stress reactions. Once the basics of these coping skills have been covered, considerable attention is devoted in the group setting to rehearsing these skills, troubleshooting as these skills are applied to ongoing concerns in patients' lives, and perfecting the use of these techniques until patients become proficient in them (for more extended discussion see Turk, Meichenbaum, & Genest, 1983).

The second psychological component of the program introduces group members to the ideas that: (a) the term *psychological* is not synonymous with psychiatric and that people with pain can and do have psychological components to the pain that are normal and predictable; (b) there are a number of "myths" surrounding chronic pain (e.g., pain is "real" or "psychogenic," there must be a cure for all pain, pain is a function of tissue damage only) of which they need to become aware; (c) their pain affects and is affected by these preexisting beliefs, as are their emotions and behavior; (d) people with pain are not typically aware of these beliefs and need to be trained to identify their occurrence in their daily lives; and (e) their emotions and behavior, as well as their pain, can be positively influenced when these beliefs are reevaluated and replaced with more realistic and rational self-statements.

As Ron entered this treatment program, the judgment of the clinical staff was that he was, indeed, clinically depressed, but was nevertheless highly motivated to be in the group and was working hard in all aspects of the program. His progress in the following areas was assessed on an ongoing basis: (a) use of medications; (b) physical activity and mobility; (c) mood; and (d) cognitive-attitudinal processes.

Upon admission, Ron was taking 6 to 8 Excedrin tablets each day, alternating with 200 mg of Advil and up to 2 Darvocet tablets as needed. He had also been prescribed 50 mg of amitryptiline each night, but had discontinued it for several days before starting treatment. The amitryptilyne was resumed at the previous dosage on admission to the program, was increased to 100 mg after two days of treatment, to 150 mg after 1 week of treatment, and to 200 mg after 1½ weeks. He was maintained on this dosage due to sleep difficulties until the end of treatment and was discharged on this same dosage. His use of Excedrin and Darvocet was discontinued within a day or two of beginning treatment. His use of Advil was placed on a time-contingent basis, rather than on an as-needed basis, and limited to 2 tablets 4 times a day until discharge, at which time this was also discontinued.

Ron's physical activity and mobility increased steadily over the course of treatment. He worked extremely hard at the physical exercises, to the point that he overexerted himself during the second week and aggravated his pain in the sacroiliac joint, necessitating a trial with a sacroiliac belt designed to provide greater support. In his work with occupational therapy, he demonstrated amelioration in his efforts to improve his body mechanics, although he was not able to markedly increase his tolerances, which were assessed at 40 minutes for sitting, 30 minutes standing, one mile for walking, 15 lb lifting from floor to waist, and 50 lb lifting from waist to chest level. He was, however, successful in correcting his antalgic gait by the end of treatment.

Ron's mood demonstrated considerable improvement over the course of the 3-week program (see Figure 6.1). By the end of treatment, his CES-D score was 13, which was lower than his score at initial evaluation (prior to the onset of the major depressive episode). This is all the more remarkable, given the fact that during the second week of treatment there was a fire in his home, which necessitated his family moving out and staying with relatives and caused further financial strain. He demonstrated great ability to reformulate this crisis by noting that "the important thing is that no one was hurt" and that "what was lost can always be replaced."

He did experience a temporary setback at the beginning of the third week, when he appeared to be quite depressed and noncommunicative. When he was seen for an individual session, he indicated that his landlord was attempting to hold him responsible for the fire damage, although it had been determined that the cause was a faulty electrical outlet. He stated that he felt "like taking my cane and wrapping it around his neck." The reason for his intense reaction was that he had done a considerable amount of extra work repairing the home prior to the fire and felt that this was not being appreciated by the landlord. However, he responded extremely well to cognitive restructuring, focusing on how his beliefs about the way the landlord "should" behave were not realistic and what he could tell himself instead. He also responded well to modeling and rehearsal that sought to convey to Ron how he could change his behavior toward the landlord in a businesslike and interpersonally effective manner.

Ron's ability to engage in cognitive and attitudinal changes over the course of treatment was excellent. Despite his lack of formal education, he demonstrated above average ability to understand psychological concepts. Noteworthy among the changes he underwent in treatment was his gradual abandonment of the idea that he "had to return to bricklaying" or his productive work career would be over and he would be totally disabled. Moreover, he spent considerable time explaining to his wife the material he was learning in treatment and, in fact, functioned as her therapeutic support when she became overwhelmed by the fire. He complied fully with all assignments and, at the staff's suggestion, purchased a copy of the book *Feeling Good* (Burns, 1980), read it during his time off in the evenings, and integrated this material into the discussions during the psychology sessions. By the end of treatment, he was able to use relaxation, problem solving, and cognitive restructuring appropriately on an ongoing basis.

## Termination

When Ron ended treatment after 3 weeks, he had made significant cognitive and behavioral changes. He was not judged to be at maximum medical improvement at discharge (that is to say, no longer in need of further medical intervention), but it was noted that he had made significant changes in his gait, had decreased his verbal and nonverbal pain behavior to the point where it was nonexistent, and he had decreased his use of analgesic medication appreciably. His level of depression had significantly improved through a combination of cognitive therapy and pharmacotherapy; he had modified his vocational goals significantly and was no longer viewing return to work as a bricklayer as his only option. He was discharged with diagnoses of: (a) mechanical back pain, secondary to original injury, improved; (b) severe posture and gait disturbance, secondary to the back pain, improved; (c) adjustment disorder with mixed emotional features, secondary to the original injury, improved; and (d) major depression, single episode, secondary to the original injury, improved. He was discharged with a recommendation to undergo 1 to 3 injections of a local anesthetic to the sacroiliac joint, followed by stretching physical therapy exercises. He was placed on a home exercise program that included walking on a daily basis, stretching exercises on a daily basis, and continued relaxation and stress management. He was also informed that he should contact the psychology staff on an as-needed basis. Ron informed the staff he was prepared to begin study for his high school equivalency certificate by enrolling in classes within a few weeks of completing treatment.

## Follow-Up

Six months after termination Ron had maintained his gains (see Figure 6.1). He was enrolled in classes to obtain his high school equivalency certificate. He continued to practice his cognitive and behavioral coping skills and was successful in preventing a recurrence of his depression. His marital relationship improved, as he continued to instruct his wife in the techniques he had learned in treatment. He also related that he had resumed relations with his father-in-law and had undertaken to share with him the skills he had learned at PETI when the father-in-law ran into some life stresses of his own and started to become depressed. As a result of his experiences at PETI and his work with his family members, Ron developed an interest in the helping professions and was contemplating going beyond the high school equivalency certificate and attending college. He also began volunteering his services at PETI and was a guest speaker at a subsequent treatment program, where he communicated his experiences to current patients in treatment.

## Overall Evaluation

Perhaps the best overall evaluation of this case is provided by Ron himself. At a guest lecture at PETI, he stated the following:

> I'm still in . . . pain; but, since I've been through this program and following all the exercises and therapy, this is what I have accomplished: It's there, I don't need to show it, I don't need sympathy or pity from anybody, it's there and I deal with it. I went for 3 years through a vicious cycle of doctor after doctor . . . nobody could pinpoint what was wrong with me. I had 16 years of construction work as a bricklayer, I was very active and physically fit until my injury, so this was very frustrating to me . . . just sitting at home, rotting away . . . nobody helping me . . . telling me what's wrong . . . correcting it. I was on hold for 3 years and . . . your mind can play some pretty funny games with you. I was getting very depressed . . . locking myself up in the house . . . causing arguments with people. What I've learned . . . is that there was a lot of negative thinking, not enough positive thinking in my mind at the time. . . . Any little problem, after a period of 3 years, I could blow it up to be this big. . . . I came this close to putting a gun to my head. . . . I'm glad I didn't do that now. I have so much to live for now. . . . I didn't like myself (then), but as I got in here, I started picking up what they were teaching me. I pushed myself hard and hurt more, but (was told) No pain, no gain. That's right! . . . I felt this was my last shot, I'm going to do it, and I did it.

## References

Burns, D. D. (1980). *Feeling good: The new mood therapy*. New York: William Morrow.

Holzman, A. D., & Turk, D. C. (Eds.). (1986). *Pain management: A handbook of psychological treatment approaches*. New York: Pergamon.

Kerns, R. D., Turk, D. C., & Rudy, T. E. (1985). The West Haven-Yale multidimensional pain inventory (WHYMPI). *Pain*, 345-356.

Locke, H. J., & Wallace, K. M. (1959). Short marital adjustment and prediction tests: Their reliability and validity. *Marriage and Family Living, 21*, 251-255.

Mayer, T. G., Gatchel, R. J., Mayer, H., Kishino, N. D., Keeley, J., & Mooney, V. (1987). A prospective two-year study of functional restoration in industrial low back injury. *Journal of the American Medical Association, 258*, 1763-1767.

Meilman, P. W., Skultety, F. M., Guck, T. P., & Sullivan, K. (1985). Benign chronic pain: 18-month to ten-year follow-up of a multidisciplinary pain unit treatment program. *Clinical Journal of Pain, 1*, 131-137.

Radloff, L. (1977). The CES-D scale. A self-report depression scale for research in the general population. *Applied Psychological Measurement, 1*, 385-401.

Turk, D. C., Holzman, A. D., & Kerns, R. D. (1986). Chronic pain. In K. Holroyd & T. Creer (Eds.), *Self-management of chronic disease*. New York: Academic Press.

Turk, D. C., Meichenbaum, D., & Genest, M. (1983). *Pain and behavioral medicine: A cognitive-behavioral perspective.* New York: Guilford.

Turk, D. C., & Rudy, T. E. (1985, October). *Pain experience: Assessing the cognitive component.* Paper presented at the annual meeting of the American Pain Society, Dallas, TX.

Turk, D. C., & Rudy, T. E. (1987). Assessment of chronic pain patients. *Behaviour Research and Therapy, 25,* 237-246.

Turk, D. C., & Rudy, T. E. (1988). Toward an empirically derived taxonomy of chronic pain patients: Integration of psychological assessment data. *Journal of Consulting and Clinical Psychology, 56,* 233-238.

Turk, D. C., Wack, J. T., & Kerns, R. D. (1985). An empirical examination of the "pain behavior" construct. *Journal of Behavioral Medicine, 9,* 119-130.

# Chapter 7

# Epilepsy

## Bruce P. Hermann

## Description of the Disorder

Epilepsy is one of the most common of the neurological disorders affecting from 1% to 2% of the population, or some 2 to 4 million Americans (Zielinski, 1982). As such, it is a disorder that a variety of mental health professionals are likely to come into contact with, especially since epilepsy is often associated with an increased risk of a multiplicity of psychosocial problems. Unfortunately, most graduate programs in the allied health sciences provide little or no training regarding epilepsy and its consequences. And practitioners and clinicians often find themselves ill-prepared to meet the needs of individuals with epilepsy whose cases are further complicated by social, behavioral, or vocational problems.

A brief description of epilepsy, its classification, and treatment will be given in this chapter. A case will be presented that illustrates many of the complexities involved in dealing with an individual with intractable epilepsy.

Seizures can be a symptom of many underlying diseases, but epilepsy per se is defined as a condition where two or more seizures occur unrelated to an acute provocation, such as meningitis, drug withdrawal, or withdrawal from alcohol. An epileptic seizure results from sudden, excessive, rapid firing of neurons (nerve cells), and produces a change in the individual's awareness of the environment, loss of consciousness, and/or uncontrollable body movements (Hughes, 1980).

Many different types of seizures exist. Table 7.1 presents the most commonly utilized international system for the classification of epileptic seizures. Briefly, most seizures can be placed into one of two major categories: partial seizures and generalized seizures. Generalized seizures refer to those attacks that involve both cerebral hemispheres from the initial onset of the seizure. As seen in Table 7.1, there are several specific types of generalized seizures including absence seizures, generalized tonic-clonic seizures, myoclonic attacks, and others. The other group of seizures refers to attacks that begin in one part of one hemisphere: so-called partial epilepsies. Partial epilepsies can be divided into three major types: simple, complex, and secondarily generalized. The difference between simple and complex partial seizures is that there is loss of consciousness in the latter. Secondarily generalized seizures refer to a generalized tonic-clonic seizure that originates from a focal lesion. Sometimes these spells are preceded by a clear-cut simple or complex partial attack. The individual in the case presented below suffered from complex partial seizures. Therefore, further information will be presented regarding this particular seizure type.

Complex partial seizures are the single most common type found in adults. They usually occur when there is abnormal neuronal activity in a part of the brain known as the temporal lobe, although these seizures can originate from other areas. The temporal lobes, for reasons yet unknown, are more susceptible to seizures than other parts of the brain. From an observer's viewpoint, when a complex partial seizure begins, it causes a change in the person's behavior. A strange look may appear on the face. The person may stare for a few seconds, may turn his or her head to one side, and may begin to have "automatisms" (i.e., movements of the body over which the person has no control). The individual may smack his or her lips, chew, rub hands, and/or walk about aimlessly. This typically occurs for a minute or two before the person gradually regains awareness of his or her surroundings (Hughes, 1980).

The major form of treatment of the epilepsies involves the administration of anticonvulsant medications. Table 7.2 lists some of the major anticonvulsants and specific characteristics of each drug. Despite the development of newer and more effective medications, only about 50% of the population of individuals with epilepsy achieve *complete* control

**Table 7.1** Classification of Seizures

---

*Partial Seizures*

A. Simple Partial (consciousness not impaired)
   1. With motor signs (Jacksonian)
   2. With somatosensory and special sensory signs
   3. With autonomic signs
   4. With psychic symptoms

B. Complex Partial (consciousness impaired)
   1. Simple partial onset followed by impaired consciousness
   2. Impaired consciousness at onset

C. Secondarily Generalized (partial onset evolving to generalized tonic-clonic seizures

*Generalized Seizures*

A. Absence (petit mal)
B. Myoclonic
C. Tonic-clonic (grand mal)
D. Clonic
E. Tonic
F. Atonic (drop attacks)

---

of their seizures. The remaining 50% continue to have seizures of varying frequency with approximately 10% to 20% of all individuals having poorly controlled seizures.

Finally, epilepsy is associated with a wide variety of significant psychosocial problems in our society (Laidlaw & Laidlaw, 1982). There still remains a considerable amount of stigma and discrimination associated with the disorder, employers are often reluctant to hire individuals with epilepsy, learning and academic underachievement problems are overrepresented among school children with epilepsy, and rates of a variety of emotional problems are elevated in epilepsy as a result of the organic, social, and other stresses associated with the disorder (see Whitman & Hermann, 1986).

In summary, epilepsy is one of the most common of the neurological disorders. It is associated with a wide spectrum of social and psychological problems. A significant segment of the population of people with epilepsy remain intractable to treatment via anticonvulsant medications.

A case of an adult with epilepsy is presented, who had a long-standing seizure disorder, continued to experience seizures despite the use of a wide variety of anticonvulsant medications, suffered from some

**Table 7.2** Properties of Commonly Used Anti-Epileptic Drugs

| Drug | Optimal plasma levels mcg/(ml) | Half-life in hours | Unwanted side effects and toxicity | Efficacy of drug in terms of seizure types |
|---|---|---|---|---|
| Carbamazepine | 4-8 | 12 ± 3 | Vertigo, diplopia, ataxia, blood dyscrasias | Generalized tonic-clonic seizures and all types of partial seizures |
| Ethosuximide | 40-100 | 30 ± 6 | Anorexia, headache, lethargy, hiccups | Absences, absence status |
| Phenobarbital | 15-40 | 96 ± 12 | Sleepiness, para-doxical excitement in children, rash | Generalized tonic-clonic seizures and all types of partial seizures |
| Primidone | 5-15 | 12 ± 6 | Sedation, nausea, ataxia | Generalized tonic-clonic seizures and all types of partial seizures |
| Phenytoin | 10-20 | 24 ± 12 | Ataxia, drowsiness, gum hypertrophy, skin rash | Generalized tonic-clonic seizures and all types of partial seizures |
| Valproic acid | 40-100 | 12 ± 6 | Nausea, vomiting, cramps, weight gain, hepatic toxicity | Absences, myoclonic, atonic seizures, general-ized tonic-clonic seizures |

significant psychosocial complications of epilepsy, and sought treatment of her epilepsy via surgical means. Through a detailed presentation of her previous history, her surgical workup, and results of neuropsychological and behavioral testing (both pre- and postoperatively), we will review the outcome of an important approach to intractable epilepsy and the psychological contributions to that treatment.

## Case Identification

Sandra is a 21-year-old right-handed female who was referred to this epilepsy center by the local chapter of the Epilepsy Foundation. She experienced her first seizure at the age of 11 months; the etiology of her epilepsy was unknown. She continued to experience some seizures in infancy, but the spells spontaneously ceased for at least a few years. The seizures then suddenly reoccurred several years later (at approximately the age of 4) and have been present ever since. Most of the seizures follow a fairly typical course. They begin with an aura described as a "strange feeling" and a warm sensation that comes over her head and face. This sensation may last only a few seconds and the patient is aware that she is beginning to have a seizure and may try to sit down or reach a safe place at this time. Shortly thereafter she loses consciousness. According to witnesses, she appears to be confused and unaware of her surroundings and will not respond if spoken to. Occasionally, she may try to talk but her verbalizations do not make sense. At times she manifests a variety of automatisms characterized by purposeless, non-goal-directed motor activity (i.e., fussing with her clothes, manipulating some object in her immediate environment, lip smacking and chewing movements). At times she may ambulate and appears to be wandering aimlessly. These seizures may last for as short a period of time as 1 minute, and have occasionally lasted for as long as 15 minutes. Once the spell ends she is very tired, has a headache, is somewhat confused and groggy, and may sleep. Her expressive speech is also dysfluent following the seizure.

In addition to these complex partial attacks, the patient experiences secondarily generalized tonic-clonic seizures in that the spells begin as above, and then proceed into a tonic-clonic seizure. On several occasions she had periods of status epilepticus (extended periods of seizure activity) and had to be hospitalized. These episodes always occurred when she stopped taking her medications. In the past, Sandra has been on a wide variety of anticonvulsant medications, none of which have satisfactorily controlled her seizure disorder. At present she is taking two medications (Mebaral and Dilantin).

Sandra most recently worked as a secretary for a brief period of time. Her last employment was approximately 2 years ago and before that she worked at a fast food restaurant for approximately 1½ years. She says that she left her job as a secretary because she had problems in comprehending and remembering phone messages. This was a recurring complaint throughout the interview in that she repeatedly mentioned problems in comprehension and memory. She stated that these difficulties were exacerbated by her medications and that, at present, she experienced approximately five seizures per month. The seizures have caused difficulties for her in that many employers are reluctant to hire her because they are afraid that she might "scare off" customers in a store if she were to have a seizure at work. Further, because of her epilepsy she cannot drive. Therefore, she has transportation problems that prevent her from taking advantage of some job openings that are some distance from her home.

Sandra came to the center seeking evaluation as a possible surgical candidate. She wanted to be evaluated for surgery so that she might be relieved of her seizures and subsequently lead a more normal life-style.

## Assessment

The patient underwent complete neuropsychological evaluation, intensive 24-hour closed circuit TV-EEG monitoring of her seizure activity with both scalp and subdural strip electrodes, intracarotid sodium amytal assessment in order to determine speech dominance and memory function, and social service evaluation. Table 7.3 lists the neuropsychological and behavioral and emotional measures that were administered as part of the assessment. As can be seen, Sandra is currently functioning in the borderline range of intellectual ability, with Verbal, Performance, and Full-Scale IQ scores of 76, 79, and 76, respectively.

Formal assessment of language function revealed deficits in the areas of reading comprehension and written fluency, with borderline performance on a measure of sentence repetition. These anomalies in language ability were noted in the context of completely intact visual-perceptual, visual-spatial, and visual-constructional abilities.

In the area of memory and learning ability, an asymmetry in performance was noted. In the delayed recall condition of the Wechsler Memory Scale, Sandra showed relatively greater impairment in the ability to recall complex verbal (prose) material relative to recall of nonverbal (visual) material. Finally, in the area of sensorimotor function, significantly slower motor speed was noted with her preferred (right) hand, and impairment with the right hand was noted on a measure of tactile form perception.

In summary, the neuropsychological evaluation was significant for a variety of signs implicating dysfunction of the presumed dominant (left) cerebral hemisphere. The important findings included: (1) significant impairment of selected aspects of language function (reading comprehension, written fluency, sentence repetition); (2) significantly more impaired long-term recall for complex verbal (prose) material relative to recall of nonverbal (visual) material on the Wechsler Memory Scale; (3) significantly slower motor speed with the preferred (right) hand; and (4) unilateral right hand deficits on a tactile form perception task. These results implicated dysfunction of the dominant

**Table 7.3** Preoperative and Postoperative Scores on Neuropsychological Tests

| Wechsler Adult Intelligence Scale-Revised (WAIS-R) Scale | Pre-Op | Post-Op |
|---|---|---|
| Information | 5 | 5 |
| Digit span | 8 | 8 |
| Vocabulary | 5 | 5 |
| Arithmetic | 8 | 8 |
| Comprehension | 4 | 8 |
| Similarities | 5 | 7 |
| Picture completion | 5 | 7 |
| Picture arrangement | 7 | 9 |
| Block design | 6 | 7 |
| Object assembly | 6 | 7 |
| Digit symbol | 11 | 10 |
| Verbal IQ | 76 | 81 |
| Performance IQ | 79 | 83 |
| Full Scale IQ | 76 | 81 |

Note: Mean of subtest scores = 10 (SD = 3) and mean of IQ values = 100 (SD = 15).

| Multilingual Aphasia Examination | Pre-Op | Post-Op |
|---|---|---|
| Visual naming | 41 | 28 |
| Sentence repetition | 35 | 40 |
| Associative verbal fluency | 40 | 42 |
| Oral spelling | 47 | 47 |
| Token test | 54 | 59 |
| Aural comprehension | 42 | 42 |
| Reading comprehension | 28 | 40 |

Note: Scale scores converted to T scores ($\bar{x}$ = 50, SD = 10)

### Thurstone Word Fluency Test

Total words produced = 28

Note: Scores less than 45 considered impaired.

| Visual Perceptual/Visual-Spatial/Visual Construction Tests | Pre-Op | Post-Op |
|---|---|---|
| Hooper Visual Organization Test | 43 | 50 |
| Judgment of Line Orientation Test | 42 | 36 |
| Facial Recognition Test | 49 | 50 |
| Rey Complex Figure (copy) | 42 | 37 |

Note: Test scores converted to T scores ($\bar{x}$ = 50, SD = 10)

(Continued on p. 117)

**Table 7.3** Continued

| *Wechsler Memory Scale* | Pre-Op | Post-Op |
|---|---|---|
| Memory quotient | 90 | 80 |
| Logical memory | 7 | 8 |
| Visual reproduction | 8 | 9 |
| Associate learning | 9 | 6 |
| Logical memory-delayed | 35% | 34% |
| Visual reproduction-delayed | 72% | 78% |

Note: Mean of memory quotient = 100 (SD = 15). Mean of logical memory, visual reproduction and associate learning subtests = 10 (SD = 3).

| *Wisconsin Card Sorting Test* | Pre-Op | Post-Op |
|---|---|---|
| Total categories | 3 | 6 |
| Perseverative responses | 21 | 3 |
| Errors | 54 | 20 |

| *Sensorimotor Tests* | Pre-Op | Post-Op |
|---|---|---|
| Pegboard (right hand) | 55 | 52 |
| Pegboard (left hand) | 53 | 51 |
| Dynomometer (right) | 43 | 54 |
| Dynomometer (left) | 47 | 61 |
| Tap (right) | 42 | 42 |
| Tap (left) | 57 | 48 |
| Tactile form perception (right) | 6 | 10 |
| Tactile form perception (left) | 9 | 9 |
| Finger identification (right) | 28 | 28 |
| Finger identification (left) | 30 | 30 |

Note: All motor measures (pegboard, dynomometer, tap) are reported in T scores ($\bar{x} = 50$, SD = 10). Tactile perceptual measures reported in terms of number correct. Total correct for tactile form perception is 10; for finger identification, total correct is 30.

| *Other Tests* | | |
|---|---|---|
| Trails A | 51 | 33 |
| Trails B | 44 | 53 |
| Phoneme Discrimination Test | 28 | 28 |
| Tonal Memory Test | 15 | 17 |
| Rhythm Test | 30 | 45 |

Note: Trail-Making Test and Rhythm Test reported in T scores ($\bar{x} = 50$, SD = 10), while scores for other tests represent number of item correct. There are 30 possible correct responses for the other two auditory-perceptual tasks (phoneme discrimination, tonal memory).

cerebral hemisphere in general, with extension into the frontal (motor ability, written fluency) and parietal (tactile-perceptual deficit) areas. Impairments in other areas of language function (e.g., repetition) and delayed recall of verbal material implicated dysfunction of the dominant temporal lobe and hippocampus.

Previous interictal (between seizures) EEGs revealed a left temporal lobe spike focus. In association with her neuropsychological profile implicating dysfunction of the dominant hemisphere, she appeared to be an appropriate candidate for focal resection of her epileptogenic lesion. She was subsequently admitted for 24-hour closed-circuit-TV EEG monitoring of her seizures. The patient was admitted to the monitoring unit for 1 week. Her anticonvulsant medications were tapered. The goal was to have the patient experience some of her typical complex partial seizures so that: (1) the exact site of seizure onset can could be determined electroencephalographically, and (2) the seizures themselves could be videotaped in order to ensure that these spells were typical of her usual attacks. Sandra did indeed have two seizures during her monitoring stay; EEG results confirmed that the onset of the spells originated from the left temporal lobe.

Since the seizures clearly appeared to be originating from the left temporal lobe, one further test was required. An intra-carotid sodium amytal test was conducted to determine which hemisphere was dominant for language ability, and to help ensure that the contralateral temporal lobe (right temporal lobe) could sustain memory function following epilepsy surgery on the dominant temporal lobe. That is, conclusive evidence was needed to document that the patient would not experience an anterograde amnesia following her epilepsy surgery.

To that end, the patient underwent an intra-carotid sodium amytal test (commonly called a Wada Test). The patient was seen in the department of radiology and 100 mgs of sodium amytal were administered to the dominant cerebral hemisphere via the internal carotid artery (transfemoral approach). Following administration of the sodium amytal, the patient manifested an immediate right-sided flaccid monoparesis. In the context of this neurologic deficit, the patient was unable to manifest any spontaneous expressive speech, she could not name objects that were presented to her. Further, she could not read simple sentences presented to her, and she showed no signs of receptive language comprehension. Following Dodrill's amytal test procedure, memory assessment began. Using this procedure it was concluded that the right temporal lobe could sustain memory functions following resection of the left temporal lobe. Following a 20-minute delay, the right cerebral hemisphere was then perfused with 100 mgs of sodium amytal and the patient manifested an immediate left-sided flaccid monoparesis. In the context of this neurologic deficit, the patient could accurately name objects presented to her and read distractor sentences. In addition, she showed good receptive language comprehension, although recall ability was poor.

Results of the intra-carotid sodium amytal test indicated that: (1) the patient's left hemisphere was dominant for language function, and (2) the right hemisphere could sustain memory functions following partial resection of the right temporal lobe.

## Selection of Treatment

As indicated above, the patient suffered from long-standing medically resistent complex partial seizures. Not only was her seizure control unacceptable, but the epilepsy had significant adverse effects on several aspects of her life. She therefore was an appropriate candidate for surgical intervention. Her work-up was consistent in pointing to a left temporal lobe origin of her epilepsy. EEG/video monitoring of spontaneous seizure activity demonstrated onset of seizure activity from the left temporal lobe. The intra-carotid sodium amytal test showed her to be left-hemisphere dominant for language; neuropsychological evaluation demonstrated compromise of the left (dominant) hemisphere. In this context, the neurosurgeon offered the patient the option of undergoing partial resection of her left temporal lobe, and she accepted this option.

## Follow-Up

Six months following her epilepsy surgery, Sandra returned for a repeat neuropsychological evaluation. Table 7.3 shows the results of the pre- versus the postoperative neuropsychological assessments. Since her left temporal lobectomy, the patient has not experienced any complex partial seizures. She does report that she has experienced some *auras* (simple partial seizures), which typically occur 1 day out of the week and tend to occur in clusters of two or three. The aura is described as before—a strange feeling over her face, (e.g., heat) sometimes associated with a rising epigastric sensation in the stomach and chest. No loss of consciousness is associated with these spells and she finds them much less disruptive than the seizures that she experienced pre-operatively.

Sandra was administered a battery of neuropsychological tests from which we derived a total of 65 cognitive indices. We compared her pre- and postoperative neuropsychological performance on each index and considered a change in performance of one standard deviation or greater to be a cognitive alteration of *probable clinical significance*. Comparing her postoperative evaluation to her preoperative neuropsychological assessment, Sandra performed at essentially similar levels on the majority of the measures (69%). Hence, she showed cognitive stability on the vast majority of cognitive indices that were administered. Conversely, she manifested significant neuropsychological alteration on 31% of the measures. Of the cognitive change that occurred, the majority of the changes (80%) reflected significant cognitive *improvements*. Improvements were noted on measures of psychometric intelligence (comprehension subtest from the WAIS-R), language ability (reading comprehension from the Multilingual Aphasia Battery), novel problem solving and abstract thinking ability (Wisconsin Card Sorting Test), improved auditory attention (Rhythm Test), improved grip strength bilaterally, and improved tactile form perception utilizing the right hand. The cognitive improvements are hypothesized to be due to the resection of the epileptic focus with subsequent reduction in the amount of abnormal interictal epileptiform activity propagated to other cortical areas. With this reduction in "neural noise" following surgery, non-epileptic cortical areas can express their neuropsychological function in a more normal manner. Relative loss occurred in the area of visual naming ability (a mild dysnomia), significantly decreased performance on the paired associate learning subtest of the Wechsler Memory Scale, and poorer performance on the Trail Making Test-A indicating some relative slowness in visual-motor tracking.

In summary, her postoperative neuropsychological profile was characterized by cognitive stability. And of the cognitive changes that occurred, the majority of changes reflected relative cognitive improvements.

With regard to pre- versus postoperative changes in emotional and behavioral functioning, Table 7.4 shows results of pre- and postoperative MMPIs, General Health Questionnaires, Center for Epidemiological Studies in Depression Inventories (CES-D), and the Washington Psychosocial Seizure Inventories (WPSI). As is evident from the table, significant improvements were noted on five MMPI scales (De-

**Table 7.4** Preoperative and Postoperative Scores on Behavioral and Psychosocial Measures

| Scale | Minnesota Multiphasic Personality Inventory (MMPI) Pre-Op Score | Post-Op Score |
|---|---|---|
| L | 40 | 56 |
| F | 80 | 55 |
| K | 49 | 53 |
| Hs | 50 | 48 |
| D | 76 | 53 |
| Hy | 49 | 47 |
| Pd | 97 | 50 |
| Mf | 45 | 45 |
| Pa | 82 | 65 |
| Pt | 76 | 56 |
| Sc | 80 | 57 |
| Ma | 65 | 73 |
| Si | 58 | 51 |

| Washington Psychosocial Seizure Inventory (WPSI) | | |
|---|---|---|
| Family background | 4 | 3 |
| Emotional adjustment | 20 | 7 |
| Interpersonal adjustment | 14 | 1 |
| Vocational adjustment | 12 | 4 |
| Financial status | 6 | 2 |
| Adjustment to seizures | 9 | 6 |
| Medical management | 3 | 0 |
| Overall psychosocial function | 36 | 7 |

| General Health Questionnaire (GHQ) | | |
|---|---|---|
| Total Score | 15 | 1 |

| Center for Epidemiological Studies in Depression Questionnaire (CES-D) | | |
|---|---|---|
| Total Score | 24 | 3 |

NOTE: For each test higher scores represent increased difficulties. The MMPI utilizes T scores ($\bar{x} = 50$, SD = 10) while the other measures utilize raw scores. For the GHQ, scores 5 and above represent significant psychological distress, while the CES-D scores exceeding 15 represent significant depressive symptomatology.

pression, Psychopathic Deviant, Paranoia, Psychasthenia, and Schizophrenia). Overall, her postoperative MMPI was characterized by significant normalization of emotional function, although these improvements need to be viewed in the context of a significantly higher Lie scale (K is essentially unchanged). This is corroborated on additional tests including significant improvement on the General Health Questionnaire and the CES-D. Specifically, Sandra moved from the pathological range preoperatively to within normal limits postoperatively. Additionally, there were improvements on the Emotional Adjustment, and Interpersonal Adjustment, Vocational Adjustment and Overall Psychosocial Functioning scales of the WPSI. In summary, behavioral and emotional measures revealed some evidence of improved self-reported behavioral adjustment, less depression, and fewer psychosocial problems. Finally, the patient is now employed and is working as a full-time secretary.

## Overall Evaluation

This case is instructive for several reasons. First, this patient is quite typical of many individuals who have intractable epilepsy. The seizures started early in life, they were not substantially controlled despite the use of a wide variety of anticonvulsant medications, and the patient experienced many psychosocial difficulties as a result of her chronic seizure disorder. Second, it is clear that despite this patient's long history of epilepsy, she experienced a significant reduction in her seizure frequency following epilepsy surgery. Finally, the patient demonstrated postoperative stability of cognitive functioning with significant improvements in many areas of cognitive function, and improved behavioral and psychosocial functioning.

In summary, it is clear that appropriately selected candidates can benefit substantially from epilepsy surgery. In conjunction with close monitoring of neuropsychological and behavioral functioning, as well as aggressive teamwork with vocational rehabilitation and social service personnel, excellent outcome can be obtained for many patients.

## References

Hughes, J. R. (1980). Epilepsy: A medical overview. In B. P. Hermann (Ed.), *A multidisciplinary handbook of epilepsy.* Springfield, IL: Charles C Thomas.

Laidlaw, J., & Laidlaw, M. V. (1982). People with epilepsy—Living with epilepsy. In J. Laidlaw & A. Richens (Eds.), *A textbook of epilepsy.* Edinburgh, Scotland: Churchill Livingstone.

Whitman, S., & Hermann, B. P. (1986). *Psychopathology in epilepsy: Social dimensions.* New York: Oxford University Press.

Zielinski, J. J. (1982). Epidemiology. In J. Laidlaw & A. Richens (Eds.), *A textbook of epilepsy.* Edinburgh, Scotland: Churchill Livingstone.

# Chapter 8

# Hearing Impairment

## Frank P. Belcastro

## Description of the Disorder

Communication is an active process, a two-way operation that permits the exchange of messages between two persons over time and space (Owens, 1986). This process is the basis for social interaction and enables interpersonal relationships to develop. People use different modes of communication: language, oral, visual, and nonverbal. Also, most individuals utilize the five senses for acquisition of information from the environment. However, for the close senses of taction, gustation, and olfaction to serve as communication receptors, they must be in close physical proximity with the communication event. On the other hand, the distance senses of vision and audition permit contact with the environment without physical proximity. The auditory channel is critical to the development of normal language and speech. Further, it is essential for comprehension and learning.

A major challenge of educators has been the teaching of language to hearing impaired children. The foremost goal of these educators is to reduce the expressive and receptive language deficits of hearing impaired children through successful intervention in order to increase their participation in normal communication (Council for Exceptional Children, 1966).

The field of special education, in general, and the area of hearing impairedness, in particular, are in a period of change in response to important new social and educational policies. The change is in the direction of expanding the practice of serving hearing-impaired children while they remain in their own homes or in their neighborhood schools. The result is a challenge to all regular school personnel, who must direct increased attention to these children, and to specialists in the field of hearing-impaired, who must now reorganize their work to include the mainstream context.

The hearing impaired are not a homogeneous group. There are different degrees of hearing loss and hearing distortions, disparate central nervous system disorders, and varying ages of onset of hearing impairment. The hearing impaired are also required to process information totally or partially through sensory channels other than hearing.

A variety of terms have been used to describe the hearing impaired. The *deaf* are those who have nonfunctional hearing for everyday purposes of life. The *hard-of-hearing* have hearing that is defective, yet still functional (Committee on Nomenclature, 1938).

The development of language from an educational perspective is a critical consideration and, thus, produces different definitions. The *prelingually deaf* are those persons who became deaf before speech and language developed; the *postlingually deaf* are those who became deaf after speech and language development (Mandell & Fiscus, 1981).

Although the degree of hearing loss is important for diagnostic purposes, classification based on level of function is essential to those involved in planning and providing instructional programs for children who are hearing impaired. One such classification system separates levels of function according to decibel loss and matches these levels with some characteristics of hearing and behavior and suggests possible implications for educational programs at each level (Downs, 1976).

Only a small proportion of hearing-impaired children are enrolled in residential and day schools and in classes for the deaf. The remainder are in regular classrooms being served by specialists for the hearing impaired; most of these children have mild or moderate hearing losses (United States Office of Education, 1979). The following case study of a child with a moderate hearing loss is illustrative of the vast majority of hearing-impaired children.

## Case Identification

This is the case of Angie, a 5-year-old girl who has a mild hearing disorder. Following complaints by her parents and teacher, she was referred for evaluation. Angie is the only child of a two-parent family. She began kindergarten at age 5 with a possible hearing loss. Early that year, her parents expressed concern about her speech and hearing as well as her difficulty following directions.

Her teacher initiated intervention in an attempt to improve Angie's attention skills in class. For 1 week, she verbally reinforced Angie each time she attended during story time. For the following 2 weeks, she placed a good listener sticker on Angie's chart when she attended during story time or other instructional time. Angie failed to attend almost all of the time, although she appeared to attend more often in a one-to-one setting in comparison to a large-group setting.

Due to the lack of success with this strategy, parents and teacher requested a full evaluation.

## History and Presenting Complaint

Angie's mother reported that Angie was born after a full-term, uncomplicated pregnancy. She crawled at 8 months and took her first step at 14 months. She was toilet trained by 2½ years.

Angie said her first words at 14 months; two-word phrases emerged at 28 months. Her parents were not concerned about this delay in speaking because Angie's father had reported that he was a "late talker." Her mother stated that Angie was a very verbal child but that she has had difficulty saying many words clearly and has tended to leave off the last syllable of many words for quite some time.

According to her mother, Angie's childhood had been healthy with no serious injuries or medical problems; she receives regular dental care. She passed her school vision screening during her first month in kindergarten.

The Adaptive Behavior Profile—Home Scale (Keystone Area Education Agency, 1983) was employed to examine Angie's level of functioning in the areas of: coping behaviors, social skills, emotional development, language skills, self-care skills, applied thinking skills, and relations with community persons and with her family.

Her parents reported that while Angie's ability to follow directions was poor, her organizational skills were comparable to her friends' and her questions were indicative of good thinking. They stated that while her language was limited, she got along well with her friends and tended to respond appropriately in social situations. Her parents also noted that she did not disrupt the family, was not aggressive, and did not seem to withdraw from social contact.

Angie's parents asserted that she expressed ideas marginally well and seldom listened attentively. However, although she communicated her needs readily, she seldom understood directions with accuracy. They reported that she was always well-groomed and that her personal belongings were usually well-maintained. In addition, she was always appropriately dressed.

The parents felt that Angie's problem-solving skills were acceptable and that she got along well with adults in her neighborhood, in the community, and in her family.

Angie's kindergarten teacher reported that her ability to follow directions was poor and that she needed constant reminders to do her work. She seldom listened attentively and had difficulty expressing ideas and understanding directions. The teacher's report was similar to that of the parents', with respect to other skill areas.

## Assessment

On referral, audiological, psychological, and speech pathology assessments were conducted.

### Audiologist

Angie was tested using the pure-tone audiometric test (American National Standards Institute, 1969) in a sound-proof booth. Results showed that she had a moderate symmetrical sensorineural high frequency hearing loss beginning with 30 dB at 1,100 Hz and dropping to 50 dB at 4,000 Hz in both ears. While tympanometry tests, which determine the health status of the ears, were within normal limits, acoustic reflexes were present only for 1,000 Hz at 85 dB and absent for 2,000 Hz and 4,000 Hz.

The informal speech audiometry test, composed of age-appropriate lists of words, revealed that speech reception thresholds were 20 dB bilaterally. Further, speech discrimination scores were 72% and 80% for the right and left ears, respectively. Both the acoustic reflex and informal speech audiometry substantiated the presence of a high frequency hearing loss.

The findings were shared with Angie's mother, and it was recommended that Angie's hearing loss be confirmed by an ear specialist. The mother reported that both she and her husband had hearing losses on both sides of the family and had often wondered about Angie's hearing. However, because she had always seemed to respond to various sounds at home (e.g., the telephone, doorbell, television), they dismissed the notion of a hearing impairment. The audiologist explained that Angie's loss falls only in the upper limits of the frequency range and that she had normal hearing for the lower-pitched sounds. Consequently, she would be aware of many environmental sounds; however, because her hearing for high pitches was defective, she would perceive speech as sounding somewhat muffled. Since the consonant sounds in speech carry a great deal of high frequency energy (e.g., /s/, /z/, /sh/), Angie would tend to miss hearing these words (Bennett, 1978; Moskowitz, 1975; Smith, 1975). He also explained that Angie would be at a disadvantage if expressive background noise was present because it would tend to interfere with her good hearing. On these occasions, she would have to rely more on her vision.

The ear specialist confirmed her hearing loss and along with the audiologist felt that Angie should be fitted with a single in-the-ear style hearing aid. After an adjustment period, she would be fitted with the second hearing aid. Both hearing aids would be monitored on a monthly basis by the school audiologist. In addition, it was recommended that Angie be assigned preferential seating in all academic situations.

*School Psychologist*

The school psychologist administered an intelligence test and a group achievement test (Belcastro, 1987). Angie's IQ score of 102, which fell within the average range, was derived from the Stanford-Binet Intelligence Scale (Termen & Merrill, 1972). Her scores on the Wide Range Achievement Test (Jastak & Jastak, 1978) were 0.1 on word recognition (18th percentile) and 0.2 on math computation (47th percentile). Though mathematical computation was consistent with intelligence testing, Angie's word recognition score reflected some weakness in this area. It was recommended that further testing of reading ability be carried out over the school year.

*Speech Pathologist*

The speech pathologist administered language, articulation, and voice and fluency tests. Angie's score on the Peabody Picture Vocabulary Test (Dunn & Dunn, 1981) ranked in the 40th percentile. Her total score of 30 on the principal subtests of the Test of Language Development (Newcomer & Hammill, 1982) converted to a language quotient of 80, which was below average.

Results of the Arizona Articulation Proficiency Scale (Fudala, 1970) and the Goldman-Fristoe Test of Articulation (Fristoe & Fristoe, 1972) revealed the following multiple sound errors: (1) substitutions in the initial position (t/k, sh/ch, s/th, and d/th); (2) substitutions in the medial position (t/k, t/sh, t/th, t/s, d/g, and b/v); (3) final-position substitutions (t/k, sh/ch, t/ch, p/s, sh/j, sh/th, d/th, and d/g); and (4) consonant-blend substitutions (sh/tr, d/gr, and f/sw). Omissions were made of nearly all final consonants in words. Among these were: k, g, t, d, f, v, sh, th, l, and s (Sander, 1972). Distortions were made of the following sounds: y, j, r, and z.

Evaluations for voice and fluency demonstrated that these were adequate. All structures of oral mechanism appeared to be functioning within normal limits. Angie's spontaneous speech and language mean length of utterance (four) were below average for her age.

The speech pathologist noted that the test results indicated that Angie had a significant disability in oral speech, which was largely due to her bilateral high frequency hearing loss. Speech therapy, in addition to specialized and intensive remedial language therapy during the academic year, with a curriculum emphasizing speech and language skills, was recommended.

## Selection of Treatment

After reviewing assessment data, the diagnostic team recommended the following:

1. Itinerant instruction from a teacher of the hearing impaired three times a week for 30-minute sessions (Young, 1983).
2. Speech and language therapy three times a week for 20-minute sessions (Osberger, 1981).
3. Preferential seating in all academic situations while being mainstreamed.

4. Fitting with two hearing aids, the second fitting after an adjustment period with the first.
5. Hearing aid monitoring and testing by the audiologist.

The short-term objective of Angie consistently wearing her new hearing aids to school every day was identified. Long-term objectives were to improve language development, enhance speech articulation, and improve attention skills.

The team's recommendations were approved by the parents. Individualized education plans for speech and language instruction and for itinerant hearing instruction were generated with parental input.

## Course of Treatment

A number of individuals were involved in developing and implementing Angie's education and remedial program. These included the classroom teacher, parents, itinerant teacher, and speech and language therapist.

### Classroom Teacher

With consultation from the various specialists, the classroom teacher carried out most of the training efforts with Angie. A 24-element procedure was implemented to enhance Angie's educational and social functioning and to ameliorate language and speech inadequacies.

1. A preferential seat was assigned to Angie where she could easily see both the teacher and her classmates; this was away from noise sources and near the teacher. Less active students were seated around Angie.
2. A positive attitude toward Angie was established with the teacher serving as the model for the other children.
3. A buddy system was devised in which another child helped to convey classroom activities to Angie.
4. The class was helped to understand more about hearing and hearing loss by having specialists visit and present information about the ear, hearing aids, noise, and famous hearing-impaired people.
5. Angie was encouraged to participate in classroom activities via verbal reinforcement.
6. The teacher spoke naturally and faced Angie when speaking to her. She spoke slightly slower than usual.

7. New topics were introduced with a short sentence or a key word so that Angie could follow changes in activities.

8. Visual aids were used whenever possible. The overhead projector was used as an alternative to the chalkboard and permitted the teacher to face the class as she spoke.

9. The teacher did not talk when she was writing on or facing the chalkboard.

10. The teacher was careful not to stand with her back to the window while talking since the shadow or the glare would make lipreading difficult.

11. The teacher kept her hands or book away from her face while talking.

12. The teacher stood still while giving directions, preferably where her face was easy to see. When dictating spelling words or problems, the teacher chose one place to stand. When she had to move, she always returned to the same place before continuing the lesson.

13. The teacher conducted class recitations and discussions from the front of the room. Whenever papers were being shuffled or passed or when students' chairs were being moved, the teacher did not speak because these background noises limited Angie's ability to hear and understand what was being said.

14. When Angie misunderstood, her teacher restated the question or statement in a different way.

15. The teacher was patient with Angie. She never passed over her in class. She always reinforced Angie for attending and for participating.

16. The teacher placed a simple lesson outline on the chalkboard and often gave a copy to Angie to review in advance. She also provided Angie with a list of all new vocabulary words and wrote key words and phrases on the board as the lesson progressed.

17. All homework assignments were written on the board.

18. Written tests were given whenever possible and were at a level that Angie could read and understand.

19. When the teacher had difficulty understanding Angie, she asked her to repeat what she had said.

20. The teacher did not call attention to Angie's speech errors in the classroom. Instead, she recorded and shared them with the speech therapist.

21. The teacher realized that Angie had a limited vocabulary and syntax difficulties in both receptive and expressive areas. She also was aware that Angie's failure to understand was related to this language deficit as well as to the inability to hear normally.

22. The teacher encouraged Angie to tell her if the aid did not seem to be working properly.

23. The teacher was alert for words that looked the same to Angie (cook-court, mom-bomb, town-down) and for sounds that are not visible (k, g, s, ng, c, z, r).
24. The teacher alternated listening activities with other activities that required less attention.

## Parents

The parents applied many of the teacher's strategies at home as well as outside the home. In addition, under the guidance of the consultant for the hearing impaired, the parents instituted a series of behavior modification procedures to control Angie's behavior outside the house. Angie learned not to wander away but to stay close to her parents whenever she was in a parking lot, in any store, at a stadium or playing field, after exiting a car, near the street, and beyond the front lawn and backyard.

Communication in these areas was accomplished by intruding in Angie's line of vision or tapping her on the shoulder, beckoning her to her parents, walking her to the least-noisy location, bringing the mouth close to one of her ears, and delivering the message.

Angie's parents knew that positive family relationships were important for progress to occur. They were accepting and supportive of her and provided a safe and trusting atmosphere. Whenever the family visited relatives who had children, child-rearing practices and rules were applied as equally and consistently as possible to all. The parents' expectations were realistic and Angie was challenged to attain realistic success.

Angie's parents granted her the same basic rights as the normal-hearing child. These included the right to privacy, the right to receive information and explanations, the right to independence by being responsible for her own decisions and by being able to participate in family decisions, and the right to be human—to become tired, bored, angry, and so on.

## Itinerant Teacher of the Hearing Impaired

The duties of the itinerant teacher of the hearing impaired were quite varied and included direct language development therapy, coordination of language development efforts among the team members, and training of teachers and administrators.

The itinerant teacher worked with the speech therapist and the class-room teacher to assure the use of appropriate techniques and adequate attention to speech-and-language development and correction.

Direct language therapy was the itinerant teacher's primary respon-sibility. The focus was on vocabulary development and the assembling of words in such an order so that they convey the meaning intended. One of Angie's receptive language difficulties was with the multiple meanings of words:

*Teacher*: "What does the word *run* mean in each of these sentences?

1. I will *run* home.

2. She will *run* out of food."

*Angie*: "In the first sentence, *run* means to go fast.

In the second sentence, *run* means not to have any left."

Angie was also asked to differentiate among the meanings of *run* in the following additional sentences.

3. The water is *running*.

4. I have a *run* in my stocking.

5. She will *run* for office.

The itinerant teacher worked on Angie's syntax. Often, Angie would omit small words, such as *of*, *a*, and *the*. In addition, the teacher attempted to maintain Angie's normal voice quality and vocal ex-pression.

The delay in expressive vocabulary was mild. Angie was asked to use vocabulary words in the context of simple sentences.

*Teacher*: "Use the word *play* in at least two sentences."

*Angie*: 1. "I *play* kick ball.

2. I *play* a tape."

The itinerant teacher provided Angie with both auditory and visual input (gestures, signs, labels, written lists) over repeated trials.

## Speech and Language Therapist

Although the speech and language therapist worked with the itiner-ant teacher and the classroom teacher to improve Angie's use of appro-priate techniques of speech and language through corrective tech-niques, her primary responsibility was Angie's actual production of sounds and words, which included auditory discrimination.

The speech therapist used several techniques with Angie for each sound to effect auditory discrimination:

1. The therapist "bombarded" Angie with the particular sound and had her count how many of these sounds she heard as the therapist said them.
2. The therapist produced the sound along with many other widely disparate sounds; Angie signaled when she heard them.
3. The therapist said several words beginning with the particular sound, which gave Angie the opportunity to hear it in this position. The same technique was used with words that: (a) ended with the sound, and (b) contained the sound in the medial position.
4. Through the use of worksheets, Angie was asked to select pictures of words that contained the sound in the initial, medial, and final positions. Next, she was asked to choose the sound in syllables, words, phrases, and especially sentences (each of these in all three positions, when appropriate).

For sound production, Angie was asked to produce the particular sound in a variety of ways. For example, she was expected to correctly produce the particular sound in isolation, in nonsense syllables, and in the initial, medial, and final positions of words. To assure that the sound was learned, Angie had to use it in one word of a short phrase, in one word of a sentence, in a short-story selection, in a short conversation with the therapist, and in a short puppet play that was presented to her class.

For Angie, the auditory discrimination portion of her remediation program required greater concentration and time. This was especially true for those sounds that are produced by unseen but specific movements of the tongue within the mouth, such as /r/.

## Follow-Up

The diagnostic team met at the end of the school year at the request of the teacher. There was a consensus that gains had not yet reached the point where intervention could be terminated. By the end of the kindergarten year, they agreed that Angie had adjusted to amplification. Consequently, she began to hear better and was benefiting from instruction.

The first- and subsequent-grade teachers stated that Angie was indistinguishable from other children in class with regard to following of directions or attending to tasks and to the teacher.

At the end of the second grade, the consultant of the hearing impaired administered the Boehm Test of Basic Concepts (Boehm, 1971) and the Brigance Inventory of Basic Skills (Brigance, 1976). Results indicated that Angie was in the low-average range on basic concepts and memory skills. In addition, she possessed average motor skills, such as the manipulation of small items (e.g., scissors, handwriting, tracing). During the third grade, Angie's mean length of utterance improved to average age levels. Itinerant instruction shifted to itinerant monitoring; frequency of instruction was faded from 30-minute sessions three times a week to one 30-minute session every 2 weeks. Also at this time, the speech pathologist readministered the Peabody Picture Vocabulary Test, Test of Language Development, and the Arizona Articulation Proficiency Scale. Scores on those measures reflected that Angie's receptive and expressive language were at the average level of achievement. Further, her substitutions, consonant blends, omissions, and distortions were reduced. However, substitutions of t/k in all three positions (initial, medial, and final) still persisted as did sh/ch and sh/th in the final positions. Also, omissions of the final consonants l and d continued, as did the distortion of the z sound.

Due to her improvements, Angie's speech and language therapy was reduced from 20-minute sessions three times a week to one 20-minute session per week. Over the course of treatment, the audiologist continued to monitor and test her hearing aids.

## Overall Evaluation

Because Angie was referred for evaluation at an early age, treatment strategy was easier to design and administer. The concern and cooperation of her parents, teachers, and specialists facilitated her progress.

Angie required the normal amount of time (about 1 year) to adjust to amplification. After that period, the recommendations of the diagnostic team proved to be useful. Angie had made progress commensurate with her intelligence, hearing loss, and age in all areas initially requiring remediation (Van Hasselt, 1983). Further, the attention directed to Angie's social and emotional adjustment, the positive attitudes of family members, teachers, and peers, and her physical development all contributed to the effectiveness of the intervention.

During her school career and as an adult, Angie will require supervision and remediation for speech and language deficits, albeit to a minimal degree. She will always need hearing aids. However, as she gains experience and knowledge, adjustments will very likely become accepted and minimally intrusive (Levine, 1981). Angie already has learned to read, write, produce highly intelligible speech, and make friends. She has the potential, as does the normal-hearing person, to become involved in co-curricular activities, attend college, pursue a career, get married, and have a happy, well-adjusted family life.

# References

American National Standards Institute. (1969). *Specifications for audiometers*. New York: American National Standards Institute.

Belcastro, F. P. (1987). Hearing impairment. In V. B. Van Hasselt & M. Hersen (Eds.), *Psychological evaluation of the developmentally and physically disabled* (pp. 93-114). New York: Plenum.

Bennett, C. W. (1978). Articulation training of profoundly hearing-impaired children: A distinctive feature approach. *Journal of Communication Disorders, 11*, 330-342.

Boehm, A. E. (1971). *Boehm Test of Basic Concepts*. New York: Psychological Corporation.

Brigance, A. (1976). *Brigance Diagnostic Inventory of Basic Skills*. N. Billerica, MA: Curriculum Associates.

Committee on Nomenclature. (1938). Conference of executives of American schools for the deaf. *American Annals of the Deaf, 83*, 501-550.

Council for Exceptional Children. (1966). *Professional standards for personnel in the education of exceptional children*. Washington, DC: National Education Association.

Downs, M. P. (1976). The handicap of deafness. In J. L. Northern (Ed.), *Hearing disorders* (pp. 31-38). Boston: Little, Brown.

Dunn, L. M., & Dunn, L. M. (1981). *Peabody Picture Vocabulary Test*. Circle Pines, MN: American Guidance Services.

Fristoe, R. E., & Fristoe, M. (1972). *Goldman-Fristoe Test of Articulation*. Circle Pines, MN: American Guidance Services.

Fudala, J. B. (1970). *Arizona Articulation Proficiency Scale*. Los Angeles: Western Psychological Services.

Harkins, J. (1987). Greeting the challenge: The impact of technological innovation. *Gallaudet Today, 18*, 38-42.

Jastak, J. F., & Jastak, S. R. (1978). *Wide Range Achievement Test*. Wilmington, DE: Jastak Associates.

Keystone Area Education Agency. (1983). *Keystone Adaptive Behavior Profile—Home scale*. Elkader, IA: Keystone Area Education Agency.

Lee, J. C. (1986). The next ten years. *American Rehabilitation, 12*(1), 16-21.

Levine, E. S. (1981). *The ecology of early deafness*. New York: Columbia University Press.

Mandell, C. J., & Fiscus, E. (1981). *Understanding exceptional people*. St. Paul, MN: West.

Moskowitz, B. A. (1975). The acquisition of fricatives: A study in phonetics and phonology. *Journal of Phonetics, 3*, 141-150.

Newcomer, P. L., & Hammill, D. D. (1982). *Test of language development*. Austin, TX: PRO-ED.

Osberger, M. J. (1981). The development and evaluation of some speech training procedures for hearing-impaired children. *Speech of the hearing-impaired: Research training and personnel preparation*. Washington, DC: Bell Association for the Deaf.

Owens, R. E., Jr. (1986). Communication, language, and speech. In G. H. Shames & E. H. Wiig (Eds.), *Human communication disorder: An introduction* (2nd ed.) (pp. 27-29). Columbus, OH: Charles E. Merrill.

Sander, E. K. (1972). When are speech sounds learned? *Journal of Speech and Hearing Disorders, 37*, 55-63.

Smith, C. R. (1975). Residual hearing and speech production in deaf children. *Journal of Speech and Hearing Research, 18*, 795-811.

Terman, L. M., & Merrill, M. A. (1972). *Stanford-Binet intelligence scale.* Boston: Houghton Mifflin.

United States Office of Education. (1979). *Progress toward a free appropriate public education: A report to Congress on the implementation of P.L.: 94-142.* Washington, DC: Department of Health, Education, and Welfare.

Van Hasselt, V. B. (1983). Social adaptation in the blind. *Clinical Psychological Review, 3*, 87-102.

Young, E. (1983). A language approach to treatment of phonological process problems. *Language, Speech, and Hearing Services in Schools, 14*, 47-53.

# Chapter 9

# Hyperactivity and Attention Deficit Disorders

Marc S. Atkins
William E. Pelham
Karen J. White

## Description of the Disorder

The treatment of the psychiatric disorder variably referred to as minimal brain dysfunction, hyperkinesis, hyperactivity, and attention deficit disorder has been the subject of considerable research and debate (e.g., O'Leary, 1980; Ross & Ross, 1982). The two most common treatments for this disorder, psychostimulant medication and behavior therapy, have each demonstrated improvement (e.g., Gittelman, Abikoff,

AUTHORS NOTES: The authors are grateful to Lee Pat Strickland, pharmacist; William Kepper, M.D.; Connie Speer, M.D.; Mary Lou Stewart; the teacher and staff of Gilchrist Elementary School, Tallahassee, Florida; and to Seth and his parents for their cooperation on this project.

Address all correspondence to Marc S. Atkins, Department of Pediatric Psychology, Suite 2307, Children's Hospital of Philadelphia, Pennsylvania, 19104.

Pollack, Klein, Katz, & Mattes, 1980; Pelham, Schnedler, Bologna, & Contreras, 1980; Rapport, Murphy, & Bailey, 1982). However, there is as yet no consensus regarding the optimal treatment for these children, and assessment of the social or academic behavior of treated children indicate that many remain deviant following treatment as compared to normative standards (e.g., Abikoff & Gittelman, 1984).

Three factors appear to contribute to reports of insufficient effects of current treatments for hyperactive children. First, the interpretation of treatment effects is complicated due to the wide range of symptoms, such as inattention, overactivity, impulsivity, noncompliance, academic difficulties, aggression and poor peer relations, which describes this population (Hinshaw, 1987). Thus, the variability across treated subjects noted in evaluations of the effects of either behavioral or pharmacological treatments for hyperactivity may reflect the inability of any one treatment to provide maximal effects on all symptoms (Pelham & Murphy, 1986).

In addition, both behavioral and pharmacological treatments of hyperactivity have demonstrated improvement on direct measures of either classroom behavior, academic performance, or both (e.g., Gittelman et al., 1980; O'Leary & Pelham, 1978; Pelham et al., 1980; Rapport, Murphy, & Bailey, 1982). Yet, few studies have included evaluations of peer relations, despite the fact that peer rejection has been shown to be a common problem for these children and an important predictor of adult adjustment (Milich & Landau, 1982; Pelham & Bender, 1982). The omission of information concerning peer relations may be allowing a misleading impression of the efficacy of current treatment strategies for hyperactivity (e.g., Pelham, Schnedler, Bender, Nilsson, Miller, Budrow, Ronnei, Paluchowski, & Marks, 1988).

A second issue relates to the failure of current treatments to maintain positive effects on follow-up evaluations. In the majority of studies, treatment regimens have been implemented for 3 months or less and follow-up data are virtually nonexistent. Thus, reports of insufficient treatment effects (e.g., Abikoff & Gittelman, 1984) may reflect the inability of short-term interventions to maintain over time. Third, considerable debate has focused on the relative effectiveness of medication *versus* behavior therapy (e.g., Ayllon, Layman, & Kandel, 1975; Gittelman et al., 1980; Rapport, Murphy, & Bailey, 1982), whereas comparatively few data are available evaluating additive combinations of the two treatments (Pelham & Murphy, 1986). However, given the complex symptom pattern exhibited by the majority of children diagnosed as hyperactive or conduct disordered, and the apparent failure of either behavior therapy or medication to effect sufficient change when used alone, combination treatments appear necessary (e.g., Wells, Conners, Imber, & Delameter, 1981).

## Case Identification

Seth was a 9-year-old Caucasian boy who was adopted prior to his third year by his current family. His biological mother was reported to be a drug abuser who frequently neglected Seth. No information was available on his biological father. Seth had no further contact with either biological parent following his adoption. His adopted family was comprised of one girl, age 14, and two boys, ages 16 and 20, none of whom had histories of academic or behavioral problems at school or home. The family was headed by two parents. The father was a salesman and the mother a homemaker. The family income was approximately $25,000 annually. All family members were practicing Mormons.

Seth obtained a full-scale WISC-R IQ of 118, (PIQ = 118, VIQ = 113). On the Woodcock-Johnson Tests of Academic Achievement, he scored in the 74th percentile in reading, the 46th percentile in mathematics, the 37th percentile in written language, and the 54th percentile in knowledge (Woodcock & Johnson, 1977).

## Presenting Complaints

On referral, Seth was described by his teacher as highly disruptive, off-task, and unpopular with his peers. At home, he was described as disruptive and argumentative with his parents and siblings. He received a rating of 16 from his third grade teacher on the Abbreviated Conners Teacher Rating Scale (ACTRS), which is above the cut-off store for a diagnosis of hyperactivity (Goyette, Conners, & Ulrich, 1978). In addition, Seth was diagnosed as having attention deficit disorder with hyperactivity (American Psychiatric Association, 1980) based on parent and teacher ratings using the SNAP Rating Scale that lists the *DSM-III* criteria (Atkins, Pelham, & Licht, 1985). A concurrent *DSM-III* diagnosis of conduct disorder, undersocialized, aggressive was indicated based on interviews with his parents and teachers and scores greater than one standard deviation above the mean for his age on the conduct factor of the Conners Teacher Rating Scale (Goyette, Conners, & Ulrich, 1978).

# History

Seth had a several year history of severe behavioral and academic problems. He was diagnosed as hyperactive and learning disabled in the first grade, retained one grade and placed in a learning disability classroom. At the end of the second grade, the school referred Seth for psychological services in lieu of retention or special placement.

# Assessment

Due to the severity of Seth's behavior problems at school, multiple school-based measures were collected, which are described below. He was enrolled in a regular third grade classroom throughout this study.

## Classroom Observations

Direct observations of on-task behavior in the classroom were obtained by trained observers using an occurrence/nonoccurrence, continuous, 10-second interval recording system. On-task was defined as any verbal behavior (e.g., answering questions, reading aloud) or nonverbal behavior (e.g., writing, reading) relevant to the currently assigned task. A male child with no academic or behavioral difficulties was selected by Seth's teacher at the beginning of the study and served as a comparison child. Seth and the comparison child were observed for an average of 60 minutes and 30 minutes respectively, each day, an average of 3 days a week. Interobserver agreement was calculated on approximately 20% of the intervals by dividing the number of agreements by the total number of agreements and disagreements. Interobserver agreement averaged 93.1% with a range across days of 75.0% to 99.5%.

## Academic Performance

Seth's class work was monitored for the accurate completion of four types of assignments: spelling, English, reading, and mathematics. Although reading was not considered a problem for Seth, as indicated by his high achievement score and by teacher report, this work was assessed daily to assure that treatment did not have an adverse effect on his reading performance. His completed schoolwork was collected and graded at the end of each school day. All curricular decisions were made by the classroom teacher. No attempt was made to influence the type or amount of work assigned daily.

*Teacher Ratings*

At least once per condition, teacher ACTRS ratings were obtained to assess the teacher's perceptions of treatment efficacy.

*Peer Ratings*

The Pupil Evaluation Inventory (PEI), a 35-item peer assessment inventory (Pekarik, Prinz, Liebert, Weintraub, & Neale, 1976), was administered to obtain peer perceptions of Seth's classroom behavior. Considerable normative and psychometric data have been reported for the PEI with estimates of test-retest reliability, internal consistency, and agreement with parallel teacher and peer ratings ranging from moderate to high (Atkins & Johnston, 1988). Empirically derived aggression, withdrawal, and likeability factors (Pekarik et al., 1976) were used as dependent measures. Factor scores represented the average percentage of same-sex peers who nominated a child on items of that factor. The PEI was administered following the treatment phases described below.

## Selection of Treatment

Alternative behavioral treatments were evaluated using multiple measures obtained in a regular elementary classroom over the course of an entire school year. Following a baseline phase, a behavioral treatment package was developed by adding increasingly more intensive components until optimal effects with an implementable package had been obtained. A reversal phase followed to establish that improved performance was controlled by the treatment package. The effect of the final behavioral treatment acceptable to school personnel was evaluated in combination with a low dose of psychostimulant medication to determine if the combination of behavioral and pharmacological treatments provided any advantages for Seth over behavioral treatment used separately. This is consistent with a clinical approach, beginning with the least restrictive treatment and moving to progressively more potent or complex treatments if improvement is insufficient, based on evaluations in the clinical setting.

## Baseline

Prior to the implementation of treatment, observational data, weekly teacher ratings, and daily academic progress were assessed for approximately 4 weeks. The PEI was administered at the end of this phase.

## Parent Training and Teacher Consultations

Following baseline, the first author met weekly in separate sessions with Seth's teacher and with his parents. Parent sessions involved the development of home-based contingency management programs, supplemented with assigned readings (Patterson, 1976), to modify problem behaviors noted by the parents. In addition, the parent sessions served to monitor Seth's behavior at home and ensure that contingencies and rewards were administered appropriately. A more detailed description of the parent training procedures is described elsewhere (Pelham, 1982). The weekly sessions with Seth's teacher were held to determine the behaviors in need of intervention, to monitor teacher perceptions of the course of treatment, and to model the appropriate use of each treatment component prior to its implementation in the classroom.

## Daily Report and Behavior Tally

Treatment began with the development of a daily report card (O'Leary, Pelham, Rosenbaum, & Price, 1976). Seth's teacher generated a list of problem behaviors from which four were targeted for treatment (out of seat without permission, bothering others, calling out in class, noncompliance with teacher requests). Another behavior, "Didn't argue with teacher during report," was added to reduce the possibility of disruption when a negative report was given. In addition, Seth was required to complete all academic work assigned during that period and to maintain an average of at least 70% accuracy. A behavior tally, located on the back of the daily report, was placed on Seth's desk at the beginning of each academic period. On the occurrence of a target behavior, Seth's teacher was instructed to place a mark in the appropriate place on Seth's behavior tally. This was intended to provide Seth with concrete and immediate feedback concerning the behaviors his teacher considered inappropriate.

The daily report was taken home each day throughout treatment. Home rewards were provided daily for appropriate evaluations consistent with performance criteria established for each behavior. In addition, Seth earned an additional reward at home if he met criteria on 4 of 5 days during that week. For 3 weeks, the daily report was used in the morning only to provide a multiple baseline analysis of the procedure across morning and afternoon. The PEI was administered following this condition.

## Playgroups

During this phase, the daily report was extended to all-day use and a school-based reward was provided in addition to the home reward. The school-based reward consisted of a playgroup for Seth and a peer he selected, contingent on his reaching criterion on the daily report. The playgroup lasted approximately 20 minutes and was supervised by undergraduate psychology students trained by the authors. At his teacher's request, Seth chose a different peer each day until all peers were selected. This phase lasted approximately 3 weeks.

## Response Cost

The next component added to the treatment package was a modification of the response cost procedure developed by Rapport, Murphy, and Bailey (1980). Each time Seth's teacher observed the occurrence of a target behavior, Seth lost 1 minute of playgroup time for that day. On days during which he lost three or fewer points, he was allowed to choose a second peer for that day's playgroup. In addition, as before, Seth was required to reach criterion on his daily report.

The response cost procedure was implemented in two phases. First, for 1 week, while the daily report/playgroup condition was in effect, the first author used the response cost procedure in the classroom during one of the morning academic periods. This served to model the procedure for Seth and his teacher and to evaluate empirically the efficacy of adding this component to the treatment package. The following week Seth's teacher used the response cost procedure in the classroom with one variation. On her request, Seth was moved to a seat closer to her desk to enable her to monitor his behavior more effectively. This phase lasted approximately 4 weeks concluding with a PEI administration.

### Reversal

Experimental control was assessed in this phase when baseline conditions were reinstated. All treatments were withdrawn and Seth returned to his original seat. This phase lasted approximately 2 weeks.

### Reinstatement of Behavioral Treatment

For this condition, Seth returned to the seat closer to the teacher's desk, the daily report card was reinstated for the entire day, playgroups were provided contingent on reaching criterion on the daily report card, and rewards were provided at home as in prior conditions. However, the response cost procedure was not utilized due to the teacher's complaint that it was interfering with her ability to perform her teaching responsibilities and her refusal to continue using the procedure. This phase lasted approximately 4 weeks.

### Pemoline plus Behavioral Treatment

The effects of 1.9 mg/kg pemoline (42 mg)[1] combined with the behavioral treatment package were assessed with a placebo-controlled, double-blind evaluation following the reimplementation of the behavioral treatment package.[2] Given the longer half-life of pemoline relative to other stimulants (Conners & Taylor, 1980), placebo days occurred on randomly selected Mondays following drug-free weekends in order to provide a two-day wash-out period. Although Seth's teacher was informed of the use of medication during this phase, neither she nor the classroom observers were aware of which days medication was administered relative to placebos. This phase lasted approximately 6 weeks and was followed by a PEI administration.

## Course of Treatment

*Classroom Observations*

Figure 9.1 presents the percentage of intervals that Seth was observed to be on-task across conditions during the morning and afternoon academic periods. Considerable variability in Seth's responding was evident during baseline in both academic periods. The mean rate of on-task behavior was 40% during morning activities and 33% in the afternoon. On introduction of the morning daily report procedure, the mean rate of on-task behavior increased to 59% with no appreciable change in the afternoon. However, Seth's on-task performance remained highly variable during the morning period. The addition of the playgroups to the daily report resulted in no appreciable change in on-task performance during the morning period (*M* = 56%), relative to the preceding condition. When the daily report was introduced in the afternoon, it resulted in an increase in the mean rate of responding (*M* = 50%) relative to the preceding condition, but also an increase in variability. Seth's on-task behavior was equivalent to baseline performance on 5 of 11 days it was observed during this phase. By contrast, when the response cost procedure was utilized, either by the experimenters or by Seth's teacher, the mean rate of on-task behavior was considerably higher and substantially less variable as compared to the prior conditions for both academic periods. During the period in which Seth's teacher used the response cost procedure, Seth's mean rate of on-task behavior increased to 83% in the morning and 81% in the afternoon.

The withdrawal of treatment during the reversal phase resulted in a dramatic reduction in the percentage of on-task behavior during both morning (*M* = 59%) and afternoon (*M* = 39%) academic periods. On reintroduction of the behavioral treatment package without the response cost component, Seth's on-task behavior increased during both academic periods as compared to the reversal phase, but was lower than that obtained with the response cost procedure (*M* = 79% for morning and *M* = 66% for afternoon periods). During the combined pharmacological and behavioral treatments phase, Seth's morning performance was slightly higher and somewhat less variable as compared to the response cost condition, with the exception of the last three data points, which were collected during the last week of the school year. In the

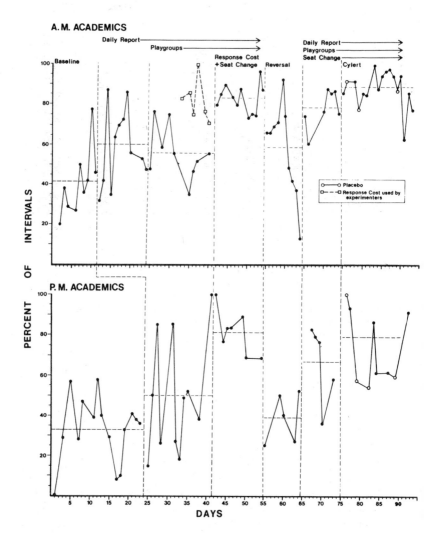

**Figure 9.1.** Mean percentage of intervals of on-task behavior for Seth in morning and afternoon academic periods.

NOTE: Means for each condition are indicated by dashed lines. Data points representing times in which the response cost procedure was used by the experimenters and data points indicating placebo days were not included in the calculation of condition means.

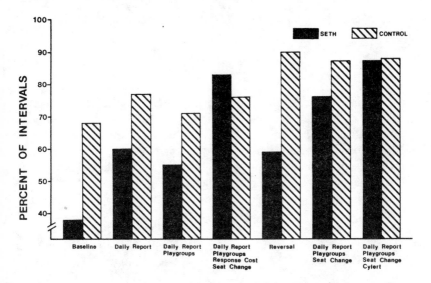

**Figure 9.2.** Mean percentage of intervals of on-task behavior for Seth and a
nonproblem comparison child averaged across academic periods.

NOTE: Data points representing times in which the response cost procedure was used by
the experimenters and data points indicating placebo days were not included in the
calculation of condition means.

afternoon, his mean rate of on-task behavior was about equal to but
more variable than the response cost condition ($M = 79\%$ on-task during
response cost and 77% on-task during the combined condition). Placebo
days appeared only slightly lower than pemoline days in both morning
($M = 81\%$) and afternoon ($M = 65\%$) periods.[3]

Figure 9.2 presents the mean percentage of on-task behavior Seth
and the comparison child averaged across academic periods. A higher
mean rate of responding was noted for the comparison child, as compared to Seth, during baseline, daily report, and reversal phases. However, during the phase that included the response cost procedure, and
during the combined pharmacological and behavioral treatments condition, the mean rate of on-task behavior appeared to be approximately
equal for Seth and the comparison child. During the response cost phase
Seth was observed to be on task an average of 83% of the time, as
compared to 76% for the comparison child. The combined pharma-

cological and behavioral treatments condition produced means of 89% for Seth and 88% for the comparison child.

## Academic Performance

Figure 9.3 presents the average daily number of problems completed correctly by Seth during morning and afternoon academic tasks, averaged across all academic tasks. For both morning and afternoon tasks, all treatment conditions resulted in an increase in academic productivity as contrasted to baseline and reversal conditions. For the morning tasks, the largest gains occurred during the condition including the response cost procedure followed by the combined pharmacological and behavioral treatments condition and the first daily report condition. In the afternoon, the response cost condition resulted in the largest amount of work produced by Seth, followed by the second all-day-report condition and the combined pharmacological and behavioral treatments condition.

## Teacher Ratings

Table 9.1 presents mean teacher ACTRS ratings for each condition that indicated the positive effects of treatment as compared to baseline ratings, but little or no discrimination among treatment conditions. Instead, a gradual decrease was apparent in mean ratings across conditions from a mean score of 14.5 in baseline to a mean score of 6.5 in the final treatment condition. In contrast to the observational and academic measures, teacher rating scores did not return to baseline levels during the reversal phase.

## Peer Ratings

Table 9.2 presents means and z scores for the aggression, withdrawal, and likeability PEI factor scores. For all third grade administrations, Seth remained over 2 SD above the mean for his class on the aggression factor, almost 3 SD above the mean on the withdrawal factor, and about 1.5 SD below the mean on the likeability factor. The only suggestion of improvement came after the 6 weeks of combined pharmacological and

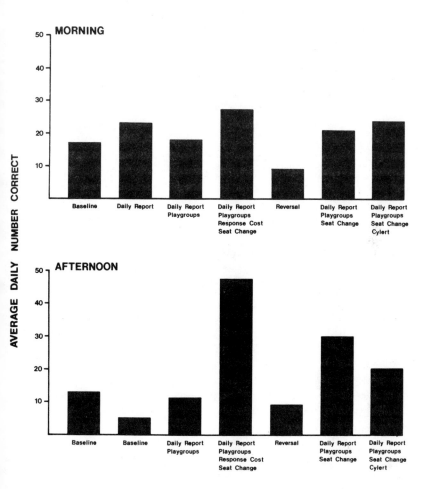

**Figure 9.3.** Average daily number of academic problems completed correctly by Seth during morning and afternoon academic periods.

NOTE: Activities during which the response cost procedure was used by the experimenters and placebo days were not included in the calculation of condition means.

behavioral treatment, when Seth's aggression and withdrawal factor scores decreased by almost 0.5 SDs.

**Table 9.1** Abbreviated Conners Teacher Rating Scale Scores across Experimental Conditions

| Condition | Score |
|---|---|
| Baseline | 14.50 |
| Daily report | 13.50 |
| Daily report and playgroups | 12.75 |
| Daily report and playgroups and response cost | 10.00 |
| Reversal | 9.00 |
| Daily report and playgroups and pemoline | 6.50 |
| Followup (12-month) | 16.00 |

NOTE: High scores denote negative ratings.

**Table 9.2** Peer Evaluation Inventory (PEI) Scores for Seth across Experimental Conditions

| | PEI Factors[1] | | | | | |
| | Aggression | | Withdrawal | | Likeability | |
| Condition | M | Z | M | Z | M | Z |
|---|---|---|---|---|---|---|
| Baseline | 68.7 | 2.88 | 50.8 | 3.09 | 15.7 | −1.42 |
| Daily report and playgroups | 59.9 | 2.67 | 29.4 | 3.27 | 15.7 | −1.45 |
| Daily report, playgroups, and response cost | 76.6 | 2.82 | 44.4 | 3.11 | 10.8 | −1.86 |
| Daily report, playgroups, and pemoline | 65.6 | 2.42 | 28.6 | 2.66 | 5.7 | −1.76 |
| Follow-up (12-month) | 42.6 | 2.23 | 12.5 | 1.00 | 7.5 | −1.04 |

NOTE: Mean scores are the percentage of male peers who nominated Seth averaged across items comprising that factor. Z scores are based on means and standard deviations for males' ratings of males on that administration. $N = 14$ on first four administrations and $N = 16$ on followup.

[1]Derived from "The Pupil Evaluation Inventory: A Sociometric Technique for Assessing Children's Social Behavior" by E. G. Pekarik et al., 1976. *Journal of Abnormal Child Psychology, 4*, pp. 83-97.

# Follow-Up

Follow-up peer and teacher ratings were obtained in the spring of the following school year (12 months posttreatment). Only 4 of the 16 males in Seth's fourth grade class also were members of his third grade class. Therefore, the follow-up peer ratings provided an assessment of Seth's sociometric status with a predominantly new set of peers.

Throughout this school year, Seth was continued on 42 mg pemoline and a modified form of the behavioral treatment was continued by his teacher. Weekly reports were sent home regarding his behavior, and rewards were provided by his parents contingent on appropriate classroom behavior. Because his fourth grade teacher thought her behavioral program sufficient, the authors were not involved in Seth's treatment during the follow-up year.

One year following treatment, Seth's fourth grade teacher gave him an ACTRS rating of 16, the same score given initially by his third grade teacher. On peer ratings (Table 9.2), Seth's withdrawal factor score decreased from more than 2 SD above class mean on the final third grade sociogram, to 1 SD above the mean on follow-up. Similarly, the likeability factor score improved from almost 2 SD below the class mean on the final third grade sociogram, to 1 SD below the mean on follow-up. However, the aggression factor score was essentially unchanged from the end of the third grade to follow-up. Both scores were more than 2 SD above the class mean.

Three years later, in the seventh grade, Seth had been returned to a special education classroom for "severely emotionally disturbed" children due to persistent and increasingly severe behavior problems.

## Overall Evaluation

These results illustrate the utility of single-subject methodology for evaluating alternative treatments for a hyperactive, aggressive boy being treated in an outpatient clinic while in a regular elementary school classroom. Increasingly more intensive components of a classroom-based behavioral treatment package appeared necessary to maximize improvement in classroom behavior for this child. The daily report, probably the most commonly used procedure in child behavior therapy, led to only moderate improvement in on-task behavior, teacher rating, and academic productivity and resulted in no change on peer ratings. The daily report had to be supplemented by a response cost program or pemoline in order to show major improvement in on-task observations and academic productivity. Only when pemoline was added did peer ratings begin to show modest improvement.

These results are consistent with the argument that "standard" clinical behavioral interventions are not sufficient treatments for hyperactive/aggressive children, and that adjunctive treatments are usually necessary (Pelham & Murphy, 1986; Satterfield, Satterfield, & Schell,

1987). At the same time, the results in the response cost condition replicate other findings regarding response cost's effects on hyperactive children's on-task behavior and academic productivity (Rapport et al., 1982), confirming that a highly structured behavioral intervention is helpful for specific target behaviors.

It is worth noting, however, that for this particular child, the addition of pemoline rather than response cost to the daily report program was the treatment of choice by the school personnel. Seth's teacher requested not to use the response cost procedure during the final treatment phase because she perceived it as an intrusion on her regular classroom activities. Seth's fourth grade teacher also used only a daily report program, along with a regimen of pemoline, electing not to use the response cost procedure. Similarly, Rosen, O'Leary, and Conway (1985) reported that teachers refused to implement behavior modification procedures following their successful cognitive-behavioral treatment of a hyperactive boy. In addition, Rapport (1981) reported that the response cost technique was not used with two of six teachers referred to his Rapport et al. (1982) study. One teacher did not want to use the response cost procedure and the other was thought to have too few behavior management skills to implement it appropriately.

These negative evaluations stand in contrast to the positive teacher appraisal reported by others using this procedure (Rapport et al., 1982). It appears that response cost and other structured behavioral procedures that may be necessary to maximize a child's improvement may not be implemented by many regular classroom teachers. Indeed, this problem is not specific to behavioral treatments for hyperactivity. Teachers' resistance to utilizing behavior-change programs in their classrooms is a concern of many school-based consultants (e.g., Kratochwill & Van Someren, 1985; Witt, 1986). Thus, problems with the implementation of highly structured behavioral programs in regular classroom settings highlight the adjunctive role that can be played by a moderate dose of a psychostimulant, which, as in this case, can yield results comparable to or better than intensive behavioral programs (Pelham et al., 1988).

The complexities involved in assessing the effects of a combined treatments approach for externalizing childhood disorders are illustrated by the differential response to treatment across dependent measures for this child. For example, despite clear effects of the behavioral intervention on classroom observations and academic performance measures, teacher ratings showed only moderate changes in Seth's behavior until the last (pemoline) phase. Her ratings failed to differentiate even between his obviously worsened behavior during reversal and his behavior during treatment. Similarly, Seth was continually rated as extremely deviant by his peers throughout treatment. Further, 1 year posttreatment, teacher ratings of hyperactivity were again above the cut-off score for a rating of hyperactivity and peer ratings of aggression remained extremely high. In addition, as noted, while in middle school, Seth had to be placed in a classroom for severely emotionally disturbed children due to continued behavior problems.

It should be noted that, in addition to the 10-month treatment described herein, Seth participated in 7-week, intensive, summer day treatment programs during the summers preceding and following the treatment described herein. Thus, the poor long-term outcome described above indicated that 14 months of intensive treatment was not sufficient to provide maximal improvement in classroom behavior for this child and, in fact, appears insufficient for children with similar symptomatology (Satterfield et al., 1987).

In summary, a modified form of a behavioral treatment package for a hyperactive/aggressive child combined with a low dose of psychostimulant medication appears to be as effective on short-term outcome as intensive behavioral treatment alone. Because the intensive treatment was not continued by school personnel, the combined procedure was the treatment of choice for this child. Further, the use of multiple measures to assess treatments for externalizing childhood disorders, and specifically the inclusion of peer ratings, appears to be an important component to future evaluations of treatments for these disorders. In addition, the lack of change in peer ratings of aggression noted in this study indicated the need for an even more comprehensive treatment that focuses on peer relationships (Pelham & Milich, 1984). Finally, the failure to effect a positive long-term outcome for this child highlights the need for effective procedures for maintaining interventions for long periods of time in children with externalizing disorders.

## Notes

1. This dosage of pemoline was found to be equivalent to .3 mg/kg methylphenidate on an analog spelling task (Stephens, Pelham, & Skinner, 1984.)

2. In addition to the placebo-controlled condition in the present study, the effects of 1.9 mg/kg pemoline on Seth's performance were evaluated in three double-blind, placebo-controlled assessments. Two were conducted prior to this study and the third in the summer following the study. One assessment focused on performance in two learning

tasks and revealed a 50% improvement in Seth's learning with pemoline relative to placebo (Stephens, Pelham, & Skinner, 1984). The other two assessments were conducted in 2 consecutive years of a summer treatment program that employed a highly structured token economy as the primary treatment modality. Assessment of incremental effects of 1.9 mg/kg pemoline in these programs revealed major changes in Seth's behavior with pemoline relative to placebo. During the first of these assessments, pemoline effected a 53% decrease in points lost for inappropriate behavior, a 79% increase in observed positive peer interactions, and a concurrent 88% decrease in time spent in time-out. Results of the assessment a year later were similar, yielding 60% to 80% increases in positive behavior and decreases in negative behavior (e.g., aggression, noncompliance, teasing) in pemoline conditions relative to placebo.

   3. The failure of the placebo data to demonstrate a clear effect of pemoline is likely due to pemoline's pharmacological properties. Once pemoline has been taken for a period of weeks, it may take as long as 1 to 2 weeks to stop having an effect (Conners & Taylor, 1980). Thus, despite the fact that placebo days occurred on randomly selected Mondays following drug-free weekends, this may not have been a sufficient period of time for the drug to wash out. However, given this child's positive response to pemoline in the three double-blind, placebo-controlled evaluations noted in note 2, we did not want to compromise his treatment by giving placebo for the lengthy period of time that might have been required for pemoline to wash out.

# References

Abikoff, H., & Gittelman, R. (1984). Does behavior therapy normalize the classroom behavior of hyperactive children? *Archives of General Psychiatry, 41,* 449-454.

American Psychiatric Association. (1980). *Diagnostic and statistical manual of mental disorders* (3rd ed.). Washington, DC: Author.

Atkins, M. S., & Johnston, C. (1988). The pupil evaluation inventory. In M. Hersen & A. S. Bellack (Eds.), *Dictionary of behavioral assessment techniques* (pp. 364-366). New York: Pergamon.

Atkins, M. S., Pelham, W. E., & Licht, M. H. (1985). A comparison of objective classroom measures and teacher ratings of attention deficit disorder. *Journal of Abnormal Child Psychology, 13,* 155-167.

Ayllon, T., Layman, D., & Kandel, H. (1975). A behavioral-educational alternative to drug control of hyperactive children. *Journal of Applied Behavior Analysis, 8,* 137-146.

Conners, C. K., & Taylor, E. (1980). Pemoline, methylphenidate, and placebo in children with minimal brain dysfunction. *Archives of General Psychiatry, 37,* 922-930.

Gittelman, R., Abikoff, H., Pollack, E., Klein, D. F., Katz, S., & Mattes, J. (1980). A controlled trial of behavior modification and methylphenidate in hyperactive children. In C. K. Whalen & B. Henker (Eds.), *Hyperactive children: The social ecology of identification and treatment* (pp. 221-243). New York: Academic Press.

Goyette, C. H., Conners, C. K., & Ulrich, R. F. (1978). Normative data on revised Conners parent and teacher ratings scales. *Journal of Abnormal Child Psychology, 6,* 221-236.

Hinshaw, S. P. (1987). On the distinction between attentional deficits/hyperactivity and conduct problems/aggression in child psychopathology. *Psychological Bulletin, 101,* 443-463.

Kratochwill, T. R., & Van Someren, K. R. (1985). Barriers to treatment success in behavioral consultation: Current limitations and future directions. *Journal of School Psychology, 23*, 225-239.

Milich, R., & Landau, S. (1982). Socialization and peer relations in hyperactive children. In K. D. Gadow & I. Bialer (Eds.), *Advances in learning and behavioral disabilities* (Vol. 1) (pp. 283-340). Greenwich, CT: JAI.

O'Leary, K. D. (1980). Pills or skills for hyperactive children. *Journal of Applied Behavior Analysis, 13*, 191-204.

O'Leary, K. D., Pelham, W. E., Rosenbaum, A., & Price, G. H. (1976). Behavioral treatment of hyperkinetic children. *Clinical Pediatrics, 15*, 510-515.

O'Leary, S. G., & Pelham, W. E. (1978). Behavior therapy and withdrawal of stimulant medication with hyperactive children. *Pediatrics, 61*, 211-217.

Pekarik, E. G., Prinz, R. J., Liebert, D. E., Weintraub, S., & Neale J. M. (1976). The pupil evaluation inventory: A sociometric technique for assessing children's social behavior. *Journal of Abnormal Child Psychology, 4*, 83-97.

Patterson, G. (1976). *Families: Application of social learning to family life.* Champaign, IL: Research Press.

Pelham, W. E. (1982). Childhood hyperactivity: Diagnosis, etiology, nature, and treatment. In R. Gatchel, A. Baum & J. Singer (Eds.), *Handbook of psychology and health* (Vol. 1): *Clinical psychology and behavioral medicine: Overlapping disciplines,* (pp. 261-327). Hillsdale, NJ: Lawrence Erlbaum.

Pelham, W. E., & Bender, M. (1982). Peer relationships in hyperactive children: Description and treatment. In K. D. Gadow & I. Bailer (Eds.), *Advances in learning and behavioral disabilities* (Vol. 1) (pp. 365-436). Greenwich, CT: JAI.

Pelham, W. E., & Milich, R. (1984). Peer relationships in hyperactive children. *Journal of Learning Disabilities, 17*, 560-567.

Pelham, W. E., & Murphy, H. A. (1986). Attention deficit and conduct disorders. In M. Hersen (Ed.), *Pharmacological and behavioral treatments: An integrative approach* (pp. 108-148). Elmsford, NY: John Wiley.

Pelham, W., Schnedler, R., Bender, M., Nilsson, D., Miller, J., Budrow, M., Ronnei, M., Paluchowski, C., & Marks, D. (1988). The combination of behavior therapy and methylphenidate in the treatment of attention deficit disorder: A therapy outcome study. In L. Bloomingdale (Ed.), *Attention deficit disorders.* (Vol. 3) (pp. 29-48). Elmsford, NY: Pergamon.

Pelham, W., Schnedler, R., Bologna, N., & Contreras, A. (1980). Behavioral and stimulant treatment of hyperactive children: A therapy study with methylphenidate probes in within-subject design. *Journal of Applied Behavior Analysis, 13*, 221-236.

Rapport, M. D. (1981). *A comparison of attentional training utilizing a response cost procedure and methylphenidate (Ritalin) on the classroom behavior and hyperactive children.* Doctoral dissertation, Florida State University, Tallahassee, FL.

Rapport, M. D., Murphy, H. A., & Bailey, J. S. (1980). The effects of a response cost treatment tactic on hyperactive children. *Journal of School Psychology, 18*, 98-111.

Rapport, M. D., Murphy, H. A., & Bailey, J. S. (1982). Ritalin vs. response cost in the control of hyperactive children: A within-subject comparison. *Journal of Applied Behavior Analysis, 15*, 205-216.

Rosen, L. A., O'Leary, S. G., & Conway, G. (1985). The withdrawal of stimulant medication for hyperactivity: Overcoming detrimental attributions. *Behavior Therapy, 16*, 538-544.

Ross, D. M., & Ross, S. A. (1982). *Hyperactivity: Current issues, research and theory* (2nd Ed.). New York: John Wiley.

Satterfield, J. H., Satterfield, B. T., & Schell, A. M. (1987). Therapeutic interventions to prevent delinquency in hyperactive boys. *Journal of the American Academy of Child and Adolescent Psychiatry, 26*, 56-64.

Stephens, R. S., Pelham, W. E., & Skinner, R. (1984). State-dependent and main effects of methylphenidate and pemoline on paired-associate learning and spelling in hyperactive children. *Journal of Consulting and Clinical Psychology, 52*, 104-113.

Wells, K. C., Conners, C. K., Imber, L., & Delameter, A. (1981). Use of single-subject methodology in clinical decision-making with hyperactive child on the psychiatric inpatient unit. *Behavioral Assessment, 3*, 359-369.

Witt, J. C., (1986). Teachers' resistance to the use of school-based interventions. *Journal of School Psychology, 24*, 37-44.

Woodcock, R. W., & Johnson, M. B. (1977). *Woodcock-Johnson Psycho-Educational Battery*. Hingham, MA: Teaching Resources Corporation.

# Chapter 10

# Learning Disabilities

## Edward S. Shapiro

## Description of the Disorder

Learning disabilities (LD) are not easily defined. The most commonly accepted definition is that developed and endorsed by the Department of Education in 1977:

> "Specific learning disability" means a disorder in one or more of the basic psychological processes involved in understanding or in using language, spoken or written, which may manifest itself in an imperfect ability to listen, think, speak, read, write, spell, or to do mathematical calculations. The term includes such conditions as perceptual handicaps, brain injury, minimal brain dysfunction, dyslexia, and developmental aphasia. The term does not include children who have learning problems which are primarily the result of visual, hearing, or motor handicaps, of mental retardation, of emotional disturbance, or of environmental, cultural, or economic disadvantage. (*Federal Register*, December 29, 1977, p. 65083).

Subsequent definitions of learning disabilities have been developed by the National Joint Committee for Learning Disabilities (NJCLD) (Hammill, Leigh, McNutt, & Larsen, 1981) and the Association for Children and Adults with Learning Disabilities (ACLD) (1984). The

NJCLD definition broadened the LD category beyond children, avoids the phrase "basic psychological processes," avoids use of terms such as *perceptual handicap* or *minimal brain dysfunction*, and recognizes that a learning disability can occur concomitantly with other handicaps. Likewise, the ACLD definition assumes a neurological origin for the learning problem and recognizes that a learning disability can affect areas outside academic skills such as social interaction.

Whichever "official" definition one ascribes to, learning disabilities are generally considered evident when there are discrepancies between an individual's ability and his or her actual achievement, and that discrepancy is not due to environmental disadvantage, mental retardation, or emotional disturbance. The result of the wide-scale disagreement about what constitutes a learning disability is a very heterogeneous population that is difficult to describe.

One of the most significant problems for defining a learning disability relates to the ability to accurately assess an ability/achievement discrepancy. Typically, the translation of this discrepancy becomes the difference between scores on tests of intelligence and achievement. Unfortunately, the high correlations between scores on these measures (mean about .70) suggests that there may be almost 50% common variance explained across these two measures. Thus, in many cases low scores on intelligence tests may only reflect the poor academic achievement the student has attained. Indeed, in such cases it is virtually impossible to really know what the student's potential or ability might be from these measures.

Additionally, a distinction must be made between a student who is diagnosed as having a learning disability and eligibility for special education services for learning disabled children and adolescents. Although discrepancies between ability and achievement may be evident in many students, it is often the degree of discrepancy that classifies the student as eligible to receive services under the category of learning disabled.

A potential alternative to using intelligence and achievement tests to identify learning disabilities has been the use of curriculum-based assessment (CBA). Many models of CBA have been described in the literature (e.g., Blankenship, 1985; Deno, 1985; Shapiro & Lentz, 1985, 1986), but all are based on examining differences between expected and actual *performance*, rather than ability and achievement, as the critical variables in identifying learning disabilities. The particular advantage of CBA measures over traditional norm-referenced assessment is their potential use as repeated measurements to examine ongoing academic progress of students.

In the case to be presented herein, a fourth-grade student who was identified as eligible for learning disabilities services will be described. This student was assessed using both traditional norm-referenced measures, such as intelligence and achievement tests, as well as using CBA. Additionally an intervention program using CBA data to examine his progress across time in reading is provided.

## Case Identification

| | |
|---|---|
| *Child's Name*: | Josh K. |
| *School*: | St. E's |
| *Grade*: | 4 |
| *Birthdate*: | 4/7/77 |
| *Date Evaluated*: | 1/14/88, 1/21/88, 1/28/88 |
| *Chronological Age:* | 7 years-11 months |

## Presenting Complaint

Josh was referred for evaluation by his mother and teacher due to his persistent problems in most academic areas.

## History

There is a long and involved educational evaluation surrounding Josh. Josh was first evaluated through the Intermediate Unit in 1983 while attending kindergarten. Mrs. K. reported that teachers indicated he was having problems soon after school began. Results of that evaluation reported severe articulation problems, a WISC-R Verbal IQ score of 78, a Performance IQ of 85, and Full Scale IQ of 80. Based on the results of the evaluation, it was recommended that Josh be retained in kindergarten and continue speech therapy. Possibilities of special education were raised with mother at this time, although the exact nature of services was unclear.

Josh was retested 1 year later again by the Intermediate Unit in an attempt to determine educational placement. At this point he was 7-1 years and attending H.S. School. Again, Josh's articulation problem was noted as severe. WISC-R results showed substantial changes with a

Verbal IQ of 69, Performance IQ of 101, and Full Scale IQ of 83. Examination of Josh's readiness skills showed that he had not yet acquired basic sight vocabulary, used incorrect pronouns, prepositions, and articles, but could identify letters of the alphabet. Recommendations for an "alternative placement" were again made to mother, but the nature of the recommendation was still unclear.

Given this feedback, Mrs. K. proceeded to contact two private schools for learning disabled children, but did not follow-through with pursuing application for Josh. Instead, Josh began to attend a private parochial school for children with mental retardation. At the point of this examiner's first evaluation of Josh, he was attending this school in the A.M., and attended a second grade class at a neighboring regular parochial school primarily for socialization in the P.M. In speaking to the principal at Josh's school, it was noted that Josh's acceptance to the school for children with mental retardation was conditional, in that he would not attend the school past first grade, since the administration felt he was misplaced and was clearly not a mentally retarded child.

Josh was assessed first by the examiner in March 1985. The results indicated that Josh attained a WISC-R Verbal IQ of 77, Performance IQ of 114, and Full Scale IQ of 92. Subtest scores on the Verbal Scale ranged from 3 to 8 and from 10 to 14 on the Performance Scale. Evaluation of reading skills at that time found him to be placed at the beginning of the first grade book in the reading series, but to be instructional at the primer book. Analysis of reading skills on the Brigance Inventory of Basic Skills showed Josh to lack basic phonetic analysis skills. In mathematics, Josh was found to be having significant problems in rate of computations.

Based on this evaluation, it was stated clearly that Josh should be considered as a learning disabled student. Given the large (37-point) discrepancy between verbal and performance subtests on the WISC-R, his significantly low levels of achievement in both reading and mathematics, and what appears to be a significant language delay, it was strongly recommended at that time that mother seek placement for Josh in a classroom for learning disabled students within the local school district.

Mrs. K. expressed a strong desire for Josh to remain outside of the public school system. After visits to several schools, it was decided that Josh could attend a parochial school with extensive support. At the time of his entrance into the school, the current administration seemed willing and eager to work closely with him. Additionally, Mrs. K.

contracted with a tutor, who began to provide weekly sessions for Josh beginning Fall 1985 and continuing until the present.

Mrs. K. asked to see this examiner again in April, 1987, due to problems her daughter, Susan, was having at school. In a visit to the school, it was determined that a change in school administrations had created a situation within which neither Josh nor Susan would be successful. As a result, Mrs. K. chose to move her children to a different parochial school beginning in Fall 1987. This move has resolved many of the problems Susan was having at school.

In November, 1987, Mrs. K. contacted this examiner again. This time, the problem centered around her decision to separate from her husband of over 10 years. Although the details will not be discussed here, it is important to know that Mr. and Mrs. K.'s marriage has been an ongoing source of conflict in the home. Throughout this, however, Mrs. K. has maintained an extremely strong commitment to her children and their education.

After several sessions with both Mrs. K. and her children, it appeared that there may be a reconciliation of the marriage. At the same time, however, the significant and substantial academic problems Josh was having at school had begun to resurface. More importantly, Josh's level of motivation for school had begun to deteriorate, a problem not noted during other evaluations.

The present evaluation was conducted to examine Josh's current educational status and to make strong recommendations for future educational planning.

## Assessment Methods

Parent Interview
Teacher Interviews
Wechsler Intelligence Scale for Children-Revised (WISC-R)
Kaufman Test of Educational Achievement (K-TEA)
Direct Academic Assessment of Reading and Math

*Test Results*

WISC-R
| | |
|---|---|
| Verbal IQ: | $74 \pm 6$ |
| Performance IQ: | $111 \pm 8$ |
| Full Scale IQ: | $90 \pm 5$ |

Subtest Scores:

| Verbal | | Performance | |
|---|---|---|---|
| Information | 5 | Picture Completion | 11 |
| Similarities | 9 | Picture Arrangement | 9 |
| Arithmetic | 5 | Block Design | 11 |
| Vocabulary | 6 | Object Assembly | 17 |
| Comprehension | 4 | Coding | 10 |
| Digit Span | 5 | Mazes | 9 |

K-TEA

| Subtest | Standard Score | Percentile |
|---|---|---|
| Math Applications | 75 | 5 |
| Reading Decoding | 83 | 14 |
| Spelling | 89 | 23 |
| Reading Comprehension | 84 | 14 |
| Math Computation | 82 | 12 |
| Reading Composite | 82 | 5 |
| Math Composite | 77 | 6 |
| Battery Composite | 80 | 4 |

*Discussion of Test Results*

Josh was evaluated across three sessions, two held in this examiner's office and one in the school setting. Within the office, the WISC-R was administered one week, with the achievement measures administered during the following week. At school, interviews were held with three of the four different teachers Josh has for reading, math, and social studies.

In reading, Josh is currently placed in the beginning of 4-1 book of the Economy reading series. He is in the lowest of three reading groups. According to his teacher, the average student in his classroom is in the middle of the 4-1 book. Thirty minutes per day are allotted for reading, with 15 minutes devoted to small group activities. Josh's reading group receives 60 minutes of reading activities beyond the allotted time twice a week. His teacher indicated that although Josh is in the lowest reading group, his skills are not the poorest of his peers.

Assessment in reading was conducted by both the administration of the K-TEA and direct assessment of reading skills taken from the reading series. Josh was found to be reading at a frustration level within the 4-1 and 3-2 levels of the basal reading series. He was instructional at the 3-1 level; however, comprehension appears to be lagging far behind his oral reading skills. On the K-TEA he was found to score at about the 5th percentile for his grade, with equally poor decoding and comprehension skills.

In mathematics, Josh is instructed in the MacMillan series. His teacher reported him to be having significant problems in basic skills. He recently scored 67% on a test of subtraction with regrouping. In computation, he was reported to still use his fingers occasionally. Students in his class are now working on multiplication and division facts, complex multiplication, and long division. Josh continues to show problems in mathematics application as well as word problems. The teacher has divided the class into two small groups for instruction in math, but both are considered average. It is planned for Josh to go into a remedial mathematics class during the second half of the school year.

Direct assessment of mathematics showed Josh to be having significant rate problems at even basic levels of addition and subtraction facts. Essentially, he performs these skills with few errors, but uses his fingers and other manipulatives to solve computations. This significantly reduces the speed at which he can perform the problems. Additionally, Josh does not always attend to signs and may mix operations. On the K-TEA, he scored at the 6th percentile for his grade in math.

In spelling, Josh shows equal problems. The class is instructed as a unit with weekly tests given to assess progress. Josh is attaining a 70% grade, barely passing. In other areas of written language he persists in having problems in all areas including mechanics, grammatical usage, and handwriting.

The one primary strength Josh shows is his behavior. He continues to be described as a pleasant and enjoyable youngster who is very "good hearted." Previous evaluations have noted a good level of motivation. Unfortunately, however, that seems to be diminished according to his teachers.

*Conclusions and Recommendations*

Every evaluation that has been conducted with Josh since he was a preschooler has pointed to the need for special education. The evaluation conducted 3 years ago identified Josh as a learning disabled student. Despite these recommendations, Josh has not received any special education services since entering school. The time is now critical for Josh to receive services for a learning disabled student.

Results of this evaluation strongly demonstrate the level of language problems Josh is experiencing. Additionally, he shows significant difficulties in memory retention and comprehension. These problems clearly affect his mathematics computation skills as well.

It is strongly recommended that Josh receive services for learning disabled children as soon as possible. It cannot be overemphasized that Josh is in serious danger of becoming an increasingly difficult academic problem as time continues. This examiner strongly believes that the level and significance of Josh's problem warrants placement in a self-contained learning disabled classroom. Josh has been maintained in mainstreamed settings with little success since school began. As evident from the results of the present evaluation that clearly echo previous assessments, Josh is not making substantial progress. Given his age (10-9) and grade (4), Josh needs to begin receiving remediation services as soon as possible. It is not suggested that it wait until the next academic year.

Further, it is suggested that tutoring continue at home to provide Josh with as much support for academic success as possible.

## Course of Treatment

Based on this evaluation, Josh was placed into a classroom for LD students within his local school district. Although apprehensive about moving her son to the public school system, Mrs. K. recognized that Josh's academic problems were reaching a critical stage.

On being placed into the LD room, it was recommended to the teacher that biweekly monitoring of Josh's progress in reading be obtained. Using CBA, Josh was instructed to read aloud a passage for 1 minute from the 3-1 and 3-2 levels of the basal reading series each week. (See Shapiro, 1987, 1989, for details on this use of this type of ongoing assessment strategy.) Passages selected for assessment were taken from the same portion of the text in which Josh was being instructed. His teacher established a goal of completing both the 3-1 and 3-2 books by the end of the school year.

Figure 10.1 shows the results of Josh's progress in reading across the first 25 weeks of the school year. The dashed line on the figure represents the slope of improvement necessary for Josh to reach the teacher's goal of having him read at 100 words correct per minute. This goal was selected based on assessing a random sample of third-grade students in the same school who were reading at the 3-1 or 3-2 levels of the basal

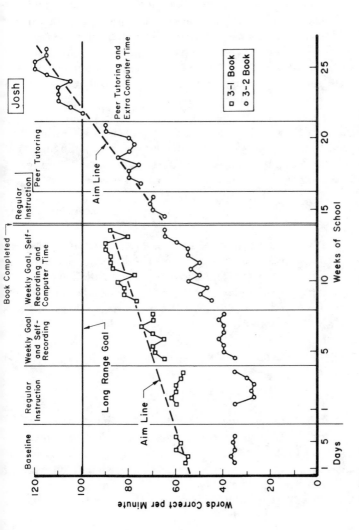

**Figure 10.1.** Progress monitoring chart (words per minute) for Josh in reading.

SOURCE: *Academic Skills Problems: Direct Assessment and Intervention* by E. S. Shapiro, 1989. New York: Guilford. Reprinted with permission.

reading series. Following 5 days of baseline data, no progress was found during the initial 3 weeks of instruction within the special education classroom. After consulting with the teacher, it was decided to have Josh meet weekly with the teacher to determine a reading rate goal for that week and to self-record his reading rate. This change resulted in an improvement over previous performance. At 8 weeks into the treatment program, earning additional computer times was added to the program, which resulted in Josh improving his oral reading rate and completing the 3-1 book after 14 weeks of school. Additionally, oral reading rates on the 3-2 book, which had not been instructed up to this point, also showed substantial improvement over baseline levels. The treatment program continued with the 3-2 book, with the teacher moving to a peer-tutoring format. Finally, at 21 weeks into school, extra computer time plus peer tutoring were instituted and resulted in Josh reaching the stated goal of at least 100 words per minute.

Similar types of data were obtained for progress in mathematical computations, spelling, and written language. In each area, a variety of intervention strategies, including self-monitoring, goal setting, using self-instructional training, contingent reinforcement, and peer tutoring, resulted in substantial improvements in Josh's academic progress.

## Follow-Up

One year after placement into the LD classroom, Josh continues to make substantial progress. Reports from both his teachers and his tutor indicate that he works very hard and is looking forward to when he does not have to attend "special classes." His written language remains a problem, however, and he continues to show more problems in the verbal area. Mrs. K. reported that she was extremely happy with Josh's progress and has some regrets over not placing him into the LD class earlier in his school years.

## Overall Evaluation

Josh's case represents a classic example of a learning disability. On standardized testing, Josh's scores showed large and highly significant differences between the intelligence and achievement tests. Further, substantial within-test differences were evident on the intelligence test, with a 37-point difference between verbal and performance subtests of the WISC-R. These types of scores are strongly suggestive of a learning disability and are important in demonstrating Josh's eligibility for LD services.

Although the results of standardized tests help to substantiate Josh's legal eligibility for services, they fail to offer suggestions about the remediation process. CBA provided a starting point for Josh's reading skills and offered opportunities to provide an ongoing assessment of Josh's progress as his teacher began the instruction process. Use of the CBA data provided strong and data-based evidence of the positive impact the special education instruction was having on Josh's reading ability. Although not shown because of space limitations, equal success was noted in Josh's performance in mathematics and spelling. Written language remained as an area of little improvement, however.

# References

Blankenship C. S. (1985). Using curriculum-based assessment data to make instructional decisions. *Exceptional Children, 52*, 233-238.

Deno, S. L. (1985). Curriculum-based measurement: The emerging alternative. *Exceptional Children, 52*, 219-232.

Federal Register. (1977). Procedures for evaluating specific learning disabilities. Washington, DC: Department of Health, Education, and Welfare, December 29.

Hammill, D. D., Leigh, J. E., McNutt, G. & Larsen, S. C. (1981). A new definition of learning disabilities. *Learning Disability Quarterly, 4*, 336-342.

Shapiro, E. S. (1987). *Behavioral assessment in school psychology.* Hillsdale, NJ: Lawrence Erlbaum.

Shapiro, E. S. (1989). *Academic skills problems: Direct assessment and intervention.* New York: Guilford.

Shapiro, E. S., & Lentz, F. E. (1985). Assessing academic behavior: A behavioral approach. *School Psychology Review, 14*, 325-338.

Shapiro, E. S., & Lentz, F. E. (1986). Behavioral assessment of academic behavior. In T. R. Kratochwill (Ed.), *Advances in school psychology* (Vol. 5, pp. 87-139). Hillsdale, NJ: Lawrence Erlbaum.

# Chapter 11

# Mental Retardation: Children

P. J. Cushing
R. A. McWilliam
Judith E. Favell

## Description of the Disorder

Mental retardation affects not only the child but all those who live with or are closely associated with him or her. Since the child's natural environments include both home and school, the ability to function well depends on the demands and opportunities those ecologies provide. In infancy and the preschool years especially, parents are considered the primary change agents (Lillie & Trohanis, 1976). During this time, the individual with mental retardation physically changes faster than at any time in adulthood. Even though cognitive progress is delayed, developmental maturation has an impact on the continuation of services. Services are often provided according to chronological age, with cutoffs at age 3, 5, and annually thereafter. These frequent transitions can disrupt the treatment children receive and cause hardships for the families. Each transition not only changes the physical demands on the family (e.g., transportation, searching for services), but also the emotional demands (e.g., worry, stress, frustration; Hains, Fowler, & Chandler, 1988).

Support to families is now acknowledged as a major component of effective services to children with mental retardation (Dunst, 1985). Historically, child-centered programs have limited their work with families to such activities as parent "training," parent involvement in program activities, and parental permission for assessment, intervention, and so on (Lillie & Trohanis, 1976). Current best practices, however, include a stronger collaboration between professionals and parents in the treatment of children. Parents have opportunities to participate actively in assessment, intervention, and evaluation processes. The child in this case study was enrolled in a program that views the whole family, rather than the "identified client" only, as both the recipient of services and the unit of analysis for evaluation of program impact.

## Case Identification and Presenting Complaints

This case was collected because it provides a fairly representative study of the development of a child with mental retardation and the affect of the child's handicaps on the entire family unit. First, like so many children with mental retardation, Amy has associated handicaps of a mild seizure disorder and cerebral palsy. None of her associated handicaps alone would constitute a severe handicap, but they can serve to complicate treatment efforts.

Second, at 13 months of age, Amy was identified as being at high risk for developmental delays and was enrolled in an early intervention program. Early intervention services are rapidly becoming a standard resource for these children and their families. Third, Amy developed behavior problems. This too is a common finding among children with mental retardation and can have a devastating effect on the family. We have been fortunate to know Amy and her family for an extended period of time. Our long acquaintance with the family allows us to provide the reader with some idea of the many transitions and adjustments a family endures in the rearing of a child with mental retardation.

This case study covers a time from when the family had a vague concern that something may not be right with their baby (history) to the transition from early intervention into the public school (termination and follow-up) which is, perhaps, the most difficult transition for parents to make in their child's early years. The major portion of the case study (assessment and selection of treatment) will focus on the time when behavior problems first became a source of stress to the family, and the reality of Amy's handicaps became apparent to the parents. These changes and realizations raised questions about the future—questions that will surface time and time again as the family adjusts to the needs presented by Amy's mental retardation.

## History

Mrs. Anderson (pseudonym) was 23 years old at the time of Amy's birth. The pregnancy was uncomplicated with the exception of a mild case of the flu (temperature 102° Fahrenheit) during the first trimester. The baby was born 1 to 2 months prematurely and weighed 5 pounds 2 ounces. Mrs. Anderson reported that "they lost the baby's heartbeat" just prior to being transferred to the delivery room. The baby cried spontaneously at delivery; her color, however, was described as being a dark purple. Difficulty in maintaining body temperature and elevated bilirubin levels resulted in an extended postnatal hospital stay. She was released after 8 days.

Soon after birth, the family's private pediatrician became concerned that Amy's head was abnormally small. When Amy was 4 months of age and again at 8 months of age, he referred her to a neurologist. Both times the neurologist felt that Amy's small head was proportionate to her small stature. Still concerned about Amy's head size at 1 year of age, the pediatrician referred the baby to our home-based, early intervention program.

Initial contact with the family and the first formal assessments of Amy's development occurred when she was 13 months old. Height, weight, and head circumference were all at or below the fifth percentile. The extremities were slightly hypertonic, with the legs more involved than the arms. Amy's primary means of locomotion was rolling, but she was just beginning to crawl. She could only sit when supported and showed poor balance reactions, suggesting mild cerebral palsy. Amy was beginning to finger-feed and could drink from a cup with assistance. Her toy play was limited to mouthing objects. An area of strength for Amy was her attentiveness to adults and her active engagement in social interactions (smiling, laughing). Amy's performance on the Bayley Scales of Infant Development (Bayley, 1969) showed her to be functioning within the range of mental retardation (mental age equivalent, 7 months; psychomotor age equivalent, 8.3 months).

**Table 11.1** Results of Assessments

| Age | Developmental Quotient | Domains in Age Equivalents | | | |
|---|---|---|---|---|---|
| | | Cognitive | Social/Adaptive | Motor | Communication |
| 13 mo | <50[a] | 7.0 mo[a] | — | 8.3 mo[e] | 7.0 mo[g] |
| 20 mo | <50[a] | 10.4 mo[a] | 13 mo[c] | 8.8 mo[e] | 10.0 mo[g] |
| 31 mo | 39[a, i] | 12.0 mo[a] | 17 mo[c] | 11.0 mo[e] | 12.0 mo[g] |
| 47 mo | 30[a, i] | 14.0 mo[a] | 20 mo[c] | 16.0 mo[e] | 14.0 mo[g] |
| 60 mo | 35[b] | 20.7 mo[b] | 25 mo[c] | 23.5 mo[f] | 21.0 mo[h] |
| 75 mo | 34[b] | 25.0 mo[b] | 27 mo[d] | 34.0 mo[f] | 22.5 mo[h] |
| 90 mo | 33[b] | 30.0 mo[b] | 32 mo[d] | 40.0 mo[f] | 22.5 mo[h] |

[a]*Bayley Scales of Infant Development: Mental Scale* (Bayley, 1969)
[b]*Griffiths Scales of Mental Development: General Score* (Griffiths, 1970)
[c]*Vineland Social Maturity Scale (Doll, 1965)*
[d]*Scales of Independent Behavior* (Bruininks et al., 1984)
[e]*Bayley Scales of Infant Development: Motor Scale* (Bayley, 1969)
[f]*Griffiths Scales of Mental Development: Locomotor Subscale* (Griffiths, 1970)
[g]*Sequenced Inventory of Communication Development* (Hedrick, Prather, & Tobin, 1975)
[h]*Griffiths Scales of Mental Development: Hearing/Speech Subscale* (Griffiths, 1954, 1970)
[i]Ratio quotient: Bayley does not specify quotients lower than 50.

At the time of this initial assessment, Mrs. Anderson was separated from her first husband, working full time, and providing and caring for a fussy baby on her own. The doctor's implications that Amy possibly had handicaps only added to the physical and emotional stress Mrs. Anderson was already experiencing. Her greatest source of support was her parents, but they lived 100 miles away, making frequent contact difficult.

Following the initial assessment by our transdisciplinary team, the family began receiving weekly home visits by a case coordinator. A private physical therapist also saw Amy but this service was gradually withdrawn as she became more proficient in locomotion. At age 3 Amy was enrolled in a classroom program 2 days a week in addition to receiving home-based services.

Over a 2½-year period in our program, Amy's microcephaly became more apparent. Periodic assessments using standardized instruments showed her to be consistently functioning within the range of mental retardation (see Table 11.1). Further complications arose at age 3½ years when Amy's steadily improving ability to walk and run independently brought with it some behavior problems. Behavior difficulties, along with her delay in speech, became the focus of the assessment and goal setting that occurred a few months later.

# Assessment

*Family Status and Concerns*

The family's fourth assessment by our program occurred when Amy was 3 years 11 months old. At this point, Mrs. Anderson had been married to her second husband for 14 months and he had adopted Amy. Mr. Anderson was a manager in a local factory. The family felt that his income was sufficient to meet their needs; therefore, Mrs. Anderson left her job to stay at home with Amy. She stated that she felt a great deal of emotional support from her new spouse and talked about the positive effects the marriage had on her and on her daughter. Observations of Mr. Anderson and Amy together left little doubt as to her fondness for her new father and vice versa. The family discussed the following concerns at the time of this assessment.

1. *Behavior in public places.* Amy was obviously "a handful" at the grocery store, the bank, a restaurant, and most other public places. She was extremely active and would not stay in one place for more than a few minutes. The family particularly worried about her running away from them in a mall or department store. They were equally disconcerted by her grabbing items off shelves. Amy was completely unresponsive to instructions by the parents in these situations.

2. *Behavior at home.* Supervision of Amy at home was, at times, quite tiresome for the Andersons. For the better part of the day Amy was "on the go." If not constantly watched, she would get into the parents' record albums, encyclopedias, baby powder, and so on. Amy also liked to climb, which gave her additional access to varied items. Of more concern, her poor coordination made climbing quite dangerous for her. Again, Amy was unresponsive to instruction or scolding.

3. *Behavior in the classroom.* Amy's activity level, distractibility, and climbing were also a problem in the classroom that she attended 2 days a week. Her interest in most activities was fleeting at best. She wandered off from group activities, and her interest in toys during free

play was severely limited. Only occasionally would she stay with one toy or activity for more than 2 to 3 minutes.

4. *Social interactions and communication skills.* The Andersons were concerned that Amy had made very little progress toward talking over the previous year. She made a few sounds that appeared to be labels for special people in her life (e.g., "ga-ga" for Daddy), but she did not use words or sounds to communicate her needs and desires. Even so, Amy had developed some functional gestures. For example, she would try to pull her parents from the living room into the kitchen and point to or bang on the refrigerator to indicate she wanted something to eat or drink. Although this type of communication gave the parents the general idea, problems arose when they couldn't guess the precise item or activity Amy wanted. The guessing game frustrated both Amy and her parents and often resulted in crying and tantrums.

Amy also manifested distractibility and "flighty" behavior in her interactions with her parents and other people. Interactions were typically fleeting and on Amy's terms. She enjoyed some roughhousing in the form of tickling, chasing, and simple teasing. She also liked to hug and kiss when she initiated it. Nevertheless, Amy made little or no eye contact with others during social exchanges and it was almost impossible to have any degree of sustained interaction with her.

5. *Amy's future.* A concern that arose during many of the discussions with the Andersons was Amy's future. Although not always specifically stated, their concerns appeared to include the following: "What will Amy be like when she grows up?" "Where will she go to school?" "Will we be able to handle her behavior?" "Will she ever speak?" "How will Amy affect our marriage as she grows older?"

### Child Assessment

Formal assessment of Amy's abilities was conducted using the following instruments or procedures (see Table 11.1):

*Bayley Scales of Infant Development* (Bayley, 1969)

*Vineland Social Maturity Scale* (Doll, 1965)

*Sequenced Inventory of Communication Development* (Hedrick, Prather, & Tobin, 1975)

Physical examination

Physical therapy evaluation

Audiological testing
Informal observation of Amy in the home, classroom, and clinic

*Physical findings.* At the time of this assessment, Amy was 39 inches tall (10th percentile), weighed 29 pounds 12 ounces (3rd percentile), and had a head circumference below the third percentile. She was found to have mildly increased tone in her shoulders, trunk, pelvic girdle, and lower extremities. Amy could walk without falling, but a lack of trunk rotation gave her walking a stiff, awkward appearance, and prevented her from shifting her weight from one foot to the other adequately as might be required in steps over objects. Amy had worsened in the "jitteriness" seen in previous assessments. The tremors in her hands, arms, and trunk made fine motor tasks very difficult and frustrating for Amy. A lack of appropriate wrist rotation also contributed to coordination difficulties. Overall, Amy was found to function at about a 15-18 month level in both gross motor and fine motor abilities. On the *Bayley Motor Scale* (Bayley, 1969), Amy's performance indicated a psychomotor age equivalent of 16.1 months.

*Cognitive/Adaptive.* On the *Bayley Scales of Mental Development* (Bayley, 1969), Amy received credit for all items through the 12.4-month level and for several items above that level. The highest item she passed was at the 17.8-month level. This item involved following directions with a baby doll by putting it in a chair and giving it a drink with a toy cup. Amy was quite adept at dumping objects from containers and placing objects in containers. She was able to place a large peg in a hole, but only with physical assistance. She was unable to place forms (circles, squares, triangles) in a simple form board correctly. In total, her score reflected a mental age equivalent of 14.0 months. No mental developmental index quotient was completed since she was more than 30 months old (the age limit of the standardization sample).

On the *Vineland Social Maturity Scale* (Doll, 1965), Amy passed all items for the birth to 1 year of age period, expect except the item "Does not drool." She passed approximately one-half of the items for the 1 to 2-year age period, with a few additional borderline passes. At this level, Amy could eat with a spoon (although messily), drink by herself from a cup, assist in undressing (e.g., taking off socks), and mark with a crayon. Items at the 1 to 2-year levels that Amy did not pass or for which she only received partial credit required speech (e.g., uses names of familiar objects, talking in short sentences) or more advanced motor skills (e.g., walking upstairs unassisted). She only passed one item ("initiates own place activities") at the 2 to 3-year age period. In total Amy's score reflected a social age equivalent of 1.68 years (20 months) on the *Vineland* and a social quotient of 43.

*Communication.* Amy's performance on the SICD (Hedrick, Prather, & Tobin, 1975) indicated that her expressive communication skills were at about a 12-month level. The parents reported that Amy used "mamma" and "ga-ga" specifically in reference to her mother and father, generally using these words in the absence of the parent, as though she was talking about her or him. The parents also reported that she used a "k"-plus-vowel sound to say "cat" and a slightly different "k"-plus-vowel sound to say "cow." Observations by the speech and language pathologist found that Amy used several consonant sounds ("p, m, t, d, g, k") and at least five different vowel sounds. Even so, Amy's vocalizations were thought to be more like babbling than verbal utterances.

Although Amy was not yet using true words consistently, she was developing some important communication skills. For example, the parents reported that she frequently imitated sounds (e.g., car motor sound) made by others. She displayed a definite "yes" head gesture in response to some questions, and the parents reported that she occasionally shook her head for "no." Perhaps Amy's strongest skill in communication was her indicating desires by physically manipulating others. She demonstrated this on the assessment day when she placed the examiner's hand on a wind-up toy to indicate that she wanted it activated again. As mentioned earlier, Amy frequently indicated what she wanted at home by pulling the parents, pointing, and grunting. On a less physical level, Amy would attempt to engage the parents in singing some songs accompanied by gestures (e.g., "Itsy-Bitsy Spider," "Wheels on the Bus") by attempting to perform the appropriate hand moves.

## Selection of Treatment

The Andersons, like so many parents of children with mental retardation, already had little time and energy to spare. Intense, complicated intervention programs would be doomed to failure. The parents did not want to be "therapists"; they just wanted ways to lessen their own and Amy's frustration in everyday routines. They wanted interventions that were easy to implement without causing more stress than they already felt. Consequently, interventions were designed to take place within the context of the family's daily routines (e.g., meals, bath, bedtime, washing dishes, and so on).

Taking into consideration all of the concerns of the parents, four major areas of intervention were identified: (a) teaching Amy to respond appropriately to simple instructions, (b) teaching Amy a method of communicating her needs and wants, (c) developing methods to bring Amy's dangerous or undesirable behavior under control, and (d) teaching Amy to be more responsive in social interactions. A general strategy for each of these intervention targets is described below. Specifications of intervention procedures are described later in the routine-based treatment plan.

### Following Instructions

Mr. and Mrs. Anderson developed a list of general instructions that could be used across routines and settings to control Amy's behavior. They decided that "Sit down" and "Come here" would be the first ones to teach Amy. It was further decided that manual signs would be combined with verbal instructions. Gestures and physical prompts would be used if Amy did not respond to instructions. Compliance (even when physically prompted) would be rewarded with hugs and descriptive praise.

### Communication

Amy's lack of significant progress in oral communication and the possibility of motor dysfunction in the oral musculature prompted us to broach the topic of augmentative communication systems. The parents liked the idea of an augmentative system and chose simple sign language and a few symbols (e.g., magnetized pictures of food items on the refrigerator). It was also decided that the first signs Amy would be taught were those that would enable her to obtain highly desirable items and fun activities.

### Undesirable Behavior

The parents rank-ordered their priorities for intervention; climbing and running away were the top two targets. A modified time-out procedure was planned in which Amy's climbing and running away would be consequated by a firm "No" and seating her immediately in a specific chair on the far side of the room. The same procedure would be used at home and in the classroom. To eliminate the need for constant supervision and to avoid too many occasions for this "sit-and-watch" procedure at home, the parents elected to put a children's safety gate across the doorway during certain daily routines (e.g., dinner preparation, washing dishes). The parents decided not to target Amy's behavior in the mall or restaurant until they achieved some success in controlling her at home.

*Social Interactions*

The parents wanted Amy to look at them during social exchanges. This was quite important to them, but they did not wish to "force" her to do it. It was suggested that they could work on eye contact during enjoyable interactions, such as singing songs, roughhousing, or affectionate exchanges. Interruption (i.e. pausing) of an ongoing fun activity might be enough of a consequence to cause Amy to look at the parent's face. Praise for "good looking" and resumption of the activity would be the reward.

## Routine-based Treatment Plan

In developing the general strategies described above, the parents identified several times of the day that were particularly difficult, as well as routines that were appropriate for learning particular skills. Together, the treatment strategies and targeted routines of the day were used to develop a routine-based treatment plan (see Table 11.2). The intervention goals and general treatment strategies were written down the left-hand side, and the daily routines were written across the top. Thus, a treatment-by-routine matrix was formed. Adaptations or specifications of the general treatment strategies as they pertain to particular routines were entered in the appropriate block of the matrix. The classroom staff used a similar matrix for scheduling intervention during school activities (e.g., circle time, meals, free play, and activity zones).

Use of the routine-based treatment matrix has several advantages over more traditional treatment plans, which are typically lengthy, noncontextually-based, with a separate plan written by each individual therapist according to his or her discipline. First, routine-based matrices are accessible to those responsible for conducting treatment (parents or

**Table 11.2** Routine-Based Treatment Plan for First Month of Treatment

Activities

| GOALS AND STRATEGIES | Getting out of the house (school, errands, etc.) | Dressing | Bath | Meals | Leisure Time (Liv. Rm. 7-8:30) | Outdoor Play | Unspecified Times |
|---|---|---|---|---|---|---|---|
| *Following Instructions*<br>Sign, prompt, and praise | *"Come here"* to leave and put on a coat *"Sit down"* to wait in small chair while Mom/Dad put on coat (1 minute) | *"Come here"* to get dressed *"Sit down"* to wait in small chair while Mom looks for clothes in drawer (1 min.) | *"Come here"* to call Amy for a bath *"Sit down"* to take off shoes/socks | *"Sit down"* when time to eat meal | *"Come here"* to tickle or rough-house *"Sit down"* to sing or read | *"Come here"* to call from across yard or when on walk (3 or 4 feet away) *"Sit down"* on swing, slide, etc. | *"Come here"* and *"Sit down"* when appropriate. Try not to overuse in a controlling manner. Use for fun activities |
| *Signing*<br>Present model and gradually require initiation | *"Car"*: sign for drive when it is time to leave *"School"*: go to school (sign several times until reach destination) | *"Shoes"* *"Sing"*: modified sign to sing favorite songs | *"Bath"*: to get into tub *"Frog"*: modified sign for favorite bath toy Question: Where frog? | *"Eat"* *"Drink"* *"More"* | *"Book"*: to be read a story or play with book *"Sing"*: modified for singing or finger plays | *"Swing"* (modified sign) *"More"*: to continue activities (e.g., swing again) *Amy badge*—bring to parents to go outside | *"Baby"* (favorite toy) *"Cat"* *"Mommy"* *"Daddy"* Bring magnets on refrigerator when hungry |
| *Social Interaction*<br>Interrupt ongoing fun activity. Resume when brief eye contact made | Brief eye contact before opening car door | Pause in dressing once in a while. Brief eye contact before resuming | Brief eye contact to resume water play | Brief eye contact before handing Amy her milk, juice, etc. | Brief eye contact to continue roughhousing, singing, or reading book | Brief eye contact to resume pushing on swing | Pause in midst of ongoing fun activities. Resume when brief eye contact is made |
| *Behavior*<br>Sit and watch<br>Safety gate<br>Redirect | *Safety gate* if Mom/Dad need to get dressed or can't monitor Amy | Walk away if Amy gets too wild or uncooperative. Try again later | | Safety gate during meal preparation and clean up if other parent unavailable | Redirect to own books when Amy pulls out Daddy's books | If wanders off too far and does not respond to *"Come here"*, Amy must sit | Safety gate if parents can't supervise or are tired *Do not overuse |
| Climbing: Say "No, get down" (sign "down"). If Amy continues to climb, sign and say "down" again and immediately put in sit-and-watch | | | | | | | |
| Running Away: Any instance of running away results in firm "No" and sit-and-watch | | | | | | | |
| *Scheduling* | | | Alternate nights responsible for giving Amy her bath. Other parent has free time for reading, sewing, etc. | On Wednesdays Mom and Dad eat late dinner after Amy goes to bed (8 or 8:30) | Dad takes Amy out for ice cream dessert or to the park on Thursday to give Mom a break | | Try to schedule errands when Amy is in classroom. In-home respite care for mall or restaurant |

classroom staff). They may be posted on the refrigerator, bulletin board, or wall where they are likely to be reviewed periodically, thus serving as a frequent and quick reminder of the child's objectives. Second, the normal routines of the home or classroom serve as a cue to conduct specific treatment procedures; additional "therapy" time is not required. This makes it less likely that the family will forget or neglect treatment. Third, the age-old difficulty of generalization is lessened because (a) treatment is conducted within the routines where change is desired (i.e., it is functional) and (b) multiple opportunities for skill learning are presented as each treatment is conducted across several routines of the day. Finally, the effectiveness of treatment is immediately obvious to those responsible for its conduct because outcomes are defined in terms of specific child behavior change at specific times of the day. Furthermore, routine-based outcomes are typically viewed by parents and teachers as being practical and therefore worthy of their commitment to implementing treatment procedures.

## Course of Treatment

The course of Amy's treatment using the routine-based plan is described next. The effectiveness of treatment strategies to achieve family goals is also discussed.

### Following Instructions

Many opportunities arose naturally for the commands, "Come here" and "Sit down," because Amy often wandered from the activity, left her seat, or simply did not respond to environmental cues. Teaching Amy to follow these two instructions was not an easy task since it was doubtful whether she even understood the instruction. The parents were therefore working on comprehension of the verbal and gestural cues in addition to compliance. Amy's high activity level and distractibility made it even more difficult for her to comply with instructions presented from across the room. The parents had to approach Amy, obtain her attention, and then give the signed and verbal instructions. For quite a long time Amy also required physical prompting every occasion an instruction was given. For example, the parents led her to the chair and patted the chair following the instruction, "Sit down." Only very gradually did she appear to understand the commands. Then, new problems emerged.

Amy began to actively resist instructions in certain situations (e.g., leaving for school/errands, dressing, taking a walk). When told to "Come here" she would run away and when told to "Sit down" she would fall to the floor. The verbal and physical tussle between Amy and her parents when she resisted appeared to maintain the behavior. Amy frequently giggled and "teased" her parents during these interactions. Moreover, she often won the struggle through her persistence and the parents' need to move on to a new activity (e.g., leave for work or school) or intervene more directly for Amy's safety (such as when she ran away while taking a walk). Changes in the original treatment plan were needed. One adaptation was to increase the number of instructions in routines where highly valued activities (tickling, reading, snacks, singing) could be used as immediate rewards for compliance. Another adaptation involved eliminating undue attention for active noncompliance by issuing an instruction only once and ignoring any instance of noncompliance by walking away from her whenever possible. These changes proved to be beneficial.

A second, and related, difficulty was Amy's apparent inability to stay in one place when instructed to "Come here" or "Sit down." Even when she complied, she was off again in a matter of seconds. Again, the parents eliminated undue attention, this time by calmly reissuing the command and ignoring any instances of noncompliance. Rewards for compliance were gradually delayed (e.g., slowly giving her a toy or cracker while talking about her good sitting or coming when called) or extended (e.g., prolonged praising or singing and periodically reminding her that she was a good girl for sitting).

Over the course of the year, Amy's instruction following slowly improved. Although they achieved far from perfect results, the parents felt as though they had gained at least a reasonable amount of instructional control over Amy's behavior. In fact, on his own, Mr. Anderson began to implement the instructional control procedures during his Thursday evening trips to the ice cream parlor and was quite successful.

*Communication*

The Andersons selected two or three words that they wanted Amy to sign during each routine where communication was specifically targeted. These routine-specific words/signs are shown on the matrix (Table 11.2). Primarily, signs were selected that the parents could immediately consequate by giving her a preferred object (frog in bath, baby doll, food, drink) or engaging in a fun activity (car ride, sing, read book, swing). A few signs were modified to make them clearer for Amy or easier for her to imitate. Not all of the signs were introduced on the same day, but within a 4 to 6 week period the parents were using most of them within routines.

Amy showed a fair amount of interest in the signs when the parents introduced them. Even so, there was no indication that she understood their meaning and Amy made no attempt to imitate the parents' signing. The parents attempted to prompt her physically to imitate the signs, but Amy resisted these prompts. Consequently, prompting was temporarily left out and only the modeling of signs continued.

After 2 months of modeling signs, the Andersons were beginning seriously to question the value of signing. One day, however, Mrs. Anderson was talking to Amy in the living room about bath time (signed). Amy walked off to the bathroom and took her frog from the side of the tub. Similar indications of sign comprehension began to emerge in other routines, but Amy made no attempt to imitate her parents' signing. Although the parents clearly wanted Amy to start signing, they made it very clear that it was not worth engaging in warfare with her (crying, tantrums) to accomplish it.

Two basic changes in procedures were made to facilitate Amy's expressive signing. First, the parents added a 10-second pause between their modeling of a sign and giving her the preferred object or activity. It was a bit difficult for the Andersons to change their patterns, but counting to 10 to themselves before giving things to her helped them wait. It was just long enough to make Amy a little impatient but not so long that she began to get really upset. Second, they played games to provide an opportunity for several repetitions of a sign in a short time period and to sneak in a few physical prompts without Amy's resistance. Amy loved roughhousing, laughing, and active social interaction (the wilder the better). Adaptations of old games and a few new games were designed so that Amy could control the game by signing. For example, one game was "Here comes the baby." This game was played with Amy's favorite doll. The parents would "walk" the doll across the floor to Amy, stopping two or three times to say: "Here comes the baby" and signing "baby." When the doll reached her, they would put it on her chest and tickle Amy, who squealed with delight. While tickling her they would pause briefly, prompt her to sign baby, and resume tickling while repeating "baby." Later, they began pausing during the baby's walk across the floor (i.e., "Here comes the . . .").

**Table 11.3** Amy's Signed and Spoken Vocabulary Following 1 Year of Signing
Procedures

|  | *Spoken* | *Signed* |
|---|---|---|
| Spontaneous |  |  |
|  | mama | balloon |
|  | gaga (daddy) | drink |
|  | gagie (doggie) | more |
|  | caca (cat) | outside |
|  | bye-bye | car |
|  | cow-cow (cow) | school |
|  | ba (ball) | sing |
|  | bubu (bath) | please |
|  | mama go bye-bye | baby |
|  |  | cookie |
|  |  | eat |
|  |  | bath |
|  |  | frog |
|  |  | shoes |
| Imitated |  |  |
|  | paw paw (grandfather) | swing |
|  | nana (nanny) | ball |
|  | baby | one |
|  | pat pat (aunt) | thank-you |
|  | baba (Barbara) | book |

Amy soon caught on to signing "baby" to control the baby's walking
and the parents' tickling.

Overall, the combination of modeling, pausing, and repetition through
game playing resulted in the desired effect. Amy began to use signs,
first in game playing, then in imitation, and finally spontaneously
within context. Her signing was inexact owing to her difficulties in
hand/arm coordination; however, those who had regular contact with
her did understand her. The parents added new signs as they felt Amy
was ready for them. Her signed and spoken vocabulary following 1 year
of signing is presented in Table 11.3.

*Social Interaction*

The procedures for increasing Amy's eye contact with adults were
reasonably successful. The routine-based treatment matrix (Table 11.2)

shows the specific activities within routines when eye contact was required for the continuation of the activity. For example, when Amy raced to the car door and started struggling with it, instead of just opening it for her, the parents would call her name quietly and pause. When Amy glanced at them, they would say "Good looking" and open the door. Pausing was successful in eliciting eye contact. Even so, her eye contact was never sustained and seldom occurred spontaneously.

## Undesirable Behavior

Procedures designed to reduce Amy's climbing, getting into things, and running away were not as successful as had been hoped. The safety gate was used during meal preparation, while the parents were getting dressed or otherwise preparing to leave the house, and sometimes when they wanted to sit and watch television in the evening without having to jump up and down to monitor Amy. Unfortunately, Amy persistently tried to climb over the gate. Her climbing, of course, was somewhat dangerous and it was decided to consequate it with the sit-and-watch procedure used for other instances of climbing. This only made matters worse.

Although sit-and-watch was reasonably effective in the classroom, it did not work well for the parents at home. Discipline in the form of a firm "No" and backed up by sit-and-watch resulted in an increase in climbing the gate and other objects at home. This initial increase (typical in behavior reduction programs) was not followed by an eventual decline in her climbing. Amy appeared to enjoy the attention she got from her parents for climbing and resisting the sit-and-watch procedure. The situation actually became more unpleasant for the parents than the original incessant monitoring of her whereabouts.

The parents discontinued sit-and-watch at home. They chose to continue using the safety gate because it at least slowed Amy down; also, she did not leave a room unnoticed while the parents were busy. When Amy started climbing the gate her parents instructed her to "Come here" and encouraged her to engage in another activity (playing with pots, pans, or her baby). If Amy did not respond to "Come here" they told her "No climbing," and physically guided her to another activity. More important, they encouraged Amy to play with toys or other objects before she climbed the gate.

A few special activities were reserved for those times when the parents were busy and the safety gate was used. For example, Amy was given a dishpan of water and plastic dishes to play with on the linoleum floor of the kitchen while Mrs. Anderson prepared dinner. This activity entertained Amy for quite a while; it was less stressful to mop up the water afterward and change Amy's shirt than it was to monitor her whereabouts or struggle with her over the issue of climbing the gate. The parents also tried to remember to interact with her periodically as they went about their own activities (e.g., talking about pictures in her book or playing a quick peek-a-boo game during commercial breaks while watching television). This revised strategy proved to be much more effective.

Over the course of a year Amy's behavior improved. At the time of her next annual assessment (age 60 months), both the parents and the classroom staff reported that Amy seemed much calmer and easier to manage. Team members who had not seen Amy throughout the intervening year also noted these improvements. Even so, Amy was relatively difficult to manage. She was still distractible, quite active, and required a considerable amount of supervision.

## Scheduling

The parents did not expect rapid relief from the stresses of constant supervision and intervention since they knew that her behavior would change very gradually. In order to provide more immediate rest for the parents and enjoyable time as a couple, they agreed upon several alternatives to their normal schedules. For example, instead of using respite care once a week, the parents chose to have dinner together on Wednesdays after Amy went to bed (8:00 or 8:30). Mr. Anderson also offered to give his wife an hour or two off one evening a week (Thursdays) by taking Amy out to a local ice cream parlor for dessert or for a walk in the community park when the weather was nice. The family found these changes quite helpful. In addition, the Andersons approached the grandparents about caring for Amy one Friday night and Saturday a month. The grandparents were pleased to be able to help. The parents planned these times out ahead of time and reestablished a few old friendships as well as seeing a number of movies. During the year following her assessment, a new in-home respite program was established in their county. The Andersons used these services once or twice a month to go to the shopping mall in the evening or out for dinner.

## Termination

At the time of her next annual assessment and intervention planning, Amy was 5 years old (60 months) and about to enter a public school program. Her placement was a self-contained classroom within a community elementary school. Our program continued to provide home visits to the family throughout this first year of public school to ensure a smooth transition. One focus of home-based services was to maintain gains and improve skills in following instructions, communication, and behavior control, as well as to teach some basic self-help skills. A second focus was to assist the parents in gaining access to needed services in the public school and to directly assist the classroom teachers in working with Amy through occasional visits to the school.

Initially, Amy adjusted quite well to her new classroom. The teachers were quite receptive to suggestions for educational programming, and Amy continued to make progress in all areas. About midway through the school year, however, Amy developed a seizure disorder that proved to be quite difficult to control. Numerous medication changes and complications caused great stress for the family, and Amy showed some regression in her development.

Amy was just beginning to regain her lost skills when it was time for her to enter a new school for first grade. Amy did not adjust easily to this new transition. She actively resisted the teachers' instructions and was aggressive (e.g., pulling hair, pushing) with the other children several times a day during the first month. One-to-one intervention was needed to bring her behavior under control. She was, however, responsive to this intervention and was soon making developmental progress once gain. Several months into first grade, another transition was necessary when Mr. Anderson was offered a new job 100 miles away, the home town of Mrs. Anderson's parents. An increase in pay and being closer to a very important source of support made the offer quite appealing, and the family decided to move. We assisted the family in identifying resources in their new community and in exploring educational placements for Amy. With the exception of an occasion phone call, we terminated services when the family moved.

Despite the stresses of transition and Amy's new seizure disorder, the family took an active role in advocating for Amy and for other handicapped children in their community. While still receiving services from our program, they were active members of our parent advisory board. When Amy entered public school they were quite assertive in obtaining services for Amy that they felt she needed. Although we provided them with information on services and the law, it was the parents who took action on Amy's behalf. For instance, the Andersons succeeded in getting the school board to approve a summer school program for the children in Amy's school so they could maintain skills over the summer. The Andersons were also instrumental, in conjunction with a community-based support group, in getting the school system to hire a full-time physical therapist.

## Follow-Up

The Andersons visited our program for a follow-up assessment when Amy was 7½ years old (90 months). Amy was in a segregated school for educable mentally handicapped children. Her teacher, speech pathologist, and the school psychologist attended the assessment with Amy and her parents. Staff present reported that Amy had made substantial progress, especially in her attention span, compliance to tasks, and her efforts to communicate. Self-help skills and fine motor skills were still weak areas, largely because of her tremors. It was also noted that her signing was difficult to read owing to her poor fine motor abilities. Overall, Amy was reported to be a much easier child to care for than in the past, primarily because of her responsiveness to verbal instructions.

The parents had quickly become involved in advocacy activities when they moved. They were instrumental in starting up a local Association for Retarded Citizens (ARC) chapter and they were in the process of requesting a summer school program at Amy's new school so that her skills (and those of other children) could be maintained between school years. Although the parents thought highly of Amy's teachers and the educational training offered by the school, they were not pleased by its total segregation from nonhandicapped children. They were formulating plans with other parents to make some changes in this area.

## Overall Evaluation

Amy's communication difficulties, seizure disorder, behavior problems, and lack of appropriate social interaction skills are representative of many children with mental retardation. Mental retardation is not, however, a single disorder with a well-charted progression of outcomes.

It is a group of disorders, many of them with unknown etiologies, that are variously affected by environmental interventions. Hence, Amy's story is unique yet representative in its very uniqueness.

Similarly, every family of a child with mental retardation is different and in need of individualized assistance from professionals. We cannot apply the same standard, patent-pending, parent-training package to all families and expect good results. Although obvious, such uniformity of service options is a surprisingly common practice.

In our case example, it was the parents who identified the targets for intervention and who decided on the methods for achieving child change. The professionals served as resources to provide information, generate options, offer direct assistance when requested, and support the parents' decisions. The routine-based intervention planning process provided a framework that was meaningful and understandable to the parents in deciding on targets and methods for intervention. The Andersons selected targets for intervention that matched their values and priorities as well as the methods of intervention that were in line with their philosophy of childrearing. This, alone, set the stage for success.

Amy is very fortunate to have parents who have the knowledge, skills, and resources to be such strong advocates for her. She will be well served throughout her life, but unfortunately not every parent can attain the accomplishments of the Andersons. Other parents' priorities, values, skills, resources, and support may not make it possible or even desirable. As so aptly stated by Wright, Granger, and Sameroff (1984), "While the professional community has a clear feeling about what defines good parenting, it has become increasingly clear that these definitions are not shared by all parents" (p.85). We are just beginning to realize that attempting to train parents to be teachers is often ineffective and may actually be harmful to the parent-child relationship (Wright, Granger, & Sameroff, 1984). Instead, we should support them as parents in accordance with their individual definitions of what a parent should be. This is best accomplished by asking them what they need rather than telling them what they need.

# References

Bayley, N. (1969). *Bayley scales of infant development*. New York: Psychological Corporation.

Bruininks, R. H., Woodcock, R. W., Weatherman, R. F., & Hill, B. K. (1984). *Scales of Independent Behavior: Woodcock Johnson Psycho-Educational Battery, Part Four*. Allen, TX: DLM/Teaching Resources

Doll, E. A. (1965). *Vineland Social Maturity Scale*. Circle Pines, MN: American Guidance Service.

Dunst, C. J. (1985). Rethinking early intervention. *Analysis and Intervention in Developmental Disabilities, 5,* 165-201.

Griffiths, R. (1954). *The abilities of babies*. London: University of London Press.

Griffiths, R. (1970). *The abilities of young children*. London: Child Development Research Center.

Hains, A. H., Fowler, S. A., & Chandler, L. K. (1988). Planning school transitions: Family and professional collaboration. *Journal of the Division for Early Childhood, 12,* 108-115.

Hedrick, D. L., Prather, E. M., & Tobin, A. R. (1975). *Sequenced Inventory of Communication Development*. Seattle: University of Washington Press.

Lillie, D. L., & Trohanis, P. L. (1976). *Teaching parents to teach: A guide for working with the special child*. New York: Walker.

Linder, T. W. (1983). *Early childhood special education: Program development and administration*. Baltimore, MD: Paul H. Brookes.

McAfee, J. K. (1987). Integrating therapy services in the school: A model for training educators, administrators, and therapists. *Topics in Early Childhood Special Education, 7,* 116-127.

Wolfensberger, W. (1972). *Principles of normalization*. Toronto: National Institute on Mental Retardation.

Wright, J. S., Granger R. D., & Sameroff, A. J. (1984). Parental acceptance and developmental handicap. In J. Blacher (Ed.), *Severely handicapped children and their families: Research in review*. Orlando, FL: Academic Press.

# Chapter 12

# Mental Retardation: Adults

## Mary Beth Johnston
## Thomas L. Whitman

## Description of the Disorder

During the past few decades, dramatic changes have occurred in our understanding of mental retardation and its many causes and consequences. Today the most commonly accepted definitions emphasize that mental retardation consists of both intellectual retardation and deficits in social adaptation, and that these deficits are apparent during childhood and/or adolescence (Grossman, 1983). The changes in our understanding of mental retardation have led to changes in social policy with respect to mentally retarded individuals as well as to the development of highly successful treatment strategies for use with this population. Recently, the "new frontier" in work with mentally retarded individuals has involved the recognition that many also suffer from mental illness.

Mentally retarded individuals appear to be slightly more susceptible to mental illness than intellectually average individuals. According to Menolascino and McCann (1983), approximately 20% to 35% of mentally retarded people who live in the community suffer from mental illness; the incidence of mental illness in the general population is approximately 16% to 20%. Biological and psychogenic factors, as well

**Table 12.1** Factors That Make Mentally Retarded Individuals Particularly Vulnerable to Mental Illness

---

1. Unresolved parental disappointment, grief, and/or guilt resulting in denial, overprotection, and/or overt or covert rejection

2. Unrealistic expectations

3. Problems in self-image and in relationships resulting from failure to integrate the normal developmental sequences at the expected time

4. Economic or stress-related family problems

5. Peer rejection

6. Stigma of attending special classes

7. Frustration and humiliation from repeated failures

8. Fears generated in trying to survive in a highly complex world

9. Language deficits making misunderstandings common

10. Inadequate understanding of social situations and lack of social skills

---

as greater exposure to stress, appear to play primary etiological roles in the development of mental illness within the mentally retarded population (Parsons, May, & Menolascino, 1984). Intellectual deficiencies play an important indirect role in the development of mental illness in this population in that they lead to complex social adjustment problems, such as peer rejection or vocational failures, while limiting the individual's ability to understand and solve these problems. Table 12.1 lists factors that make mentally retarded individuals particularly vulnerable to mental illness. Mentally retarded adults experience the full range of mental illness. The disorders commonly seen in clinical practice are depression, schizophrenia, antisocial behavior, and personality problems, such as lack of self-confidence, nonassertiveness, and problems with anger and/or anxiety in social situations. Manic-depressive illness, anxiety disorders and phobias, and eating disorders are also seen, although less frequently.

In the case study presented below, the client is a mentally retarded young man who was experiencing problems with anger of such proportions that his continued residence in the community was at risk. This case study illustrates the complex problems faced by mentally retarded–mentally ill persons and their need for and receptivity to psychological treatment.

## Case Identification and Presenting Complaints

Frank, a 21-year-old single male, was a client of a community agency working with mentally retarded adults. Four months prior to coming to the clinic, he and his siblings were removed from their home by the Department of Public Welfare because the authorities believed that their parents were not adequately providing for their needs. Subsequently, Frank moved into a group home for mentally handicapped adults. His social worker referred him for psychological assessment and treatment because he was having frequent angry outbursts and the group home staff and residents were both afraid of and bewildered by him. In the group home, a behavioral program had been arranged in which Frank was encouraged to "take a time-out" when angry. Despite this program, his angry outbursts continued and he had not learned alternative, more acceptable strategies for managing anger.

## History

Frank was the oldest of the three children of his parents, both of whom have developmental and emotional disabilities. His mother had been given the diagnosis of schizophrenia for which she had received treatment periodically. In describing his mother, he said, "She's a nice person . . . I'm proud to have her for my mother." Frank idolized his father who, according to his report, had had a brief career as a professional boxer. He wanted to be a boxer like his father. His 16-year-old sister was residing in a foster home. "They say that dad raped her." His 15-year-old brother was institutionalized in a school for adolescents with severe behavior problems. "He got problems; when dad whipped him, he laughed . . . it didn't affect him." Frank attended elementary and high school at the local school for mentally handicapped individuals with behavior problems. For 2 years during adolescence, because of recurrent angry outbursts and family problems, Frank was placed in a residential treatment center for adolescents with serious behavior problems. After high school, Frank worked at the local sheltered workshop and lived at home.

Frank's problems at the group home began shortly after he arrived there. The group home staff found him to become easily and unpredictably angry. When angry, he engaged in a variety of behaviors including swearing, throwing things (including furniture), slamming doors, refusing to do what he was asked, and physically hurting others. Major outbursts occurred several times per week. The intensity and unpredictability of these outbursts stressed the group home staff to the point that his continued placement there was being questioned.

## Assessment

The assessment team consisted of a social worker, a psychologist, and a psychiatrist. The initial phase of assessment included interviews with Frank and his group home supervisor, psychological tests, and a psychiatric evaluation. These procedures were designed to: (a) establish rapport; (b) identify the general nature of any problems; (c) obtain a broad picture of his history, family functioning, group home and vocational functioning, and strengths and weaknesses; and (d) develop preliminary hypotheses concerning factors precipitating and/or maintaining behavior problems. An attempt was made to enlist the support of Frank's parents in the assessment process but they declined to participate.

*Mental Status*

Frank presented himself as a polite, cooperative, and rather naive individual. He made good eye contact. His speech was easily discernible despite his relatively simple sentence structure and concrete use of language. When Frank had difficulty understanding questions posed during the interview, rather than asking that they be repeated or explained, he responded according to his interpretation of what was asked, with little recognition that he had missed the point. Occasionally, he seemed to have his own agenda to talk about, and did so regardless of the topic at hand. Frank's affect was appropriate to the content of his speech, occasionally reflecting underlying anger, defensiveness, and a need to project a "macho image." His mood appeared stable, with occasional flashes of anger that were evident in changes in tone of voice, posture, and facial expression. At times he presented a somewhat threatening and frightening appearance. These episodes were brief, and usually in the context of his description of his temper and how he handles anger toward others. At other times, Frank was quite personable, smiling, chatting, and exhibiting a sense of humor.

There was no evidence of psychosis or of any other thought disorder. His judgment seemed impaired both in terms of his expectations of what he might achieve in the field of professional boxing as well as in his assessment of how his behavior affected others. His insight was poor regarding the things he could do to make his life run more smoothly. He could not see his role in the conflicts that occurred, and, in fact, blamed others for getting him upset whenever this happened.

Frank's desire to become a professional boxer was a primary theme throughout the mental status interview. He was intent on explaining how strong he is, how quick his temper is, and how intolerant he is of those who upset him in any way. He supported these allegations with mean-looking facial grimaces, clenched teeth, and cinched fists. He said that his temper problem was long-standing and was getting worse. He seemed proud that he was not in control at times, though he said that he did not intend to hurt anyone. He could not describe how he tries to control himself when angry.

Frank said that he had a number of friends. When asked about relationships with women, he became embarrassed. While describing one young woman with whom he apparently had some sort of sexual encounter, he asked, "Can we drop this?" He returned to the theme of wanting to learn more about sex later in the interview.

### Adaptive Behavior

Jan, the supervisor at Frank's group home, provided information about his behavior and served as informant for the Vineland Adaptive Behavior Scales (VABS) (Sparrow, Balla, & Cicchetti, 1984). Frank's scores on the VABS indicated significant deficits in adaptive behavior; these were more severe than would have been predicted from his overall cognitive functioning (see below). Frank attained an Adaptive Behavior Composite standard score of 38 and standard scores of 33, 46, and 43 on the communication skills, daily living skills, and socialization skills scales of the VABS, respectively. More significant than his deficiencies in adaptive behavior were his numerous maladaptive behaviors. Jan described Frank as overly dependent, withdrawn, socially isolated, anxious, unhappy, impulsive, inattentive, overly active, angry, defiant, inconsiderate, physically aggressive, and stubborn.

She also described a number of family problems. She believed that Frank's parents used his earnings at the sheltered workshop to help support them and that they were missing that added source of income. She also believed that Frank felt that he was hurting his parents by not living at home. On several occasions, he had taken food and other supplies from the group home and had run away to his parents' home.

Jan said that Frank found working at the sheltered workshop very frustrating; he did not identify with the other workers and saw them as nuisances. Riding the bus to and from work was particularly difficult for him. Jan said that the group home staff and residents liked Frank when he was not angry. He had been a sought-after companion when he first came to the group home. She also related that in some ways he seemed to enjoy the group home. She noted that he took daily baths and sometimes did so for hours at a time. Personal hygiene and grooming were very important to him.

Jan indicated that Frank had decided to pursue a career in boxing. Frequently, he got group home residents in a boxing situation and hurt or, at least, frightened them. At the "least provocation," Frank "exploded" (e.g., slammed the door, threw things, pushed a staff person). These episodes occurred unpredictably in the group home, at the sheltered workshop, or during community activities. Group home staff had become reluctant to take Frank to community activities since, if he became angry, he required considerable attention and it was difficult to supervise other residents at these times. His angry outbursts resulted in several job changes and prevented him from being considered for competitive employment. Jan was candid in saying that sometimes the group home staff was not consistent in handling Frank's angry outbursts. She provided a copy of the group home log that documented his behavior during the previous 8 weeks. The log documented instances in which Frank pulled a door off the hinges, threw a table, stormed upstairs and slammed the door, wrestled with another resident, physically assaulted a park supervisor, and called an operator in order to get an ambulance because he felt that group home staff were unsympathetic regarding a headache he had at the time.

*Cognitive Functioning*

Frank's cognitive abilities were assessed by the Wechsler Adult Intelligence Scale (WAIS-R) (Wechsler, 1981). He achieved a Verbal Scale IQ of 83 and a Performance Scale IQ of 70. His Full Scale IQ of 66 indicated that he functioned within the upper limits of the mildly mentally retarded range of intellectual functioning. On the Peabody Picture Vocabulary Test-Revised (Dunn & Dunn, 1981), a test that assesses receptive language skills, Frank attained a standard score of 48, a score significantly below average and lower than would have been predicted for his overall IQ but consistent with his score on the Vocabulary subtest of the WAIS-R. Particular deficits identified by the cognitive testing included Frank's limited ability to understand and use language, his deficient fund of culturally significant information, and his poor understanding of social conventions. Frank was at a considerable disadvantage in social situations because his understanding of what was happening and what was expected, and his ability to express his desires and frustrations appropriately, were quite limited.

## Social and Emotional Functioning

Frank's projective drawings and Rorschach responses supported the finding of the mental status interview that Frank had a very poor understanding of others, and, as a result, was uncomfortable in interpersonal situations, had difficulties in creating and sustaining relationships, and preferred distant to close relationships. In addition, he seemed to experience such strong emotion that most attempts at delaying its expression were likely to be ineffective. Frank appeared to distance himself from emotional situations in order to avoid problems in emotional control. Furthermore, he seemed unconcerned about making socially acceptable responses, even when such responses could be easily identified. He oversimplified situations in order to make them less threatening and/or demanding. He experienced frequent social difficulties because this style promotes a neglect of the demands and/or expectations of the environment. Finally, Frank set goals for himself that were beyond his functional capacities.

## Psychiatric Consultation

Because of the possibility that Frank's aggressive behavior was associated with temporal lobe epilepsy, a seizure workup was done that was positive with a borderline normal record being obtained. There were a few slow transients in the right anterior temporal area and a rare sharp transient in the right parietal area. A review of his history revealed that although a seizure disorder had been diagnosed and treated in early childhood, anticonvulsant medication had been discontinued when Frank was 7 without recurrence of seizures. He was started on a course of Tegretal to determine if it would decrease his overexcitability.

*Assessment summary.* Frank, Jan, Frank's social worker, the assessment team, and representatives of the treatment team attended a meeting at which the results of the evaluation were presented. Table 12.2 con-

**Table 12.2** Summary of Assessment Findings

| Strengths | Problem Areas |
| --- | --- |
| likable | frequent and dangerous angry outbursts |
| motivated to please | deficient social perception |
| goal oriented | poor social judgment |
| willing to work | limited social skills |
| concerned about hygiene and appearance | avoidant interpersonal style |
| empathy for his family | unrealistic vocational goals |
| | limited vocational skills |
| | history of chaotic family environment |
| | enmeshment with family of origin |
| | inadequate fund of information |
| | limited leisure skills |
| | low self-esteem |

*Diagnosis*

| | |
| --- | --- |
| Axis I: | Intermittent explosive disorder |
| | Family problems |
| | Occupational problem |
| Axis II: | Personality disorder with prominent aggressive, avoidant, and paranoid features |
| | Mild-moderate mental retardation |
| Axis III: | Partial complex seizure disorder |

tains a summary of the assessment findings. After agreeing that Frank be referred to a physician for regular monitoring of his seizure medication, the group defined two areas for in-depth behavioral assessment: (a) angry outbursts, and (b) deficits in social judgment and social skills.

*Behavioral Assessment*

Naturalistic observation, cognitive debriefing, and analogue assessment were used to gather additional information regarding the target behaviors. First, group home staff were trained to collect data regarding

Frank's angry outbursts, which were defined as abusive language, refusal to comply, threats, fights, and property destruction. They noted when an outburst occurred, the setting in which it occurred, the duration, what had happened before, and what happened following the outburst. In addition, they interviewed Frank briefly after each angry outburst and recorded his explanation of what had happened and why it had happened. Each day for a 2 week period, the social worker called the group home to get a report on his angry outbursts and to reinforce the staff for compliance with the data collection procedures. Twenty-two angry outbursts were reported during the first week and 18 were reported during the second.

Frank's social judgment and knowledge of problem-solving skills were assessed through a series of questions regarding situations that required social judgment and problem-solving skills. For example, Frank was asked how he should respond: (a) if while in the movies, he were the first to see smoke and fire; (b) if he got lost while traveling; (c) if a male friend lost one of his valued possessions; (d) if a woman friend borrowed money and didn't repay it; (e) if he had a disagreement with his father; (f) if a co-worker unfairly blamed him for a work problem; and (g) if a salesperson gave him incorrect change. When appropriate, he was asked to speculate about the motives of the other person in each situation.

Frank's social skills were assessed by role-plays of six situations representing common difficult situations including: (a) his mother's anger over his failure to keep a promise; (b) a boss's criticism of his work; (c) a group home resident's taking money from his room; (d) a group home staff person's accusation that he had not done his chore, and assignment of a penalty; (e) a woman's refusal of his request for a date; and (f) an unfamiliar person's crude and critical remarks.

On the basis of naturalistic observation, cognitive debriefing and analogue assessment, it became clear that Frank's angry outbursts: (1) occurred two to three times per day, (2) were more likely to occur when he was with more than one or two others, and (3) occurred when he interpreted a situation as potentially threatening (regardless of the actual threat involved). Further, he reacted similarly to both insignificant and significant provocation. Also, his angry outbursts occurred more frequently after family visits. It was observed that besides aggressive solutions, he knew few other methods of problem solving. Finally, his social skills were limited, especially in situations that involved more than two persons, authority figures, or women.

## Selection of Treatment

Following behavioral assessment, Frank, the group home supervisor, and the social worker met with the primary treatment team, which consisted of a psychologist, an occupational therapist, and a vocational rehabilitation specialist to establish treatment goals and to determine a treatment plan. Frank's parents were invited to this meeting but declined. Because of the seriousness of Frank's problems and the high probability that their continuation would result in institutionalization, it was decided to begin with fairly intensive treatment. Frank agreed to participate in a day treatment program with other mildly mentally handicapped individuals and psychiatric patients who were of relatively comparable functional level. Treatment was divided into four phases: the first phase emphasizing orientation to treatment, the second addressing basic anger-management and social skills, the third phase involving more complex anger-management and social skills and vocational skills, and the fourth phase emphasizing family relationships and maintenance and generalization of treatment gains. It was decided that it was important to keep Frank's family informed about his treatment despite their unwillingness to participate. The social worker agreed to call the parents every other week to inform them of Frank's progress and to invite them to the regular meetings for relatives of treatment participants.

## Course of Treatment

*Phase One*

Phase one of treatment involved 2 weeks of ½ day participation in the day treatment program. Frank's involvement consisted of morning community meetings, individual therapy, observation of social skills training, and meetings with the occupational therapist and work crew supervisor to orient him to his occupational therapy (OT) and prevocational training programs and to assess his interests and skills with respect to these programs. In addition, some changes were made in his program at the group home. The major components of this treatment phase are described below.

*Community meetings.* Community meetings were held at the beginning and end of each day's program. Morning meetings provided an opportunity to orient new members, share happenings of the previous evening/weekend, review the schedule of the day, anticipate problems, provide instructions, celebrate birthdays and other memorable occasions, and involve the group in decision making. Community meetings at the end of each day served to review the day's events, recognize good performance, remind participants of homework assignments, and anticipate upcoming events. Both meetings included staff and clients and provided an opportunity for informal social interaction. The extent and quality of these interactions served as an informal means of assessing generalization of skills acquired in the various components of treatment.

*Individual therapy.* Initially, the primary goal of Frank's individual therapy was to establish a therapeutic relationship with his individual therapist. This was accomplished through a review of Frank's family history, educational and work backgrounds, prior treatment experience, discussion of his life in the group home, clarification of his understanding of his anger problems, and identification of his strengths and weaknesses. Additional goals were to provide him with information regarding situations likely to arise in treatment, thereby improving his social judgment and teaching him the skills needed for active participation in treatment.

*Group home program.* A meeting of Frank, his individual therapist, and the group home supervisors resulted in important modifications in Frank's group home program. The goal of these changes was to reduce the demands on him until he acquired skills needed for handling complex, possibly stressful situations within the group home. Because of his intensive participation in treatment, Frank was relieved of responsibility to participate in group home activities/programs. Furthermore, his chore was changed to one that he could complete alone or with the help of one other person. Group home staff continued to monitor his angry outbursts; when they occurred at the group home, Frank was asked to go to his bedroom for 15 minutes. If an angry outburst occurred during an activity in the community, he was grounded for ½ day during the weekend. No discussion or other attention followed an angry outburst. In addition, group home staff agreed to spend 1 hour with Frank in an activity of his choice whenever he went 2 days without an angry outburst. A behavioral contract was signed that specified these changes as well as the overall structure of treatment. During this period, Frank's angry outbursts decreased from an average of 20 per week to an average of 16 per week. At the end of the 2 weeks of phase one, the behavioral contract was reviewed and modified in accord with the structure of phase two of treatment.

*Phase Two*

Phase two marked the beginning of Frank's full participation in the treatment program. Table 12.3 includes the schedule for this phase of treatment. The components of treatment during phase two are described below.

*Individual therapy.* The primary goal of individual therapy was for Frank to develop a more complex, accurate, and positive view of himself. Time was spent identifying his skill areas and charting his progress during treatment. In addition, he was complimented for appropriate social skills in each session.

The second goal was to assist Frank to learn about his feelings. He was helped to identify his feelings, associate names with his feelings, and express feelings in a safe environment. He was taught that feelings and behavior are related but not the same, that feelings can be expressed in a variety of behaviors, and that different behaviors have different consequences. Particular attention was focused on teaching Frank to talk about his frustrations. Role-playing was used to accomplish this goal.

A third goal was to identify what Frank was thinking about a variety of situations and to assist him in talking more clearly about his thinking. This was done to enhance the likelihood that he would succeed with the cognitive components of the social skills and anger-management training.

*Social skills training.* Social skills training was carried out in a group context. Typically the group included three males and three females, although the composition changed as various members left or joined. A male and a female therapist shared responsibility for training; they were occasionally assisted by a group member who had "senior status" by virtue of his or her mastery of the social skills being targeted.

Basic communication and assertive skills were taught via a training program composed of cognitive and behavioral components, the former being particularly important in Frank's case. In the cognitive component, training was provided in recognizing important dimensions of social situations, understanding social situations, and learning and

**Table 12.3** Frank's Schedule During Phase Two of Treatment

| | Monday, Wednesday, Friday | | Tuesday, Thursday |
|---|---|---|---|
| 9:00 | Community meeting | 9:00 | Community meeting |
| 9:30 | Individual therapy | 9:30 | Individual therapy |
| 10:00 | Break | 10:00 | Break |
| 10:15 | Social skills training | 10:15 | Work crew |
| 11:15 | Break | 11:15 | Break |
| 11:30 | Anger-management training | 11:30 | Anger management training |
| 12:00 | Lunch | 12:00 | Lunch |
| 1:00 | Occupational therapy | 1:00 | Psychoeducational workshop |
| 3:15 | Break | 3:15 | Break |
| 3:30 | Community meeting | 3:30 | Community meeting |

remembering social conventions. This was accomplished through discussion of situations that arose in treatment, at the group home, or in the community. Occasionally, a game was played in which each participant picked a card describing a commonly occurring social situation and discussed rules/expectations operative in the situation. They predicted the outcomes of various approaches to the situation and rated the desirability of these outcomes.

In the behavioral component, training including instruction, *in vivo* and/or videotaped demonstrations, coaching, and feedback. An introduction was given to orient the group to the purpose of each training session. A description of the skill being taught and a rationale regarding the importance of the skill were included. A discussion followed during which group members asked questions or made comments relating the information to other topics/skills. After the introduction, a therapist modeled the appropriate skill in several role-plays. Sometimes the group members viewed a videotaped demonstration of the social skill. The actors in the videotapes were staff members and current and/or former group members. Next, group members practiced the skill they had observed in a role-play with prompting and feedback. Prompts were faded until group members were able to respond appropriately without the help of a therapist. When a group member became proficient at a skill, his or her performance was videotaped for subsequent review by group members and a therapist. Periodically, videotaped role-plays that were particularly effective were played during a community meeting and/or replaced those that were used during training. The therapists reinforced the appropriate demonstration of the target social skills. Group members were trained to identify and praise each others' appropriate behavior. Therapists gave homework assignments so that group members could practice the target social skill during various program activities or at home.

*Anger-management training.* Besides the general social skills training program during which some anger-management skills were taught, Frank and his individual therapist met daily to work on anger-management skills. Training included: a rationale, assessment, skills acquisition, and skills application. To counter Frank's association of anger with strength and masculinity, it was emphasized that: (1) talking his way through problems is not indicative of cowardice, (2) whereas violence may have been effective when he was a child, it surely was not now; in fact, it was likely to create new problems including loss of jobs and relationships, punishment, and even institutionalization.

With the therapist's assistance, Frank collected data regarding people and situations that aroused his anger, what he said to himself when angry, how he felt during the early stages of provocation, how he behaved when provoked, and the consequences of his various behaviors. An "anger diary" was kept that documented the date and time, place, anger incident, thoughts, feelings, actions, consequences, degree of anger, and degree of anger management. It became clear that Frank often became intensely angry because of two factors. First, he failed to identify low levels of anger and therefore did not attempt to manage his anger before he lost control. Second, he often interpreted relatively harmless comments/actions as intentionally motivated against him. He was asked to report to his individual therapist or to his occupational therapist or work crew supervisor whenever he experienced feelings of anger, especially low levels of anger. He was reinforced for doing so with social praise. Those to whom he reported such feelings asked him to rate the intensity of his anger; then they asked him how he might reduce this.

Frank learned deep-breathing skills, relaxation, and use of calming images as ways of diminishing angry feelings. Next, a number of self-statements were developed for use during anger-arousing situations: to prepare for provocation ("Easy does it . . . Don't take it personally."), to cope with provocation ("Relax. Take a deep breath. There's no point in getting mean."), and to evaluate his behavior afterwards ("Not bad . . . I'm getting better." ). Frank practiced using these self-statements in imagined and in role-played situations. The situations used in the imagery and role-plays were taken from his anger diary. He was instructed to use these skills during OT, work crew activities, and at his group home. He agreed to tell his individual therapist, work crew supervisor, or occupational therapist whenever he experienced success in anger management.

Whenever Frank had an angry outburst during the day treatment program, he was instructed to take a time-out and to practice relaxation exercises and calming images, and then to report the incident to the appropriate staff. He then role-played the incident that provoked the angry outburst until he demonstrated skill at managing it. He was praised for handling situations in this manner.

*Occupational therapy.* The initial goal of OT was to identify leisure activities that Frank might enjoy. His knowledge of leisure activities was very limited. Consequently, he experimented with several activities. He expressed an interest in sports, especially basketball and softball, although he was generally unskilled in athletics. At first, he and his occupational therapist played these sports by themselves. Later, a third player was occasionally invited to join them. Frank also decided to work on a leather-working task. While playing sports or working on the leather-working task, he discussed and practiced self-control skills, such as developing a plan for his work, sticking to a task, and asking for help. In the sports activities, he learned to handle competition.

*Work crew participation.* Frank's initial goal in work crew activities was similar to his goal in OT (i.e., to identify work activities he enjoyed). After rotating through the various work activities, he chose to become a member of a work crew that did routine maintenance at the clinic. He typically worked alone, cleaning bathrooms, sweeping floors, emptying trash, and so on.

*Psychoeducational workshop.* Education was an important component of treatment based on the assumption that lack of information or misinformation often creates problems for mentally retarded and/or mentally ill persons. Through the psychoeducational workshop, education was provided regarding drugs and alcohol, religion and values, sex, family life, mental retardation, mental illness, leisure activities, community resources, and current events. This was done through films, lectures, discussions, art, and field trips.

*Group home program.* The group home staff continued to implement decisions made during phase one of treatment. Minor changes were made in Frank's group home program. For example, a staff member would spend time with him in an activity of his choice when he went 3 days, rather than 2, without an angry outburst.

At the end of the 12 weeks of phase two, Frank and the treatment team met to review his progress and to develop goals for the next phase of treatment. His parents were invited to this meeting but again declined. By this point, Frank was: acclimated to the treatment environment; had begun actively and, in general, appropriately participating in the intervention, and was demonstrating improved social and anger-management skills. He had a firm treatment alliance with his individual therapist. His angry outbursts occurred five or six times per week at the group home. His behavioral contract was reviewed and modified in accord with the structure of phase three of treatment.

*Phase Three*

During phase three, Frank continued in individual therapy, social skills training, anger-management training, and OT, although these activities were scheduled less frequently. He began to participate in group therapy, received more formal prevocational training, and increased his participation in work crew activities. Finally, he began to participate again in activities at the group home. Table 12.4 includes the schedule adopted by the treatment team. The components of Frank's treatment program as well as his progress are described below.

*Individual therapy.* Identity issues became the focus of Frank's individual therapy. His personal and vocational plans were discussed as were his feelings about being mentally retarded. Frank began to see himself as having a variety of roles (e.g., group home resident, friend, worker, son) and as having different levels of competence in each of these. At this point, it became possible to point out his personal limitations without arousing excessive anger. The unreality of his desire to become a professional boxer was confronted. Other vocational options were explored. A second focus involved Frank's relationships with women. He was provided advice regarding heterosexual social situations that concerned him. Frank had received sex education during the psychoeducational workshop; sexual information and values were reviewed so as to ensure his understanding of these important issues and to answer questions. Finally, communication skills (e.g., topic identification, monitoring of relevance, topic initiation) needed during group therapy, were discussed and practiced. As in previous phases, Frank's

**Table 12.4** Frank's Schedule During Phase Three of Treatment

| | Monday, Wednesday, Friday | | Tuesday, Thursday |
|---|---|---|---|
| 9:00 | Community meeting | 9:00 | Community meeting |
| 9:30 | Individual therapy | 9:30 | Prevocational training |
| 10:00 | Break | | |
| 10:15 | Social skills training | 10:30 | Break |
| 11:15 | Break | 10:45 | Work crew |
| 11:30 | Anger-management training | | |
| 12:00 | Lunch | 12:00 | Lunch |
| 1:00 | Occupational therapy | 1:00 | Work crew |
| 2:00 | Break | | |
| 2:15 | Group therapy | | |
| 3:15 | Break | 3:15 | Break |
| 3:30 | Community meeting | 3:30 | Community meeting |

use of social skills was reinforced in order to increase them and, more generally, to improve his self-image.

*Social skills training.* The cognitive component of Frank's social skills training continued to be very important. In this phase of treatment, group members viewed videotapes of correct and incorrect responses in social situations. They identified failures in social skills and provided explanations for these. Then, group members remade the videotapes with appropriate social skills. The behavioral component of Frank's social-skills training dealt with relationships within the group home, with women, and with authority figures.

*Anger-management training.* Attention was focused on the use of anger-management skills in situations that occurred frequently during treatment or at the group home. Frank's occupational therapist and work crew supervisor periodically participated in role-plays of anger-arousing situations likely to occur in OT and work crew settings. In addition, staff participated in role-plays of situations likely to provoke Frank's anger at the group home. These latter activities served the dual function of allowing Frank to practice skills in a situation that closely approximated the group home environment and of assisting group home staff in learning Frank's anger-management program. Group home staff were told to provoke him one time per week and to report on his response to this provocation.

Frank was taught to cope with failures in self-management by developing self-statements for coping with small errors or less than perfect performance during role-plays and in other program situations. He also learned and practiced apologizing for angry outbursts.

*Group therapy.* Group therapy included 10 to 12 members of relatively similar functional levels at varying stages in treatment. The group was facilitated by a male and a female leader. Group therapy provided an opportunity for Frank to relate to his peers in a less structured, more complex setting. It also provided an opportunity for him to practice such social skills as expressing his opinions, listening to others' opinions, handling differences of opinion, sharing feelings, providing support, and receiving support. The group process also facilitated the development of peer attachments. Finally, it increased Frank's awareness of experiences/feelings of others, thereby fostering greater empathy.

Group therapy typically began with a discussion of problems of immediate concern to the group members. For example, on one occasion after Frank became very angry during a work assignment when his supervisor had, in his view, unfairly criticized him, he discussed the situation with the group and talked frankly about how angry and hurt he felt. He was reinforced for his willingness to bring this problem to the group. Group members advised him to how they handled similar situations.

The concerns of individual group members typically precipitated discussion of a wide range of issues. Developmental and psychiatric handicaps and the stigma associated with these was discussed. Other difficulties, such as problems in relationships, fears about job interviews, experiences of being physically and sexually abused, need for medication, and experiences of institutionalization were also addressed. Individual treatment goals (e.g., greater impulse control, increased self-esteem, improved peer relationships, learning alternatives to "acting out") were shared with the group. Group members supported each other's efforts to achieve their goals and confronted each other for unacknowledged failures or lack of effort. One of the group therapists had considerable experience with psychodrama. She regularly employed this technique to assist group members in understanding themselves and their situations and in getting in touch with their feelings.

Frank's initial goals in group therapy complemented his work in individual therapy and social skills training: improving his self-concept, learning about others' impressions of him, and learning skills of group participation. He was able to express his opinions, share his feelings, and provide support to others. Learning and using these skills in individual therapy and social skills training helped Frank to adjust quickly to the group experience.

*Occupational therapy.* Frank continued to work on his basketball and softball skills and acquired some proficiency in these activities; he regularly included other clients in these activities. He also began a jogging program. Occupational therapy provided an opportunity for him to practice social and anger-management skills. Low levels of frustration were induced by having Frank wait for something, share, or fail at a task. He was taught to use these situations as cues to practice social skills and anger management.

*Prevocational training.* In prevocational training, the vocational rehabilitation specialist provided structured training in job-related skills. Group members were trained in such skills as interviewing for a job, discussing the fact that they are handicapped, accepting criticism from employers, accepting compliments from employers, accepting suggestions/instructions from employers, explaining a problem to a supervisor, initiating requests of a supervisor, refusing unreasonable requests from co-workers, initiating requests to co-workers, complimenting co-workers, and making suggestions regarding a task to co-workers through methods similar to those used in social skills training. The group also discussed problems that arose in the various work crew sites.

*Work crew participation.* Frank's participation in work crew activities was expanded, providing the opportunity for exposure to several different jobs, working with larger work crews, and closer supervision. He had the opportunity to practice anger-management and other social skills during his work crew assignment when his supervisor criticized his work, changed his assignment, made suggestions, and/or added unexpected tasks. Occasionally during these activities, the supervisor deliberately provoked Frank, providing an opportunity to practice anger-management skills.

*Group home program.* During phase three, Frank became more active in group home activities. His chore was changed to involve activities with others. Joe, a client he met during treatment, requested a transfer to Frank's group home and, toward the end of phase three, he moved there and became Frank's roommate. The two became jogging partners.

After 8 weeks of this phase of treatment, Frank's social skills had greatly improved and his angry outbursts, though occurring two or three times per week, had markedly decreased in intensity. He recognized failures in anger management and apologized when they occurred. He was actively participating in group home activities and had demonstrated social skills needed for competitive employment. Frank recognized his new skills and began to take much more initiative in his social skills training group and in group therapy.

## Phase Four

During the final phase of treatment, Frank worked 3 days per week in work crew activities at one of the off-campus work sites. He continued to participate in individual and group therapy, social skills and anger-management training, and OT, though with less frequency. Table 12.5 provides Frank's schedule for phase four.

*Individual therapy.* Here, Frank's feelings about separation from his family and, more generally, independence/dependence issues were discussed. He talked about how he was similar to but also different from his parents and siblings. Through role-plays in which Frank talked to various family members (portrayed by his individual therapist) he got in touch with his feelings about family experiences. In addition, he reflected on changes in himself with respect to anger management, relationships, and vocational goals. Videotapes of Frank from early phases of treatment were viewed to increase his awareness of the progress he had made. He recognized that his support system had expanded to include his therapist, program staff and clients, and group home staff and residents. Plans for follow-up after his completion of the day treatment program, were made.

*Social skills training.* Frank's goal in social skills training was to learn, practice, and utilize assertive skills in his relationship with his parents. The cognitive component of this training emphasized his rights and responsibilities as an adult. The behavioral component involved role-plays of situations likely to arise in his interactions with family members. Frank's homework assignments included stating his opinions and preferences and expressing his feelings while visiting his parents. Eventually, he was advised to refuse requests they made if he did not want to comply with them.

Besides working on these skills, Frank was given assignments to talk about different topics at community meetings and to organize various program activities. Problems that arose as he assumed greater respon-

**Table 12.5** Frank's Schedule During Phase Four of Treatment

|       | Monday, Friday            |       | Tuesday, Wednesday, Thursday |
|-------|---------------------------|-------|------------------------------|
| 9:00  | Community meeting          | 9:00  | Community meeting             |
| 9:30  | Individual therapy         | 9:30  | Work crew                     |
| 10:00 | Break                      |       |                               |
| 10:15 | Social skills training     |       |                               |
| 11:15 | Break                      |       |                               |
| 11:30 | Anger-management training  |       |                               |
| 12:00 | Lunch                      | 12:00 | Lunch                         |
| 1:00  | Occupational therapy       | 1:00  | Work crew                     |
| 2:00  | Break                      |       |                               |
| 2:15  | Group therapy              |       |                               |
| 3:15  | Break                      | 3:15  | Break                         |
| 3:30  | Community meeting          | 3:30  | Community meeting             |
| 7:00  | Group therapy (Monday only)|       |                               |

sibility were discussed and role-played. Frank achieved "senior status" in the social skills training group, and in this capacity, was called on to model basic social skills for new members. In particular, he was asked to instruct new members in the rules governing social situations. He received much reinforcement for this activity. Frank recognized his own proficiency on a number of social skills and his self-confidence grew.

*Anger-management training.* Problems that arose with respect to anger management were discussed and role-played. By this phase in treatment, lapses in anger management occurred infrequently. Frank and his therapist devised ways of teaching new clients about anger management; Frank demonstrated these skills for new clients, at his group home, and during community meetings.

*Group therapy.* Frank's main goal in group therapy was to use the group for support and advice with problems that arose in his daily life. This was considered very important as participation in group therapy was to be the mainstay of his follow-up program.

Frank presented his autobiography in group therapy. He shared with the group the joys and disappointments of his family life and received support from group members. He learned from listening to others' accounts of similar situations. Further, he shared with the group his difficulty expressing differences of opinion with his parents and behaving independently of their wishes. Group members supported his reasonable movement to increased independence while encouraging him to continue to visit his family regularly.

*Occupational therapy.* Frank continued to gain skill in basketball, softball, and jogging, and he began to regularly engage in these activities during his leisure time. He was able to handle winning and losing with equal grace.

*Work crew participation.* Frank worked three days per week in a variety of maintenance activities and he was paid for his participation. Frank's supervisor continued to provoke anger on a random basis. Whenever Frank failed to manage anger appropriately, he used the procedures described earlier. In addition, he forfeited his wage for that day. This happened three times during this period of treatment.

*Group home program.* Frank and his therapist met several times with the residents and staff at the group home. During these sessions, Frank described his treatment experience and residents and staff asked questions. He demonstrated relaxation skills and the use of self-talk in anger management. The residents and staff participated in role-plays of social situations and anger-arousing situations likely to occur in the group home.

After 12 weeks in phase four, Frank had sufficiently acquired the skills needed to manage anger to make competitive employment feasible. With the assistance of the vocational rehabilitation specialist, he secured a position at a local distribution center for retail products where he loaded and unloaded trucks and did light janitorial work. His behavior in the group home had improved such that his skills at handling anger were equal to or better than those of the other residents. The VABS was readministered and Frank attained an Adaptive Behavior Composite standard score of 75, a score reflecting impressive improvements in all areas. Frank was on a waiting list for an apartment in a less structured setting. While still visiting his family regularly, he did so less frequently and with less distress after visits.

## Termination and Follow-Up

For the first three months after termination of Frank's intensive treatment, he worked four days a week at the distribution center, and participated one day a week in the day treatment program and one evening a week in group therapy. Occasional misunderstandings occurred at the distribution center. These were resolved through discussion with Frank's therapist and/or the vocational rehabilitation specialist, or through meetings between Frank, his employer, and the vocational rehabilitation specialist. Some problems also arose at the group home. These occurred, however, with no greater frequency than they occurred with other residents. They were resolved through methods used to resolve difficulties within the group home. Subsequently, Frank worked full time and participated weekly in evening group therapy sessions. He met with his vocational rehabilitation specialist counseling on an "as-needed" basis.

After six months Frank was transferred to the "continuing care team" of the clinic. He was considered to be a client who would occasionally require support/brief treatment. As such, he was assigned a case manager who monitored his progress through observation at group therapy sessions, periodic meetings, and review with his social worker. Frank had developed a positive relationship with the clinic staff and he often called his case manager to discuss problems. He also attended social activities sponsored by the continuing care team.

Six months after completing the day treatment program, Frank and his friend Joe secured an apartment in a recently constructed apartment complex with subsidized apartments for individuals with similar disabilities. They required minimal supervision and support from Frank's social worker. His relationship with his family continued to be problematic on occasion. However, he regularly brought these problems to his therapy group, case manager and/or his social worker for advice and support. He continued to perform satisfactorily on his job.

## Overall Evaluation

Frank's assessment and treatment illustrate the complex problems encountered by mentally retarded–mentally ill individuals. His difficulties were long-standing and were probably the result of an interaction between his proneness to overexcitability caused by his seizure disorder, and his family environment in which neither anger-management nor social skills were consistently demonstrated. The impact of Frank's poor verbal skills and limited fund of cultural information, limitations common among mentally retarded individuals, were exacerbated by his aggressive manner, which provoked punishment and resulted in alienation, greater misunderstand, and low self-esteem; a vicious cycle ensued. Frank's intensive treatment program, based on a careful assessment and a thorough task-analysis of target skills, consisted of treatment that was comprehensive, extended, and redundant; further, generalization was programmed from the beginning. Such treatment lead to remediation of many of Frank's problems and to the opportunity for him to live and work in the community, to make a contribution by his work, and to give and receive support in relationships.

## References

Dunn, L. M., & Dunn, S. (1981). *Peabody Picture Vocabulary Test-Revised*. Circle Pines, MN: American Guidance Service.

Grossman, J. H. (Ed.). (1983). *Classification in mental retardation*. Washington, DC: American Association on Mental Deficiency.

Menolascino, F. J., & McCann, B. (Eds.). (1983). *Mental health and mental retardation: Bridging the gap*. Baltimore, MD: University Park Press.

Parsons, J. A., May, J. G., & Menolascino, F. J. (1984). The nature and incidence of mental illness in mentally retarded individuals. In F. J. Menolascino & J. A. Stark (Eds.), *Handbook of mental illness in the mentally retarded*. New York: Plenum

Sparrow, S., Balla, D. A., & Cicchetti, D. V. (1984). *Vineland Adaptive Behavior Scales*. Circle Pines, MN: American Guidance Service.

Wechsler, D. (1981). *The Wechsler Adult Intelligence Scale-Reviewed*. New York: The Psychological Corporation.

# Chapter 13

# Multiply Disabled Children

## Lori A. Sisson
## M. Joanne Dixon

## Description of the Disorder

Multiply disabled children form an extremely heterogeneous group comprised of those with various combinations of the following disorders: mental retardation, psychiatric disturbance, deafness, blindness, speech deficit, neurological dysfunction, or orthopedic impairment. Medical problems, such as heart disease or diabetes, also may be present. Each handicap may be congenital (the condition started prenatally, or at birth) or adventitious (the disorder developed subsequent to birth); mild, moderate, or severe in degree; temporary or permanent; static or progressive. While the potential functioning levels of multiply disabled children vary considerably, often they perform within the mentally retarded range of intellectual and adaptive abilities. Factors related to each disorder affect conceptual, motoric, and social develop-

AUTHOR'S NOTE: Preparation of this manuscript was facilitated by grant number MH18269 from the National Institute of Mental Health. The authors wish to thank Denise Frank who served as feeding trainer, staff of the John Merck Multiple Disabilities Program who implemented unit behavior management programs, and the University of Pittsburgh undergraduate students who served as behavioral raters.

ment, both singly and in combination, to cause impediments to normal growth that are more detrimental than each impairment alone. Further, multiply disabled children frequently exhibit inappropriate social responses, self-injurious behavior, stereotypies, and/or aggression, which also interfere with learning and performance.

This group of children presents special challenges to the clinician and researcher. Each multiply disabled child has unique needs related to remediation of skills deficits and modification of problematic behaviors. Interventions must be individualized, and often gains accrue only after prolonged time periods. Nonetheless, the past two decades have witnessed an increase in clinical and investigative endeavors for multiply disabled children. Several factors contributed to heightened activity in this area. First, descriptions of the degrading conditions that prevailed in many institutions for the severely handicapped (e.g., Blatt, 1968) incited many to lobby for closer scrutiny of programs and greater accountability on the part of professionals providing services to these individuals.

Second, the rubella (German measles) epidemic that swept across the United States in 1964 and 1965 directed further attention to the multi-handicapped population. As a result of this epidemic, an estimated 30,000 children were born with one or more physical anomalies, including visual disorders, hearing impairments, mental retardation, and a variety of other handicapping conditions (Griffing, 1981). Moreover, with advancements in medical technology, and reduction of infant mortality through improved medical and surgical care, the number of multiply disabled children is likely to continue to rise over the next several years.

Third, improved services have resulted from changing public and professional opinion about the potential for behavioral and vocational skill acquisition in these individuals. In particular, a number of interventions have been shown to be effective in managing inappropriate and disruptive behaviors (e.g., Sisson, Van Hasselt, Hersen, & Aurand, 1988), teaching social and self-help skills (Sisson, Kilwein, & Van Hasselt, 1989; Van Hasselt, Hersen, Egan, McKelvey, & Sisson, 1989), and promoting competence in vocational settings (Luiselli, 1985).

These factors have culminated in legislation that has articulated the rights of handicapped individuals. The case of *Wyatt v. Stickney*, in 1971, was the first major litigation involving the rights of mentally retarded citizens and provided the first standards of care and habilitation. The Education for All Handicapped Children Act of 1975 extended the right to free, appropriate public education to all children regardless of the nature and degree of their handicaps. By mandating that adequate services be provided, demanding program accountability, and providing funding, such legislative initiatives have been most influential in facilitating the involvement of service providers and researchers with multihandicapped persons.

## Case Identification

Annie was a 15-year-old, white female who was the fifth of six children born to her middle-class parents. She was the 6½ pound product of a full-term gestation complicated by maternal edema and poor weight gain. Although no serious medical problems were identified immediately following birth, the family regarded the infant's appearance as being quite unusual, including "oriental features and wrinkled and peeling skin." She also was described as "unaffectionate and irritable." By 1 year of age, Annie still was unable to sit, grab for objects, or maintain adequate head control. Achievement of developmental milestones was quite delayed, although Annie's mother could not be more specific. When she was approximately 1 year old, a series of medical problems occurred, including the development of hydrocephaly and a serious and continuing major seizure disorder.

Annie was educated in specialized classrooms for mentally and physically disabled children. She generally was cooperative at school and made slow but steady progress in self-help and preacademic skills areas. However, Annie often was noncompliant and disruptive at home, necessitating several time-limited residential and hospital placements. Currently, Annie resided on a hospital psychiatric treatment program for multiply disabled children and adolescents. The program served 24 inpatients and provided assessment and treatment across a wide variety of disciplines, including medicine/psychiatry, psychology, social work, education, physical therapy, and speech therapy. During a typical day, Annie participated in classroom activities with 5 additional multihandicapped peers. One teacher and two classroom aides carried out individual and group instruction in self-help, communication/social, and academic areas. Supervised group activities, free time, and individual therapy sessions were scheduled across the remainder of the day.

Educational and psychological tests and observations of adaptive behavior revealed that Annie exhibited skills typical of a 5- to 6-year-old child, placing her in the moderately mentally retarded range. A history of impaired social interactions and continuing deficits in this area suggested a diagnosis of pervasive developmental disorder. Finally, Annie was treated for seizure disorder with the following medications: Dilantin, Depakene, and Tegretol.

## Presenting Complaints

Hospitalization was precipitated by an increase in oppositional, aggressive, and self-injurious behavior. Hitting, hair pulling, and biting frequently occurred when limits were set and were directed primarily toward herself, her mother, or her 12-year-old brother. Annie also became disruptive when parental attention was given to others, especially her younger brother. In addition to these descriptive responses, Annie's parents were concerned about their daughter's deficient social behaviors. Not only were social interactions severely limited, but they also were inappropriate when they occurred. Annie became sexually intrusive with others, touching them and stimulating herself in their presence. Finally, Annie had developed an unusual preoccupation with food. Specifically, she limited her food intake to a restricted range of items (including sausage, bread, tea, chocolate milk, and soft drinks) and refused all others. Associated with the decreased food intake was an increase in verbalizations about food. Annie perseverated on the time and content of the next meal. She repeatedly commended that she was "on a diet" and wondered whether she was "getting fat" despite the fact that her height and weight were significantly below norms for her age.

## History

It was mentioned above that Annie had a long history of developmental delays and medical problems. Perhaps because of her failure to acquire skills and her fragile medical condition, Annie's parents and four older siblings were protective of her and placed few demands. Later, when Annie was required to do something for herself, or when the attention of her caretakers turned from her to her younger brother, she became aggressive and destructive. This pattern of responding led to temporary removal from the home on at least five occasions. When she was 3 years old, Annie's family placed her in a residential program for severely mentally retarded children, where she remained for 1 year. She was enrolled in residential treatment for 1-year periods two other times during her early childhood years. As an adolescent, Annie was hospitalized twice for short-term treatment. Although improvements were noted following each placement, Annie's behavior always deteriorated shortly after the return to her family. Her parents had attempted to use time-out procedures for aggression. However, they were unable to elicit compliance with time-out requirements and eventually discontinued the behavior management program. Instead, they allowed Annie to do as she pleased and curtailed interactions with their son in her presence in order to avoid tantrums.

Social deficits also were apparent from an early age. As an infant, Annie was unresponsive to affection from adults. When she was older, she initiated interactions only when she needed something from others. Then, her approach was inappropriate. She would stand too close and pull and tug at the other individual. She spoke in an expressionless monotone, and conversation was limited to her own interests and desires. Approximately 2 years ago, Annie began to go up to others and touch or pinch herself or the other person in sexually provocative ways. Interruption of these responses led to tantrums. When these intrusive behaviors began, Annie's parents severely limited her contact with persons outside of the family.

The third problem was extreme food selectivity and food refusal. Although Annie was described as a "finicky eater" during childhood, the range of foods she consumed was gradually but significantly reduced over the preceding 2 to 3 years. Preferred foods were limited to sausage, bread, and several beverages at the time of admission to the hospital. As previously noted, many conversations centered on food-related topics. Initially, Annie's parents attempted to force her to consume a healthy variety of foods by serving the items prepared for other family members and requiring certain portions to be completed in order to leave the table or earn dessert. Annie foiled these attempts by refusing to eat and becoming loud and aggressive when limits were set. Eventually, Annie's parents complied with their daughter's requests for specific foods, to avoid tantrums and discourage weight loss. They typically responded to her incessant comments about meals and dieting with rationales regarding healthy eating. Records indicated that Annie always lagged behind age peers in growth rate. Currently, she weighed 86 pounds and was 58 inches tall, placing her at the 5th percentile for both height and weight, according to National Center for Health Statistics norms.

## Assessment

Three primary target behaviors were identified based on history provided by Annie's parents and referral complaints: tantrums (including noncompliance, aggression, and self-injury), social deficits, and food refusal. The first step in treatment of these problem behaviors was to determine baseline (pretreatment) levels of occurrence. Thus, during the first 2 weeks of hospitalization, Annie's behaviors were monitored with no contingencies in effect. Of course, it was necessary to interrupt aggression, since there was potential for harm to other individuals.

### Tantrums

Informal observations confirmed the parents' reports that she exhibited tantrums in demand situations and when adult attention was directed toward another child. However, in contrast to the high rates of intense disruptive behavior at home, Annie was fairly cooperative at the hospital, showing low-to-moderate levels of noncompliance, aggression, and self-injury. For purposes of data collection and treatment, these three behaviors were defined as follows: Annie was considered to be *noncompliant* when she failed to begin action on a command given by an adult within 20 seconds of that command. Sometimes noncompliance was passive, where she simply did nothing. At other times, Annie indicated refusal to comply verbally (by saying "No!") or physically (by stomping away). *Aggression* was defined as Annie bringing arms, legs, teeth, or head into forceful contact with another person, such as in hitting, kicking, biting, or head-butting. When such aggressive behavior was directed toward herself, *self-injury* was coded.

Assessment of tantrum behavior involved day-long monitoring of incidents of these three problematic responses, yielding frequency counts. Nursing staff and teachers carried tally sheets with them and marked target behaviors as they occurred. Across the first 2 weeks of hospitalization (the baseline period), Annie displayed mean daily rates of 6 (range: 4-8) noncompliant episodes and 3 (range: 0-6) aggression acts. Self-injury was observed 15 times on both the first and second days of hospitalization, and then decreased across subsequent days to 0 by the end of the second week.

## Social Deficits

Social skills deficits were characterized by sexually intrusive behaviors and low rates of peer interactions. *Sexually intrusive behaviors* included incidents in which Annie touched staff members or peers on the breast or crotch or stood within 3 feet of another person and touched herself in these areas. *Peer interactions* were positive, age-appropriate social responses directed toward a peer. Examples of social responses were talking to another child, sharing materials, and playing a game with others. Measures of intrusive and interactive behaviors were obtained with the procedures described above; that is, staff members tallied occurrences across the day. During the baseline period, Annie engaged in a mean of 10 (range: 5-13) sexually intrusive behaviors per day and a mean of 3 (range: 0-7) peer interactions per day.

## Food Refusal

Because the referral complaint included an eating problem, Annie was included in a group of four inpatient children who displayed problematic mealtime responses. This group ate breakfast and lunch in the hospital dining area with other residents on the unit. Six to 12 children, with three to five supervising staff members, ate meals together at four tables. Dinner (Monday-Friday only) was served in a special room designed for unobtrusive observations. This room was equipped with a large plexiglass one-way observation window and a camera and microphone for videotaping. The 40 children with feeding problems ate dinner together with one adult. All meals were prepared by the hospital dietary staff and were consistent with the regular hospital diet providing approximately 1,600 calories per day, across three meals and two snacks. All food was served family style. Children passed serving bowls and dished out portions, with adult supervision and assistance as necessary.

During baseline, Annie was required to serve herself a small amount of each food item provided at the meal. Portions were not standardized. Instead a supervising adult monitored the amount of food Annie placed on her plate. Second helpings were allowed when the first was consumed, and dessert was provided when at least one bite of every item was tried, in keeping with the unit policies.

The amount of food Annie ate was estimated by counting the number of bites she took. A *bite* was defined as Annie placing at least $\frac{1}{2}$ teaspoonful of food in her mouth and swallowing it. For the dinner meals, bites were counted from videotapes of the feeding session. Since it was impossible to determine how much food was on Annie's fork or spoon from the videotapes, the supervising adult was instructed to interrupt feeding responses when Annie attempted to take bites smaller than $\frac{1}{2}$ teaspoon. Data also were taken in the hospital dining area during lunch. These data were collected via direct observations in that setting. Only those bites that met the $\frac{1}{2}$-teaspoon criterion were counted.

Undergraduate research assistants collected all data on feeding responses. Use of independent observers offered several advantages: (a) educational and nursing staff were freed of time-consuming data collection activities and were able to attend to the needs of Annie and other patients; (b) raters were able to record objectively the target behavior since they had little investment in treatment outcome; and (c) a sensitive and reliable measure of amount of food consumed was obtained via the interval recording technique. Raters wore earphones connected to a cassette tape player. An audiotape had been prepared to assist in behavioral observations. A verbal cue signaled raters to observe Annie for 10 seconds. During this observation interval, raters watched her and recorded each bite taken. Consecutive 10-second intervals were signaled, and bites were recorded in this way throughout the entire meal. Usually one rater observed Annie. However, a second rater independently recorded bites periodically across baseline and treatment sessions during lunch and dinner meals. The extent to which the two raters agreed on the occurrence of the target behavior was calculated by dividing the number of bites recorded in agreement by that number plus the number recorded in disagreement, then multiplying by 100. Agreement was reached when both observers marked a bite in the same interval. This measure of percentage occurrence agreement provides an index of the reliability of the observation system. Percentage occurrence agreement in this case always exceeded 82%.

Baseline data on number of bites of food taken during dinner indicated that Annie consumed fewer then 20 (mean: 9, range: 0-19) bites per meal. Baseline probes during lunch revealed that Annie ate less than 11 (mean: 5, range: 0-10) bites per meal. Informal reports indicated that Annie ate small quantities of meat or bread items. Weekly weight monitoring showed that Annie lost 6 pounds during the 2-week baseline period.

## Selection of Treatment

*Token Reinforcement and Time-Out Strategies*

Staff on the inpatient unit routinely employed a combination of behavioral treatments to promote prosocial responding. First, a simple token program was used with each child to foster compliance, social interaction with peers, and completion of daily self-care activities. Implementation of this procedure involved providing the patient with a card on which three categories of behavior were listed: "Following Directions," "Playing with Others," and "Taking Care of Responsibilities." There were 10 boxes beside each category. When the child engaged in a physical behavior related to one of the categories on the card, a staff member commented on it, offered praise, and initialed the card in one of the boxes. When all of the boxes were initialed, the card was exchanged for a previously chosen back-up reinforcer. Then, a new card was issued. This token system was effective because: (a) target behaviors were listed to alert the child and staff members to desired responses; (b) positive reinforcement was immediate and ongoing; and (c) the procedure was extremely flexible, allowing reinforcement for virtually any prosocial behavior, at whatever rate was necessary to foster and/or maintain appropriate responding, with events preferred by the individual child.

The second component of the unit behavior management program was time-out. Whenever a child was disruptive, he or she was moved away from the group to a designated area and remained there until quiet behavior was exhibited for a prespecified period of time. Variations of the procedure were sometimes required. For example, immobilization time-out, in which the child was firmly held in the time-out area, was employed with patients who did not demonstrate compliance with the time-out requirements. Time-out had the advantage of separating the individual from the group so that the activity was not disrupted. Further, the offender was unable to participate in pleasurable unit activities or earn initials for the token card while in the time-out area.

In Annie's case, token reinforcement seemed appropriate for encouraging compliance and promoting positive peer interactions. The token program was supplemented with compliance training and group social skills instruction. According to compliance training procedures, specific commands were given across the course of the day, and Annie was expected to carry out the requested behaviors prior to engaging in subsequent activities. When this was insufficient to motivate Annie to comply, graduated manual guidance was employed. That is, Annie was physically guided through the response, with only the amount of force necessary to complete the behavior. Social skills training involved daily sessions, carried out by the classroom teacher, in which children were taught to initiate play, share, and maintain conversation via instructions, modeling, behavior rehearsal, and feedback on performance (Sisson, Babeo, & Van Hasselt, 1988). Inappropriate social responses, such as intrusive sexual behaviors, were also defined in the sessions. Annie's participation in social skills training lessons ensured that she possessed the skills necessary to earn reinforcement for engaging in positive peer interactions.

Time-out was indicated for disruptive behavior, including tantrums, aggression and inappropriate sexual responses. (No treatment appears to be necessary for self-injurious behavior since it was reduced significantly during the baseline phase simply through extinction procedures.) For Annie, time-out involved verbally instructing her to go to a designated spot and to remain there until summoned, after 1 minute of silence. Due to her age and size, physical assistance was applied only when there was danger to Annie or another patient. However, if Annie delayed time-out, the requirement for nondisruptive behavior was extended.

## Edible Reinforcement for Food Intake

A number of medical and behavioral methods for treating food refusal are available (Luiselli, in press). While cases of immediate risk from dehydration or severe malnutrition may require intrusive procedures (forced, intravenous, or tube feeding), behavioral methods offer effective alternatives to such interventions. Typically, this approach requires that preferred foods are delivered contingent on eating nonpreferred ones. In the first step of such a program, Annie was served one bite (approximately $\frac{1}{2}$ teaspoonful) of each food item from the meal. For example, if dinner consisted of meat, vegetable, fruit salad, and bread, one bite of each was placed on Annie's place. When she had completed this amount of food, she was given access to second helpings of whatever she desired, offered dessert, and provided with a preferred beverage (tea, chocolate milk, or soft drink—items generally unavailable to patients on the children's unit). Gradually, the amount of food required for reinforcement was increased to two bites of each, three bites of each, and so on. Staff were instructed to simply state the contingency at the start of the meal and to ignore comments related to eating during the meal or at other times.

## Course of Treatment

Annie was hospitalized on the inpatient unit for 3 months. During this period, target behaviors were monitored continually, treatments were applied, and efficacy of the interventions was evaluated.

*Tantrums*

The token and time-out programs were effective in reducing numbers of noncompliant and aggressive episodes Annie exhibited. Annie's interest in the token card began during the baseline period, when she observed other patients receiving reinforcement for prosocial responding. She was pleased to receive her own card, eager to earn initials, and proud to show her card to staff. Annie was able to identify verbally preferred events to earn by filling a token card. Foods and beverages were not used for this purpose to ensure that the potency of the reinforcer for food intake was not compromised. However, Annie enjoyed earning the opportunity to stay up later than the 9:00 P.M. unit bedtime and to apply and wear make-up. Time-out provided a efficient, non-negotiable consequence for maladaptive behavior. Generally, Annie retired to the time-out area when verbally directed to do so. She was distressed by the fact that she was unable to earn initials for her token card while in time-out. Equally upsetting was the fact that she was unable to continue the routine unit activities.

Apparently, many of Annie's problematic responses were described to elicit attention from adults in the environment or excuse her from complying with a command. At home, tantrum behavior led to these positive consequences. In contrast, the token system functioned to cue child and staff to appropriate, rather than inappropriate, actions. Further, tantrums led to time-out rather than escape from a demand situation. As a result, noncompliance was reduced to a mean of 3 (range: 0-5) episodes per day across the final 2 weeks of hospitalization, and aggressive acts occurred only 3 times during this time period.

Although there was no specific treatment for self-injury, this response was monitored throughout the time Annie was in the hospital.

Periodically, self-hitting was noted in association with noncompliance. At these times, Annie looked directly at the nearest staff member and slapped her own face, leaving a reddened area. This action was quite distressing to observe, and occasionally Annie was reprimanded or restrained by naive or simply compassionate workers. However, any staff response predictably led to an increase in self-injury, while ignoring the behavior resulted in its elimination. During the last 2 weeks of hospitalization, Annie exhibited 13 face-slaps on 1 day and 0 on all other days.

## Social Deficits

The token and time-out systems also addressed social deficits by providing an incentive to engage in play interactions with peers and mildly aversive consequences for inappropriate sexual responding. Although a reluctant participant in group social skills training, Annie often initiated social contact with peers in the classroom and on the hospital unit. Anecdotal observations revealed that these social approaches were limited in complexity and duration and designed with one purpose: to attract staff attention so they might initial Annie's token card. Thus, the criterion for earning initials was altered to encourage extended and meaningful social exchanges. The data indicated that peer interactions increased to a mean daily rate of 7 (range: 3-10) during the 2 weeks immediately preceding discharge from the hospital. With application of time-out, sexually intrusive behaviors were decreased to near-zero levels (range: 0-3) during the final 2 weeks of hospitalization.

## Food Refusal

Due to the severity of the problem and the potentially detrimental long-term effects on health, treatment of food refusal was evaluated in a carefully controlled manner. Thus, food refusal initially was treated during the dinner meal only. Figure 13.1 (top panel) shows the effects of reinforcement for consuming one bite of each food item (days 10-12), two bites (days 13-15), and three bites (days 16-18). Annie immediately responded to the program by clearing her plate in order to earn a preferred beverage. Although eating was accompanied by complaining and gagging, Annie often requested additional portions of certain items and occasionally sampled dessert. In order to rule out the possibility that some other uncontrolled variable could account for the change in

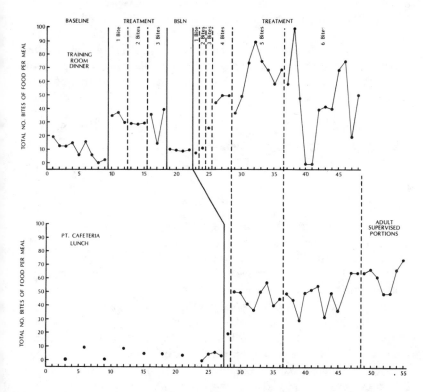

**Figure 13.1.** Total number of bites taken during dinner (top panel) and lunch (bottom panel) across baseline and treatment phases.

amount of food consumed, treatment was withdrawn briefly (days 19-22). Eating returned to baseline levels. Reinstitution of treatment (day 23) increased eating again, thus replicating earlier effects. The controlling effects of treatment were demonstrated using the withdrawal single-case design during the dinner meal (Barlow & Hersen, 1984).

Once amount of food consumed was increased during dinner, treatment was introduced during breakfast and lunch (day 28). Data obtained during lunch, as well as anecdotal reports from breakfast, suggested that application of the reinforcement program resulted in clinically significant behavior change in these settings. This again documented the controlling effects of treatment with a multiple-baseline design across meals (Barlow & Hersen, 1984). The amount of food placed on Annie's plate was increased gradually from four to six bites of each item (days 28-48). Then, Annie was allowed to serve herself portions, with supervision. The preferred beverage was allowed only when Annie cleared her plate of the food. When food intake was increased sufficiently, the dinner meal was used to train improved table manners (Sisson & Dixon, 1986). Although Annie ate an increased amount and variety of food, she regained, but did not exceed her weight at admission to the hospital. Food-related comments, complaining, and gagging diminished over the course of treatment.

## Termination

Throughout Annie's hospital stay, her parents were involved in parent training sessions with a psychologist and social worker. The purpose of these contacts was to teach her parents to apply contingencies found to be effective in managing Annie's behavior in the hospital. Unfortunately, due to the distance the family lived from the hospital and their other responsibilities, sessions were conducted on an irregular basis. Didactic instruction related to token reinforcement, time-out, and edible reinforcement for food intake was completed; however, parent participation in supervised application of the procedures was limited. To help facilitate behavioral gains at home, Annie's family was referred to an outpatient clinic for ongoing treatment. Therapists at this clinic were provided with written instructions regarding application of the behavioral treatments in order to continue parent training on an outpatient basis. Annie was discharged from the hospital to her home.

## Follow-Up

The hospital program had no formal follow-up procedures. Telephone contact with Annie's parents and outpatient therapist revealed that Annie was doing well at 1 week following discharge. However, the therapist was concerned that Annie's parents were unable to provide the structure at home necessary to facilitate successful implementation of the behavior management procedures. Thus, the family was referred for in-home behavior management training in addition to weekly clinic visits. In-home training would enable professionals to evaluate the environment and family schedule as well as offer instruction and supervision regarding applying behavioral principles in the home setting. This was considered to be essential to ensure maintainence of behavioral gains seen in the hospital.

## Overall Evaluation

Overall, Annie responded well to inpatient treatment for behavior problems and food refusal. Tantrums and social deficits were quickly remediated with routine unit behavioral procedures. Noncompliance was reduced by 50%, and aggression and self-injury decreased to near-zero levels. Accurate use of the token card and time-out was facilitated by the fact that staff members had been trained and supervised in their implementation. Annie also responded to the edible reinforcement program for food intake, increasing both the amount and variety of food consumed, and decreasing the food-related comments that had occurred throughout the day. While she consumed less than 20 bites per meal prior to treatment, Annie ate up to 100 bites per meal with the reinforcement program. This straightforward approach was easily administered by a variety of hospital staff with minimal input related to contact of the procedures. It must be noted that in order to maintain the short-term gains described above, Annie's caretakers in the community must follow through with behavior management techniques. The prognosis for continued improvement is considered to be guarded, with appropriate behavior most likely if Annie's parents are able to make a commitment to active participation in outpatient parent training.

## References

Barlow, D. H., & Hersen, M. (1984). *Single-case experimental designs: Strategies for studying behavior* Elmsford, NY: Pergamon.

Blatt, B. (1968). The dark side of the mirror. *Mental Retardation, 6,* 42-44.

Griffing, B. L. (1981). Defining the multihandicapped deaf population. *Viewpoints in Teaching and Learning, 57,* 1-7.

Luiselli, J. K. (1985). Behavioral training in the acquisition of skills for blind, severely retarded adults. *Journal of Visual Impairment and Blindness, 79,* 293-297.

Luiselli, J. K. (in press). Behavioral assessment and treatment of pediatric feeding disorders in developmental disabilities. In M. Hersen, R. M. Eisler, & P. M. Miller (Eds.), *Progress in Behavior Modification.* Newbury Park, CA: Sage.

Sisson, L. A., Babeo, T. J., & Van Hasselt, V. B. (1988). Group training to increase social behaviors in young multihandicapped children. *Behavior Modification, 12*, 497-524.

Sisson, L. A., & Dixon, M. J. (1986). Improving mealtime behaviors through token reinforcement: A study with mentally retarded behaviorally disordered children. *Behavior Modification, 10*, 333-354.

Sisson, L. A., Kilwein, M. L., & Van Hasselt, V. B. (1988). A graduated guidance procedure for teaching self-dressing skills to multihandicapped children. *Research in Developmental Disabilities, 9*, 419-432.

Sisson, L. A., Van Hasselt, V. B., Hersen, M., & Aurand, J. C. (1988). Tripartite behavioral intervention to reduce stereotypic and disruptive behaviors in young multihandicapped children. *Behavior Therapy, 19*, 503-526.

Van Hasselt, V. B., Hersen, M., Egan, B. S., McKelvey, J. L., & Sisson, L. A. (1989). Increasing social interactions in deaf-blind severely handicapped young adults. *Behavior Modification, 13*, 257-272.

*Wyatt v. Stickney.* 325 F. Supp. 781 (M.D. 5 Ala.) and 344 F. supp. 1341 (M.D. Ala. 1971).

# Chapter 14

# Spinal Cord Injuries

## John A. Jubala

## Description of the Disorder

Spinal cord injury is a devastating disruption of human life, but most individuals do survive such injuries and go on the lead often satisfying, and at times even creative, lives. The spinal cord is the main pathway between the brain and the rest of the body. All sensory and motor messages are mediated through the cord, and damage to the cord is similar to damage to the main trunk line of a telephone system. Messages that are sent never arrive at their destinations, whether they be the brain or the muscles and sensory organs of the body.

This disruption can happen at any level of the spinal cord, and the level can range throughout the cervical, thoracic, lumbar, or sacral spine. Each vertebrae is numbered in each of these sections, and each level has different implications for how that individual's body will be affected. For a complete description see a major medical text, such as Guttman (1976), or a summary chapter such as Jubala and Brenes (1986). A brief summary is as follows: The cervical segments (C1-T1) control the neck and arm muscles and the diaphragm; the thoracic segments (T2-T12) control chest and abdominal muscles; the lumbar segments L1 through L4 control the hip and knee muscles; lumbar and sacral segments L5 and S1 control hip, knee, ankle, and foot muscles; and the sacral segments S2 to S4 control the bowel, bladder, and reproductive organs.

All injuries will involve varying degrees of motor or sensory impairment (or both), depending on whether the injury is complete or incomplete. This means that some injuries can lead to a complete blockage or disruption at one level or another, while other injuries are only partially disruptive, and some neural messages can get through. Whenever a level of impairment is noted, it should be kept in mind that *all levels below that level will also be impaired.*

One must keep in mind that a spinal cord injury disrupts much more than just the ability to walk or use one's arms and hands. Sexual functioning is almost always compromised, and the bowel and bladder are usually dysfunctional at best, and in many cases nonfunctional. Quadriplegics often suffer from autonomic dysreflexia, a syndrome where neural stimulation below the level of injury causes dangerous autonomic processes to occur in the body. These include uncontrolled sweating and a significant increase in blood pressure that can lead to death if not treated. Furthermore, uncontrolled spasms of the paralyzed muscles are not uncommon, and at times can be severe enough to throw people from their wheelchairs. The spinal cord injured are very susceptible to skin pressure sores because of the long periods of sitting or lying without movement. Frequent weight shifts are necessary to prevent such complications.

While spinal cord injured individuals can and frequently do live "normal" lives, it is not unusual for them to have several hospital admissions over the years because of breakdowns in the biological systems outlined above. This is best prevented by expert rehabilitation that starts as soon after the injury as possible, and by a very strong sense of independence and responsibility for one's self on the part of the injured individual.

## Case Identification

The case we will be describing is Mr. P., a 32-year-old married, white male who was injured in the summer of 1981. The accident occurred approximately 2 months prior to Mr. P.'s admission to the rehabilitation hospital. While he was riding his 750 cc motorcycle one day he came on some clutter in the road (dirt and gravel), and after he ran over this he lost control of the bike and hit a guard rail.

At the time of his initial admission to the rehabilitation hospital, Mr. P. presented himself as a well-groomed, pleasant individual of medium height who was very open about the emotional sequelae of his traumatic injury. He propelled his own wheelchair, in which he was seated uncomfortably because of the presence of a Jewett brace that rigidly held his entire thoracic area in place. Aside from this, he was in no acute distress. He was very interested in his comprehensive rehabilitation program and asked appropriate questions.

At the time of his admission Mr. P. was essentially paraplegic with little or no movement in the musculature below the T10 neural distribution.

## Presenting Complaints

Mr. P., as is usual for spinal cord injury victims, had two hospital admissions subsequent to his trauma. The first was from the scene of the accident via ambulance to a large, metropolitan acute care facility with a trauma unit. Presenting complaints at that time were of bilateral subcutaneous emphysema, bilateral multiple rib fractures, a suspected thoracic-aortic tear, multiple facial lacerations, right knee abrasion, and total flaccid paralysis of the lower extremities with a sensory level of T10.

After surgical intervention and medical treatment, Mr. P.'s condition stabilized, and he was transferred to a comprehensive rehabilitation hospital with a spinal cord unit and treatment team. Presenting complaints at that time were of a T10-T11 incomplete, spastic paraplegia secondary to a compression fracture of the T10 vertebral body and of the right lamina. He had a neurogenic (i.e. essentially uncontrolled) bowel and bladder and pressure sores on both of his feet. Psychologically, Mr. P. complained of periods of depression and crying, but claimed that these passed. He had no memory of the accident, or of the several days immediately following.

## History

*Social and Vocational History*

Mr. P. was employed as a shipper in a manufacturing concern for over 13 years, after having graduated from high school and serving a

4-year term in the Navy with an honorable discharge. He described himself as happy in his vocation with no plans or desires for changing his status. After injury he was supporting himself with sick benefits that would last until he was eligible for disability insurance as well as Social Security Disability at 6 months following onset of disability.

At the time of injury he was married to his 26-year-old wife for 1½ years. They had no children. The marriage was described as close and supportive, although some tension was noted between Mrs. P. and her father-in-law that was apparently centered around issues of who was the most "important" family member to the patient. Mrs. P. was employed in a clerical position in a financial institution.

Mr. P.'s extended family consisted of his father, age 66, and two older sisters ages 34 and 39 who were both married and living in their own households. His mother had died from heart disease the previous year. He described his childhood as being "normal," with no particular familial dysfunction.

## Medical History

Mr. P.'s medical history did not include any diseases aside from the usual childhood ones. He had one previous surgery as a child on his left tympanic membrane. The medical history since the time of the injury becomes more complex, however. After admission to the acute care hospital Mr. P. underwent an arch aortogram because of suspected aortic tear; however, this was negative. Xrays of the spine showed a compression fracture of the T10 vertebral body, and a myelogram showed a high grade but incomplete block at the T9-T10 level. Twelve days after admission, Mr. P. underwent an open reduction and internal fixation of his fractured vertebrae. Orthopaedic fixating devices known as Luque rods were inserted for stabilization.

After surgery, the presence of a fever and shortness of breath led to a pulmonary workup, which revealed pulmonary emboli (blood clots in the lungs) and anticoagulation therapy was started. Mr. P. also began to develop an abdominal distension that eventually led to abdominal surgery and the placement of a gastrostomy tube in order to drain intestinal secretions. Some liver dysfunction was also noted, possibly secondary to blood transfusions.

Mr. P. was transferred to the rehabilitation hospital 67 days after his admission to acute care. At that time he was controlling his urinary output by catheterizing himself 4 times a day. He was independent in feeding himself and in dressing his upper extremities. He was dependent in lower extremity dressings and in transferring himself from one surface to another. His sitting and standing tolerance were limited.

## Assessment

At the time of Mr. P.'s initial interview and testing sessions in the psychology department at the rehabilitation hospital he was alert, oriented in all three spheres, pertinently responsive, and pleasantly cooperative. His affect was appropriate and his mood ranged from normal to depressed. There was no evidence of a thought disorder, major affective disorder, or of any other form of major psychopathology. There was no homicidal or suicidal ideation. He appeared to have a relatively good understanding of the nature of his injury, but was uninformed as to what to expect in the immediate and long-term future. His motivation toward the rehabilitation program was very good.

Psychological testing was undertaken with an eye toward assessing Mr. P.'s intellectual abilities (as well as to screen for neuropsychological dysfunction since there was a history of concussion and amnesia), personality dynamics, and current emotional status.

The first test to be administered was the Wechsler Adult Intelligence Scale–Revised (WAIS-R). This is an adult assessment of intelligence that results in verbal, performance and full scale IQ's. The results can be seen in Figure 14.1. As can be seen from these results, Mr. P. was functioning in the average range of verbal ability and the low-average range of performance ability, with an overall IQ in the average range. The intrasubtest scatter was not pronounced *within* the respective divisions of verbal and performance subtests, but there was a significant difference noted between the two. This *can* be suggestive of neuropsychological dysfunction, but the examiner must be careful about stating this as a fact. In Mr. P.'s case there was no indication that he was having any difficulty with functional motor activities, a CAT scan of the brain taken while in acute care showed no lesions, his performance on the Bender Gestalt Test (see Figure 14.2) showed no signs of perceptual motor dysfunction, and his performance on *each* of the performance subtests was remarkably even.

This is where interpretation must also include the behavioral observations of the examiner. In Mr. P.'s case, it was noted that he approached all tasks in a slow and deliberate manner. This caused scoring penalties on the block design, object assembly, and digit symbol subtests, even

**WAIS-R** RECORD FORM

WECHSLER ADULT
INTELLIGENCE SCALE—
REVISED

NAME___MR. P._____

ADDRESS_____

SEX _M_ AGE _32_ RACE_____ MARITAL STATUS _M_

OCCUPATION___SHIPPER_____ EDUCATION___HIGH SCHOOL GRADUATE___

PLACE OF TESTING_____ TESTED BY_____

|  |  | Year | Month | Day |
|---|---|---|---|---|
| Date Tested | | ___ | ___ | ___ |
| Date of Birth | | ___ | ___ | ___ |
| Age | | 32 | 10 | 9 |

### TABLE OF SCALED SCORE EQUIVALENTS*

| Scaled Score | Information | Digit Span | Vocabulary | Arithmetic | Comprehension | Similarities | Picture Completion | Picture Arrangement | Block Design | Object Assembly | Digit Symbol | Scaled Score |
|---|---|---|---|---|---|---|---|---|---|---|---|---|
| 19 | — | 28 | 70 | — | 32 | — | — | — | 51 | — | 93 | 19 |
| 18 | 29 | 27 | 69 | — | 31 | 28 | — | — | — | 41 | 91-92 | 18 |
| 17 | — | 26 | 68 | 19 | — | — | 20 | 20 | 50 | — | 89-90 | 17 |
| 16 | 28 | 25 | 66-67 | — | 30 | 27 | — | — | 49 | 40 | 84-88 | 16 |
| 15 | 27 | 24 | 65 | 18 | 29 | 26 | — | 19 | 47-48 | 39 | 79-83 | 15 |
| 14 | 26 | 22-23 | 63-64 | 17 | 27-28 | 25 | 19 | — | 44-46 | 38 | 75-78 | 14 |
| 13 | 25 | 20-21 | 60-62 | 16 | 26 | 24 | — | 18 | 42-43 | 37 | 70-74 | 13 |
| 12 | 23-24 | 18-19 | 55-59 | 15 | 25 | 23 | 18 | 17 | 38-41 | 35-36 | 66-69 | 12 |
| 11 | 22 | 17 | 52-54 | 13-14 | 23-24 | 22 | 17 | 15-16 | 35-37 | 34 | 62-65 | 11 |
| 10 | 19-21 | 15-16 | 47-51 | 12 | 21-22 | 20-21 | 16 | 14 | 31-34 | 32-33 | 57-61 | 10 |
| 9 | 17-18 | 14 | 43-46 | 11 | 19-20 | 18-19 | 15 | 13 | 27-30 | 30-31 | 53-56 | 9 |
| 8 | 15-16 | 12-13 | 37-42 | 10 | 17-18 | 16-17 | 14 | 11-12 | 23-26 | 28-29 | 48-52 | 8 |
| 7 | 13-14 | 11 | 29-36 | 8-9 | 14-16 | 14-15 | 13 | 10 | 20-22 | 24-27 | 44-47 | 7 |
| 6 | 9-12 | 9-10 | 20-28 | 6-7 | 11-13 | 11-13 | 11-12 | 5-7 | 14-19 | 21-23 | 37-43 | 6 |
| 5 | 6-8 | 8 | 14-19 | 5 | 8-10 | 7-10 | 8-10 | 3-4 | 8-13 | 16-20 | 30-36 | 5 |
| 4 | 5 | 7 | 11-13 | 4 | 6-7 | 5-6 | 5-7 | 2 | 3-7 | 13-15 | 23-29 | 4 |
| 3 | 4 | 6 | 9-10 | 3 | 4-5 | 2-4 | 3-4 | — | 2 | 9-12 | 16-22 | 3 |
| 2 | 3 | 3-5 | 6-8 | 1-2 | 2-3 | 1 | 2 | 1 | 1 | 6-8 | 8-15 | 2 |
| 1 | 0-2 | 0-2 | 0-5 | 0 | 0-1 | 0 | 0-1 | 0 | 0 | 0-5 | 0-7 | 1 |

*Clinicians who wish to draw a profile may do so by locating the subject's raw scores on the table above and drawing a line to connect them. See Chapter 4 in the Manual for a discussion of the significance of differences between scores on the tests.

### SUMMARY

| | Raw Score | Scaled Score |
|---|---|---|
| **VERBAL TESTS** | | |
| Information | 23 | 12 |
| Digit Span | 15 | 10 |
| Vocabulary | 44 | 9 |
| Arithmetic | 12 | 10 |
| Comprehension | 25 | 12 |
| Similarities | 22 | 11 |
| **Verbal Score** | | 64 |
| **PERFORMANCE TESTS** | | |
| Picture Completion | 13 | 7 |
| Picture Arrangement | 8 | 7 |
| Block Design | 22 | 7 |
| Object Assembly | 30 | 9 |
| Digit Symbol | 40 | 6 |
| **Performance Score** | | 36 |

| | Sum of Scaled Scores | IQ |
|---|---|---|
| VERBAL | 64 | 101 |
| PERFORMANCE | 36 | 81 |
| FULL SCALE | 100 | 92 |

**Figure 14.1.** Patient's WAIS-R profile.

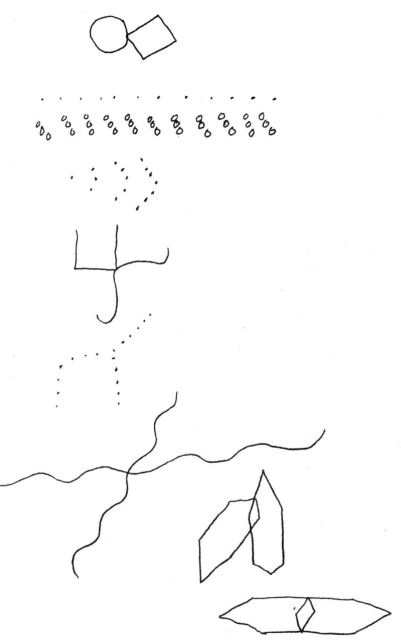

**Figure 14.2.** Patient's Bender-Gestalt protocol.

though he was able to complete most of the tasks. Furthermore, discussion with Mr. P.'s family revealed that he was always a slow, deliberate individual, sometimes "maddeningly" so, and that they noticed no change in this postmorbidly. High school transcripts were also obtained, and test scores recorded there further corroborated current levels of function. Preliminary conclusion was that while a neuropsychological dysfunction could not be ruled out entirely, it was also possible that Mr. P. was manifesting his "personal style" while taking the test. As long as he was able to function in his daily life without difficulty, which he was, further investigation was not going to be undertaken. If this were not the case, then a full-scale neuropsychological battery such as the Halstead-Reitan or Luria-Nebraska would be administered (cf. Hamsher, 1984; Lezak, 1983). Also, if he were ever to experience any difficulties in the future, this same procedure would be followed. The ideal follow-up would be to readminister the WAIS-R in one year's time and see if the performance scores changed at all.

The Minnesota Multiphasic Personality Inventory was also administered, and the results were Welsh coded as follows: 731″28′490-5/6# FK/L. For a graphic representation, please see Figure 14.3.

The configuration of the validity scales (L, F, & K) show that Mr. P. answered the questions nonevasively, and that the clinical profile is valid. The elevation of the first three clinical scales is a very typical part of an MMPI profile of a spinal injured person (Jubala & Brenes, 1988). In a noninjured person this usually indicates the so-called conversion-V form of the neurotic triad, which is associated with individuals who may be presenting with medical symptoms, but whose main dynamic is the somatic expression of psychological symptoms or processes. If there were to be a computer-generated report, no notice would be made of the individual's spinal cord injury, and a provisional description of the person would include something along the lines of "conversion disorder" or "somaticization disorder." This is simply wrong, and for a number of reasons. The 2 scale (depression) is too high for histrionic dynamics, and the person taking the test has a neurological disorder. Many of the questions that make up scales 2 and 3 address vague physical symptoms that would be very unlikely in the general population, but which are very common in the neurologically impaired. This is true for other neurological impairments, such as multiple sclerosis, as well.

Interpretation should be cautious here. The only real conclusion that can be made is that Mr. P. is experiencing mild to moderate depressive

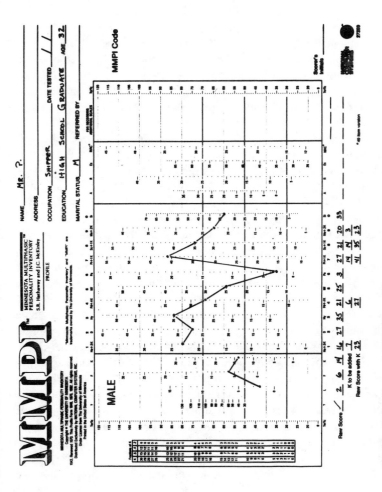

Figure 14.3. Patient's MMPI profile.

symptoms. Scale 4 is somewhat elevated, indicating that Mr. P. is most probably responding to a situational conflict at this time. This is actually lower than many spinal-injured individual's scale 4 scores. Scale 5 shows an average masculine interest pattern. Scale 6 is very low, and could be showing the paradoxical effect that can be manifested in individuals who are very sensitive toward the opinions that others have of them, and who may tend toward blaming others for their own difficulties (Duckworth, 1979). However, Greene (1980) disagrees with this interpretation and would tend toward seeing the low point 6 as an individual with narrow interests who tends to be insensitive to and unaware of the motives and feelings of others. This fits Mr. P. much better.

The high score on scale 7 shows obsessive-compulsive tendencies that would fit with the "slow and careful" behavior pattern noted on the WAIS-R. It also indicated a fairly high degree of anxiety, possibly of a chronic nature. Scale 8 is difficult to interpret in this range, and might be suggestive of simply current emotional conflict that results in feelings of alienation and remoteness from the environment. This is also not unusual in spinal injured individuals. Scale 9 is somewhat lower than what is usually seen in spinal-injured individuals, for many of them experience a "restlessness" that translates well into an elevation on this scale. Mr. P. may be experiencing some of his depression in the form of a lowering of energy, or this might simply be with his normal energy level. Scale 10 shows an average balance between social introversion and extraversion.

Overall, the profile is very similar to that of other spinal-injured individuals with the above noted exception on scale 9, and a somewhat lower scale 4. The 4 scale is often very elevated in younger spinal injured males, reflecting the very tendency to act out that often helps them to be in an accident in the first place. However, one must be careful when generalizing about the MMPI profiles for a group as heterogeneous as the spinal injured, as Trieschmann (1984, pp.131-134) warns us.

An incomplete sentences blank similar to the Curtis Completion Form was also administered, and the results show how a recently traumatized individual perceives himself and his world. Some of Mr. P.'s responses are as follows.

*My future* seems as though it will be difficult.
*I frequently* think about the future.

*If I could only* walk.
*I worry* about the future.
*If I were not* injured I would be happier.
*At times, I feel* helpless.
*I can hardly wait* till the day I can walk.
*I'd like to forget* my accident!

This focus upon the immediate problems of life, and their implications for the future is not at all unusual, and Mr. P. is an excellent example of some of the dynamics that people experience after a trauma.

## Selection of Treatment

Mr. P.'s problem list can be formulated as follows:

1. Mild to moderate feelings of depression and anxiety secondary to his traumatic injury; in *DSM III* terminology that would be 309.28, Adjustment Disorder with Mixed Emotional Features (American Psychiatric Association, 1980, p. 301).
2. Sexual dysfunction secondary to spinal cord injury.
3. Multiple body changes with a resulting change in body image.
4. Having to learn a new way of life at age 32 that includes even the smallest of the activities of daily living.

While Mr. P. also faced many other problems as a result of his injury, these are the primary psychological problems. For further discussion of these and other problems see Jubala and Brenes (1988) or Trieschmann (1980, 1984).

To address these problems the following treatment plan was devised:

1. Individual psychotherapy to help the patient with achieving and maintaining a positive adjustment, and for reducing the symptoms of secondary anxiety and depression.
2. Individual sexual education and counseling for post-SCI dysfunction.
3. Attendance at the spinal cord injury group therapy sessions for exposure to the therapeutic milieu of the SCI Unit, and for contact with other individuals undergoing the same trauma and treatment.
4. A combination of self-hypnotic relaxation training augmented by electro-myographic biofeedback to record progress.

This combination of treatment modalities is an effective program that not only helps individuals find a way to cope with their disability, but prevents many psychological problems in the future.

## Course of Treatment

*Individual Psychotherapy*

There are very few references in the spinal cord injury literature on psychological treatment. Summaries can be found in Jubala and Brenes (1988) and Trieschmann (1980). The approach outlined here was developed through a combination of general psychotherapeutic principles and experience with a large number of spinal injured individuals.

The first session is very important and sets the tone for what is to follow. Unless the therapist is disabled, it is possible that the injured patient will have some difficulty with credibility. This issue is best addressed at the initiative of the therapist, and can be approached as follows:

> *Therapist*: I'm sure you're wondering why you're seeing a psychologist. Let me assure you that it's not because we think you're mentally ill. I am a rehabilitation psychologist. My goal is to help people such as yourself to get through very difficult situations. You may wonder how I can be of any help when I myself and not disabled. All I can say is that I can give you all the knowledge that has been given to me over the years by people such as yourself. People who have survived spinal injury, and who have gone on to build satisfying lives.

This will set the therapeutic tone, and can usually transform any hostility into a sense of wondering "what this guy might have to offer."

It was not necessary to work on establishing a therapeutic alliance with Mr. P., as he was very open to the possibility of receiving emotional help from the beginning. The next step is to try to "undo" any negative messages the person may have received while in the acute care hospital. This is where a good fund of knowledge about spinal cord injury in general is of vital importance. In Mr. P.'s case, his surgeon was fairly realistic, and did not make any wild promises about his recovery. At the same time, he did not take away all hope by saying that Mr. P. would never have any return of function. Recovery from spinal injury is very difficult to predict, and many times the surgeons pronouncements turn out to be wrong. This leaves the patient feeling very suspicious of the health care professions in general.

A good approach toward instilling a sense of realistic hope in a freshly traumatized individual could sound something like the following:

> *Therapist*: I know this may make no sense to you right now, but you will feel remarkably better in the future. In many ways the worst part of this experience is over, and now you will have a say in what happens to you. Your efforts will not go unrewarded, and who knows, your body may change as well. It's well known that neurological return can continue for up to 1 year after the injury, sometimes even longer. I want you to just tuck this knowledge away in the back of your mind for now.

This may well be the dominant theme throughout psychotherapy, with frequent reframing of the rigors of rehabilitation into the accomplishments of the individual. Mr. P. was able to respond very well to this approach, and he quickly began to take pride in his accomplishments in rehabilitation.

In many ways, the rest of the individual therapy followed patterns similar to those of the cognitive-behavioral theorists (e.g., Beck, 1976), wherein Mr. P. was taught to recognize his negative and irrational beliefs about life after spinal cord injury, and was helped to analyze and challenge those chronic patterns. In addition to this, the entire process of adjustment to disability was reframed from "giving in to loss," to the more positive view of learning to surmount the greatest difficulties on one's own and feeling proud of the accomplishment.

Within a month's time, Mr. P.'s symptoms of depression and anxiety were significantly decreased. No psychotropic medication was used. His sleep and appetite improved, as did his physical activity level. While it is sometimes necessary to refer to a psychiatric consultant when symptoms are more uncontrolled, it was not necessary for Mr. P.

### Sexual Counseling

Mr. P. was experiencing erectile dysfunction secondary to the spinal injury. Since his level of injury was T10, that meant that he would be more likely to have reflex erections but not psychogenic erections. The difference between these two are that reflex erections occur as a direct result of stimulation to the penis, psychogenic erections occur as a result of general sexual arousal. Furthermore, he would have difficulty with orgasm since the sensation in the penis was absent. This meant, in effect, that Mr. P. would be able to achieve an erection and have intercourse, but he would not be able to feel the sexual stimulation or arrive at orgasm.

The main focus of sexual counseling with spinal-injured males is to encourage the person and his partner to explore the possible erotic encounters and feelings that were still available to them, and to work toward overcoming the absence of sex as it was remembered. This is difficult work, and sometimes requires an orderly approach such as the sensate-focusing techniques in order to help the couple through the adjustment phase. Sexually explicit films that show a paraplegic man with his nondisabled partner were shown to help Mr. P. envision how sex was possible in his condition. He was reluctant to address this with his wife at first, but later reported successful sexual experiences. For more information on sexual counseling see Jubala and Brenes (1988) and Trieschmann (1980).

*Group Psychotherapy*

Mr. P. was started in the spinal cord unit's group psychotherapy program immediately. This is a 1-hour group that meets once a week, and consists of anywhere from 8 to 15 spinal injured individuals and a therapist-cotherapist team of psychologists. Mr. P. was a willing participant in this group, where all of the individuals share their experiences, thoughts, and feelings about what has happened to them and what they are going through. A unique aspect of this group is that there are usually some patients on the unit who are being readmitted for advanced rehabilitative techniques, and they are able to show the freshly injured how much can be accomplished with time and effort.

There is a definite milieu present on such specialty rehabilitation units, and the patients frequently take responsibility for not only themselves but also each other. Such "bonding" not only helps the loneliness and despair of the participants, but also holds those who are not putting forth an effort responsible. Mr. P. was always impressed by the patience of the high quadriplegics who would have to spend 45 minutes to just brush their teeth. Group continued throughout Mr. P.'s stay, and occasionally included special presentations on such topics as research on spinal injury cure, with a discussion period afterward.

*Biofeedback and Relaxation*

Mr. P. was started on relaxation after his first few weeks in the program. The technique used is a variation on a hypnotic induction wherein the patient is asked to close his eyes, and begin to picture the various muscles in his body in an orderly, progressive fashion. This is all closely paced by the psychologist. Mr. P. was also asked to concentrate on his paralyzed muscles as well, offering him a chance to reintegrate his body image to some degree. Then, when the muscles have all been imaged, a deepening technique such as counting backwards from 10 to 1 while imagining oneself on and elevator or escalator is utilized. Mr. P. was able to enter a mild to moderate trance in this manner. An old but excellent text on hypnotic techniques is Cheek and LeCron (1968). For the most modern and up-to-date version of the hypnotherapy, see Rossi (1987).

Once Mr. P. was capable of achieving a relaxed state on his own, electromyographic biofeedback was utilized to increase his control over autonomic phenomena. The equipment used was an Autogen 1700 EMG device and an Autogen 5100 integrator that would measure the percent of time that Mr. P. was able to keep the microvolt level in his frontalis (forehead) muscles below a certain setting. After 10 sessions he was able to consistently keep the EMG below 1.5 microvolts for 100% of a 20-minute work period. For further information on the possibilities of biofeedback see Olton and Noonberg (1984) or Basmajian 1983).

*Termination*

Termination of psychotherapy on an inpatient unit is always difficult, because the discharge often precedes successful closure of treatment. If the patient can return on an outpatient basis this is no problem, but very few can. In Mr. P.'s case, termination was much less difficult since he was able to arrive at a sense of closure.

Treatment spanned a 16-week stay, with 26 sessions of individual treatment and 14 sessions of spinal cord group therapy. Mr. P. was free of depressive symptoms at the time of discharge, and his anxiety level was comparable to what it was premorbidly. Plans were made for a follow-up visit when he returned for his annual urological workup the following year. Mr. P. was also informed that he could contact his psychologist anytime prior to that for an appointment if he felt the need. While he returned to the rehabilitation hospital on several occasions for medical appointments, he continued to remain psychologically stable throughout the year until his first formal reevaluation.

## Follow-Up

One year after discharge Mr. P. was admitted for a 5-day urological workup and comprehensive reassessment. At that time no symptoms of depression or undue anxiety were noted throughout the year. He felt that there was some strain between him and his wife, but felt that this was due primarily to boredom on his part. This is a common problem immediately following injury, and it was felt that vocational planning was now in order. He was free of medical complications.

The next follow-up occurred 6 months later when Mr. P. was re-admitted for further urological workup and physical therapy to regain strength. His wife had left him 2 months prior to this readmission, and Mr. P. was distressed about this. He was seen for 15 sessions of individual psychotherapy over the next 10 weeks and was able to accept the termination of the marriage with some equanimity. Emotional status was greatly improved at the time of discharge.

The next follow-up was in 18 months. Since his last admission his divorce was finalized, and he returned to his former place of employment in a new capacity. He was surprised at how much he came to enjoy his work, and was more mobile in general. He was driving his own automobile with hand controls, and had begun dating for the first time since his divorce. Psychological status was stable.

Mr. P. returned for another brief admission 9 months later because of skin breakdown on the buttocks. He continued to be employed full time and remained psychologically stable.

The last, and most recent, follow-up finds Mr. P. in the same condition. He remains employed (although at times this is difficult with his skin condition), and satisfied with his social life. He has not been seen for almost 2 years since then, and no reports of any difficulties have been heard.

## Overall Evaluation

Overall, the case of Mr. P. was very exemplary of the process of rehabilitation and return to life that many paraplegics experience. It is not a spectacular case in some ways, but when one considers how much effort and pain were involved in the process one could be justified in seeing these individuals as heroes in their own lives.

Mr. P. brought with him some strengths, such as his patient persistence and willingness to admit to emotional distress, and he built on those strengths until he was able to obtain his goals. It was a long process, as rehabilitation always is, but it was successful

# References

American Psychiatric Association. (1980). *Diagnostic and statistical manual of mental disorders, third edition.* Washington, DC: Author.

Basmajian, J. V. (1983). *Biofeedback: Principles and practice for clinicians.* Baltimore, MD: Williams & Wilkins.

Beck, A. T. (1976). *Cognitive therapy and emotional disorders.* New York: International Universities Press.

Cheek, D. B., & LeCron, L. M. (1968). *Clinical hypnotherapy.* New York: Grune & Stratton.

Duckworth, J. (1979). *MMPI interpretation manual for counselors and clinicians* (2nd ed.). Muncie, IN: Accelerated Development.

Greene, R. L. (1980). *The MMPI: An interpretive manual.* New York: Grune & Stratton.

Guttman, L. (1976). *Spinal cord injuries: Comprehensive management and research* (2nd ed.). Oxford: Blackwell.

Hamsher, K. deS. (1984). Specialized neuropsychological assessment methods. In G. Goldstein & M. Hersen (Eds.), *Handbook of psychological assessment.* Elmsford, NY: Pergamon.

Jubala, J. A., & Brenes, G. (1988). Spinal cord injuries. In V. B. Van Hasselt, P. S. Strain, & M. Hersen (Eds.), *Handbook of developmental and physical disabilities.* Elmsford, NY: Pergamon.

Lezak, M. (1983). *Neuropsychological assessment* (2nd ed.). New York: Oxford University Press.

Olton, D. S., & Noonberg, A. R. (1984). *Biofeedback: Clinical applications in behavioral medicine.* Englewood Cliffs, NJ: Prentice-Hall.

Rossi, E. L. (1987). *The psychobiology of mind-body healing: New concepts of therapeutic hypnosis.* New York: Norton.

Trieschmann, R. B. (1980). *Spinal cord injuries: The psychological, social and vocational adjustment.* Elmsford, NY: Pergamon.

Trieschmann, R. B. (1984). Psychological aspects of spinal cord injury. In C. Golden (Ed.), *Current topics in rehabilitation psychology.* New York: Grune & Stratton.

# Chapter 15

# Stroke

### Gerald Goldstein
### Christopher Starratt
### Elaine Malec

## Description of the Disorder

A stroke may be produced when there is sudden occlusion of an artery in the brain. The condition has also been known as apoplexy or cerebral vascular accident, but stroke is the preferred term at present. A single stroke may involve both sides of the brain, but more commonly it only affects either the left or the right cerebral hemisphere. Thus, the most common presentation of the disorder is rapidly occurring paralysis of one side of the body, typically the side opposite to the site of the occlusion. Occlusions are generally produced by buildups of atherosclerotic plaques, and so stroke patients frequently have histories of general cardiovascular disease. Hypertension and diabetes are important risk factors for stroke. From the standpoint of the psychological aspects of this disorder, a crucial consideration is the side of the brain affected by the stroke. In most people, a stroke involving the left hemisphere produces not only paralysis of the right side of the body, but may also be associated with blindness of the right visual field and some disturbance of the ability to speak or understand spoken or written language. The terms used to describe these conditions are *right homonymous hemianopia* and *aphasia*. It may also be noted that because most people are right handed, paralysis of the right side of the body may be particularly disabling because it impairs the ability to write efficiently and to perform other motor activities in which handedness is important. A stroke involving the right cerebral hemisphere may produce paralysis of the left side of the body and a *left homonymous hemianopia*, but typically does not cause aphasia. Rather, it is more likely to produce impairments of a number of skills that require visual-spatial abilities. Spatial orientation may be involved, as well as the ability to construct objects in space or interpret complex visual stimuli. The condition is generally referred to as *constructional apraxia*. Aside from these cognitive changes, personality changes may accompany stroke. Some patients with left-hemisphere stroke may develop a depression that is not entirely based on perceived impairment of cognitive or motor function. Patients with right hemisphere stroke may experience flattening of affect or indifference.

## Case Identification

At the time of admission for the treatment described here, the patient was a 59-year-old right-handed man with a 12th grade education who was unemployed, but who previously worked actively as a carpenter. He had recovered from the medical consequences of his strokes, described below, but was in treatment at an outpatient clinic for depression. He lived with his wife and has a daughter and a son who no longer live with them.

## Presenting Complaints

The patient had recovered from the acute, life-threatening phase of his strokes 3 years before he was seen for the treatment described here. Thus, the presenting complaints were associated with the long-term outcome of his illness. Since having the strokes, the patient became increasingly inactive and chronically depressed. His wife indicated that his major occupation was sitting at home and watching television. He was also reported to demonstrate affective lability, ranging from episodes of tearfulness to outbursts of anger over events that would never have bothered him before his strokes. He was admitted to an inpatient cognitive rehabilitation program for purposes of assessing the current level of neuropsychological function, attempting to remediate his outstanding residual deficits and more intensive treatment of his depression and his deteriorating relationship with his wife.

## History

At age 54, the patient sustained a major stroke, manifested by sudden onset of left-sided weakness and neglect while he was cooking at an outdoor barbecue. He was taken to an emergency room and a CT scan was performed, showing an infarct involving the right-middle cerebral artery. He had recently been diagnosed as diabetic, may have been at least mildly hypertensive and had a history of alcohol abuse. Two years later he sustained a second stroke, also involving the left side of his body. Prior to the strokes, the patient was an active man who worked as a carpenter. He was unable to return to work after the first stroke, and after the second one he essentially became totally inactive. He suffered from an apparently persistent major depressive disorder that was treated with nortriptyline. Since the time of the strokes, the patient became totally dependent on his wife. Guilt feelings about this dependency were apparently associated with the depression, as well as the irritability and outbursts of anger.

## Assessment

### Medical Evaluation

The patient was not extensively evaluated medically at the time of his hospitalization because he was being followed at the outpatient clinic where he was being carefully monitored medically. It was noted that he walked with a cane, his diabetes and hypertension appeared to be under control, and he needed to be maintained on anticonvulsant medication because of a seizure disorder that developed after his first stroke. His EKG showed a sinus bradycardia and the EEG was diffusely abnormal, with focal slowing in the right temporal region. He was placed on a 1,200-calorie ADA diet.

*Clinical Assessment*

His mental status was described as intact with the exception of rambling speech and poor short-term memory. His mood was described as dysphoric, and he reported difficulty in sleeping. He was described as having "given up on everything" and was apparently experiencing a major depression, with symptoms of hopelessness, tearfulness, and some suicidal ideation. Evaluation of the wife indicated that she was developing a significant stress reaction, with possible bleeding ulcers.

*Neuropsychological Assessment*

A neuropsychological examination was conducted to assess the patient's motor, sensory-perceptual, language, memory, and conceptual abilities. It was noted that the patient continued to have substantial weakness of his left side. Performance with his right hand was relatively more intact, but difficulty with fine motor coordination was impaired. On the sensory-perceptual examination it was found that he neglected both visual and auditory stimuli to his left side. He also showed substantial difficulties with rapid visual scanning. As would be expected of patients with right-hemisphere brain damage, he had substantial difficulties with complex visual, perceptual, and constructional tasks. Tests involving matching faces and the relative positions of lines in space were done poorly. His copying of figures from models was accurate, but was accomplished in a fragmented, piecemeal, manner. The examination of language yielded essentially normal results, except for a mild articulation problem, but memory was significantly impaired. Recall of verbal material, such as stories, was done moderately poorly for a man of his age, but recall of nonverbal material, such as geometric designs, was found to be exceptionally poor. It was felt that the basis of this difficulty was an inability to properly perceive, and thus to efficiently encode, visual-spatial information. General intellectual functioning was found to be in the low-average range, but nonverbal reasoning skills were found to be substantially less intact than verbal skills.

In summary, the neuropsychological assessment indicated that the patient was a man of low-average general intelligence and relatively good preservation of language-related skills but significant impairment of visual perceptual and constructional skills. Impairment of memory in general was noted, but nonverbal memory was found to be more deficient than verbal memory.

*Summary and Recommendations*

The results of the assessment indicated that the patient was, in general, medically stable, but was suffering from a significant depression. His relationship with his wife, on whom he was very dependent, was problematic and deteriorating. The neuropsychological assessment pointed to significant visual-spatial memory deficits, but many areas of well-preserved function. The treatment recommended included medical management of his diabetes by dieting, continued pharmacological treatment of his depression, counseling with the patient and his wife, and cognitive rehabilitation, focusing on his nonverbal memory deficit. These plans would be implemented while the patient was in the hospital, with follow-up after discharge.

## Selection of Treatment

The selection of pharmacological treatment with nortriptyline was based on previous good response to this drug. It was also felt that his wife had to be involved in the program because of the problematic nature of their relationship at home. There appeared to be at least three behaviors that were contributing to his sustained depression. He had overall low general activity level, with few opportunities for rewarding interpersonal interaction. He was also unable to engage in previously rewarding instrumental activities, such as manual labor and "working with his hands," because of the cognitive and physical deficits resulting from the strokes. He had yet to replace these with alternative activities. Finally, when opportunity for social interaction did occur, he tended to engage in behaviors that others found aversive. For example, his participation in conversations usually focused on his disabilities, which were not usually relevant to the ongoing theme of the discussion. His statements concerning his disabilities were generally emitted in an angry and bitter affective tone. Others often found his poorly modulated affect and "crying spells" puzzling and uncomfortable to watch.

Within the marriage, his wife had assumed the role of primary caretaker and assisted the patient with many tasks that he could perform independently, though slowly and effortfully. The wife appeared to be making an honest attempt to encourage independence by closely monitoring the patient's progress during a task, making nonspecific comments, and providing unsolicited assistance. The patient reported mixed feelings about these episodes. He was grateful for the assistance, yet irritated by her apparent nagging. The wife reported feeling overwhelmed by the responsibilities of continual care and assistance, and was annoyed that her husband did not seem to be trying to improve. She became resentful because she felt she no longer had a life of her own.

The decision to employ a cognitive rehabilitation program was based primarily on the results of the neuropsychological assessment. Cognitive rehabilitation is thought to be of maximum benefit with patients who have relatively medically stable conditions, and who have specific deficits surrounded by areas of intact function. This patient met both of those criteria, and it was felt that if his cognitive deficits could be remediated to some extent his quality of life at home might be significantly improved. Restoring the patient to the level of employability did not appear to be realistic, but it was felt that his activity level could be increased and that he could achieve a more satisfactory home life.

Memory was identified as the specific area in need of rehabilitation. It was noted that the memory deficit, while of significant proportions, was set in the context of average general intellectual function (basically normal language and relatively intact sensory-perceptual function with the exception of impaired motor ability on his left side). Because he was right handed, he was therefore capable of handwriting and other activities benefited by intact use of the preferred hand. In patients with unilateral brain damage, an important strategy developed for cognitive rehabilitation involves utilizing the intact resources of the noninvolved hemisphere to compensate for the abilities normally mediated by the damaged hemisphere. The efficacy of this strategy was probably best illustrated in a study by Gasparrini and Satz (1979), in which a method of memory training based on functions thought to be mediated largely by the right cerebral hemisphere was found to be effective in the remediation of patients with left hemisphere strokes. Since this patient had right hemisphere brain damage, the reverse strategy was used, and the memory training program designed was oriented toward utilization of the skills maintained by his relatively intact left hemisphere. What this means in effect is that nonverbal memory, which is normally supported by the verbal-spatial information processing capacities of the right hemisphere, might be restored to some extent if the patient somehow learns to make extensive use of verbal mediation in the recall of nonverbal material. Correspondingly, the learning of verbal material should be best accomplished through utilization of verbal mnemonics rather than through the application of visual imagery based techniques.

## Course of Treatment

### Memory Training

Memory training consisted of two components: one aimed at improving accurate recall of item lists and the other at learning the names of people. It was hoped that the training exercise would provide the patient with compensatory strategies that might be of assistance to him in learning new material in natural settings. Such strategies are generally in the nature of mnemonic devices. In normal individuals, utilization of these devices may allow for performance of extraordinary feats of memory (Lorayne & Lucas, 1974), but in brain damaged patients they may improve (to a greater or lesser extent) impaired memory abilities. The use of visual imagery, or depicting the items to be recalled in the form of a single picture, is often a powerful mnemonic, but in the case of patients with right hemisphere brain damage, visual imagery is often significantly impaired and would not constitute a satisfactory mnemonic. However, memory may also be supported by placing of individual items into some form of contextual structure. Such a strategy can be implemented verbally by placing individual items into a grammatical structure, such as a sentence or paragraph. For example, Kovner, Mattis, and Goldmeier (1983) have shown that amnesic patients can substantially increase their recall of words when those words are embedded into a meaningful story.

The list learning procedure for this patient followed the paired-associate learning method, but the two members of the word pairs were placed into sentences. For example, if the pair was "house-laundry," the sentence might be "John's house was located right across the street from the laundry." The idea is that when the first word of the pair is presented to the patient, his recall of the second word will be supported by the embedding context of the sentence. When conducting training of this type, it is generally necessary to initially provide the patient with the mnemonic material, in this case the sentences. But it is hoped the patient will eventually learn to generate his own material, since that is clearly necessary if the training is to have any potential for generalization to learning of new information. The data for the initial training during which the sentences were provided are presented in Figure 15.1. It may be noted that the patient could not recall any of the 10 pairs during three baseline sessions. However, with initiation of training, performance improved, with 90% correct recall at one of the sessions. However, after that point there was a great deal of variability, with session scores ranging from 40% to 80% correct. Following the first six training sessions, the patient was also given pairs of new associates and was told to apply the sentence method independently. Three sessions were held utilizing five pairs, and four sessions were held using 10 pairs. As can be seen in Figure 15.1, the first two five-pair sessions were done reasonably well, but the patient never exceeded 30% correct during the 10-pair sessions. It would appear that this training, while generating some change from essentially no capacity to perform the task to some capacity, did not substantially improve the patient's memory for lists. Some of his peak performances, however, might have revealed the capacity for some potential that might have been realized with more extensive training.

Training to learn and remember names of new acquaintances was accomplished by attempting to teach the patient to associate names with a series of photographs of unfamiliar people. The mnemonic used involved encouraging the patient to relate the name to some characteristic of the face. For example, a person with a great deal of hair might be called Harry, or the face might resemble some celebrity known to the patient. This task is more easily accomplished when the name is assigned by the learner rather than by the trainer. However, we rarely assign names of our choice to individuals, and so it is ultimately necessary to master the task with trainer-provided names if the technique is going to generalize. Therefore, we began the training with names provided by the patient, in order to familiarize him with the technique, but gradually phased in trainer-provided names until toward the end of the training all of the names were trainer provided. Training itself consisted of showing the patient a different set of photographs at each session, and coaching him to make associations between names and faces. Following an interpolated task, actually the list-learning training, the patient was shown the eight photographs again, and was asked to provide the names. The data presented in Figure 15.2 show the number of correct delayed recalls at baseline and at each training session. At the three baseline evaluations, the patient did not recall more than half of the names. Over the course of training there were sessions

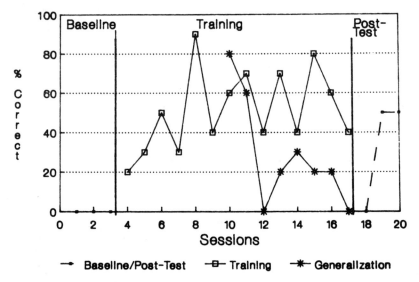

**Figure 15.1.** Paired-associate learning training.

during which he did substantially better, but again there was marked variability. However, he showed potential for improving with training, which might be better realized with more sessions and perhaps greater amelioration of his affective disorder described below.

*Ward Treatment Program*

The major issues in this program were the patient's affective lability and his difficulties with managing activities of daily living. He was assigned to group therapy with other patients on the unit, with the goals of assisting him with appropriate expression of affect and improvement of his interpersonal relationships. By mutual agreement of the group, the patient did not receive group attention during crying spells or when engaging in self-demeaning verbalizations. The group leaders made it a point to avert their gaze from the patient when he engaged in those behaviors. He was praised for each occurrence of an "other-oriented" comment or appropriate self-disclosure. The group leaders also monitored frequency of crying and provided verbal praise when at least 5 minutes had elapsed without a crying episode. There were initially numerous episodes of crying during the group sessions, but that number diminished as time elapsed. The patient gradually became more able to

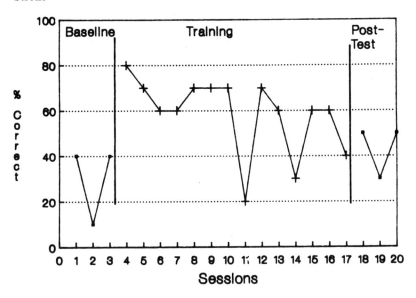

**Figure 15.2.** Name learning training.

listen to difficulties expressed by others and became less preoccupied with his own losses. On the ward, the treatment team systematically praised the patient for increased activity levels. His self-care improved, and he participated regularly in off-ward activities, including regular weekend passes spent with his wife. He was also active in occupational therapy, which emphasized hobbies that he could perform independently and that approximated in a simplified way his vocational skills.

*Family Therapy*

The patient and his wife were seen regularly during hospitalization and for about a year after discharge. Sessions were held at 3-week intervals. In general, adjustment following hospitalization was not good. Gains were made in independent self-care through the use of homework assignments while on weekend pass. These were intended to begin facilitating transfer of in-hospital gains to the home. However, while the patient succeeded in a cooking class on the unit, his wife was reluctant to allow him to prepare a meal on his own at home. When home cooking was "prescribed" as a home assignment, the patient generally completed the task, but his wife was unable to consistently support those efforts. Amount of social interaction and leisure activity increased gradually following discharge, but on 1-year follow-up, both the patient and wife reported declines in activity to near pretreatment levels. The wife was disappointed that the patient was not more active than he was, and the patient felt that excessive demands were being made of him. The wife's stress and frustration increased to the point at which she developed bleeding ulcers. This conflict over expectations continued during the course of the sessions and never really became resolved. The wife attempted to develop social activities independently of her husband, in reaction to which the patient developed feelings that he was being abandoned. He complained that his wife was "never at home anymore."

## Termination and Follow-Up

The case has not been terminated at this writing. The patient and his wife continue to be seen, and the patient's medication status continues to be maintained and periodically evaluated. While he still lives at home with his wife, their marital situation continues as what has been described as a "stalemate." The wife's efforts at increased independence have led to increased conflict and bitterness on the part of the patient.

## Overall Evaluation

This case is not reported as an example of successful treatment, but rather as an illustration of the contrast between medical and psychosocial outcomes that sometimes occurs in stroke patients. On the one hand, this patient had two serious, potentially life-threatening major strokes and recovered medically from both of them. But on the other hand, there was a marked deterioration of his quality of life and that of his wife. It is the opinion of some clinicians that outcome is typically worse for patients sustaining strokes in the right cerebral hemisphere than in the left cerebral hemisphere, possibly because of the importance of the right hemisphere for modulation of affect. This patient did not display the more typical flatness of affect or indifference found in right hemisphere stroke patients, but rather developed severe affective lability. Little is known of his premorbid personality, but apparently he was a hard-driving, industrious man with no significant psychiatric difficulties, except for some history of alcohol abuse. It would appear that the disabilities produced by the strokes would be particularly devastating for a person with his drive and activity level.

The memory-training component of the treatment can be viewed as demonstrating that the patient had some potential for new learning, but did not appear to fully realize that potential in the form of practical results. Perhaps the lesson to be learned here is that the training should have been lengthier, with efforts made to promote generalization to real-life situations. The pharmacological treatment seemed adequate in terms of controlling the major symptoms of the depression to a substantial extent. Apparently, the patient had a generally successful course of in-hospital treatment, but even the preparatory work done with him and his wife prior to leaving the hospital did not fully deter the development of a deteriorating family situation. There would appear to be no simple solution to that difficulty, and continued treatment with the husband and wife seem to be the only viable alternative.

To summarize, the case presented illustrates the kinds of treatment efforts often needed for patients who suffer a major stroke. Generally, such treatment should include attempts at remediating the cognitive and functional activities of daily living deficits produced by the stroke, as well as management of emotional and interpersonal sequelae that may involve both patient and family. While the medical prognosis for stroke is often good because of the very adequate treatments available for the acute and subacute stages of the condition, the long-term prognosis in terms of quality of life may often be problematic. It is thought by some that outcome for patients with right hemisphere stroke, as was the case here, tends to be less benign than what is found for left hemisphere stroke.

## References

Gasparrini, B., & Satz, P. (1979). A treatment for memory problems in left hemisphere CVA patients. *Journal of Clinical Neuropsychology*, *1*, 137-150.

Kovner, R., Mattis, S., & Goldmeier, E. (1983). A technique for promoting robust free recall in chronic amnesia. *Journal of Clinical Neuropsychology*, *5*, 65-71.

Lorayne, H., & Lucas, J. (1974). *The memory book*. London: W. H. Allen.

# Chapter 16

# Visual Impairment

Louise E. Moore
Vincent B. Van Hasselt
Michel Hersen

## Description of the Disorder

Mental health professionals have become increasingly attuned to the problems and special needs of individuals who are blind or visually impaired (see reviews by Boyd & Odos, 1981; Hoover & Bledsoe, 1981; Van Hasselt, 1987). The growing awareness of the value of psychological services for this population is related to several factors. First, there is a convergence of evidence indicating that a disproportionate number of visually impaired children and adults evince difficulties in social adaptation (e.g., Scott, 1969; Van Hasselt, 1983; Van Hasselt, Hersen, Kazdin, Simon, & Mastantuono, 1985). Such findings have been attributed to: (a) inadequate modeling of social behaviors due to the inability to utilize visual cues (Farkas, Sherick, Matson, & Loebig, 1981); (b) inadequate or adverse feedback from sighted peers regarding interpersonal performance (Richardson, 1969); (c) a relative lack of actual social experiences (Van Hasselt, 1983); and (d) negative attitudes toward the visually impaired and other persons with physical disabilities (Dion, 1972); Kleck, 1983).

Another reason for the upsurge of clinical and investigative efforts with visually impaired individuals is the realization that many have severe deficits in adaptive living skills (e.g., self-dressing, mobility skills, transportation usage, money exchange) and emergency safety responses (e.g., fire, evacuation, accident prevention, emergency telephone dialing) that are requisite to successful community living (see Van Hasselt, 1987). With the acceleration of legal and legislative initiatives emphasizing integration of disabled individuals in normative, nonrestrictive settings, training of such skills is now of paramount importance in habilitative endeavors with the blind.

Preliminary formulations suggesting that visually impaired children and adolescents are at high risk for psychological dysfunction have also played a major role in the heightened activity in this area. In their review of research concerning the emotional adjustment of visually impaired children, Ammerman, Van Hasselt, and Hersen (1986) found considerable data attesting to cognitive limitations, maladaptive personality profiles, behavior problems, and psychopathology (e.g., anxiety, depression) in a large proportion of this population. These findings underscore the importance of early psychological assessment and treatment for at least a subset of visually impaired children and youth.

In this chapter, an overview of disorders of the visual system will be presented. This will be followed by a case study involving the utilization of a broad-based approach to evaluation and intervention with a behavioral disordered, visually impaired child and her parents. Finally, an overall evaluation of the case material and treatment outcome will be provided.

Approximately 11.5 million persons in the United States have some form of visual impairment (National Society to Prevent Blindness, 1980). Nearly 500,000 of these individuals are legally blind (i.e., their degree of corrected vision in the better eye is 20/200 or worse, or there is a severe restriction in the visual field). Further, it is estimated that almost 37,000 children in this country carry the diagnosis. According to the National Society to Prevent Blindness (1980) the principal causes of blindness in the United States in order of frequency are glaucoma, macular degeneration, senile cataract, and optic nerve atrophy. Further, diabetic retinopathy is the leading cause of new cases of blindness for the age group 20 to 75. These disorders are described here briefly. (For a comprehensive review of disorders of the visual system, the reader is referred to Biglan, Van Hasselt, & Simon, 1988.)

*Glaucoma* involves a substantial increase in intraocular pressure, which diminishes blood supply to the retina and destroys nerve cells. This condition causes blindness if not identified and treated early. The goal of medical treatment is to reduce the intraocular pressure and halt permanent eye damage. This is typically a slowly progressing condition with visual acuity unaffected in the earlier phases, except for peripheral vision. *Macular degeneration*, a retinal disorder, causes damage to the blood vessels in the macular area, the section of the retina responsible for sharpest and clearest vision. This disease affects both eyes and makes it difficult for the afflicted individual to see into the distance, distinguish faces and objects, and perform close work.

In *cataracts*, lens opacity clouds and finally blocks vision if untreated. The condition occurs usually in the elderly, but may also strike earlier in life as a result of maternal rubella in the first trimester of gestation, genetic inheritance, or a trauma that involves the lens being struck. Intervention consists of surgical removal of the opaque lens and is successful in 90% to 95% of all cases. *Optic atrophy* involves a deterioration of the optic nerve, which may occur for a number of reasons, including degenerative diseases. This disorder may appear at any age, although it is more common in youth and middle age.

*Diabetic retinopathy* has become a major cause of blindness in the United States and Europe. This disease affects the retinal blood vessel. Blindness results from the unchecked blockage and hemorrhage of retinal capillaries that leak fluid, thus thickening and blocking the retina. Retinopathy may be delayed or deferred with early diagnosis and control of diabetes. However, once the progress of the disease is started, control of the diabetes has minimal impact. The course of the disorder is extremely difficult to predict.

## Case Identification

Jean is a 15-year-old female who was born with optic nerve hypoplasia. This is a congenital abnormality involving the small optic disk, which may be surrounded by a double ring (scleral halo) and often by an epithelium halo where vision is reduced (Biglan, Van Hasselt, & Simon, 1988). She was also diagnosed as having Leber's congenital amaurosis, a congenital defect that is transmitted as an autosomal recessive trait and is associated with an atypical form of diffuse pigmentation and attenuation of the retinal vessels. Her amaurosis is characterized as bilateral near blindness, occurring early in her life with a marked reduction in retinal functioning. Her only useful vision is light perception and minimal discrimination of shadowed images.

Jean also carries a diagnosis of mild mental retardation. Further, she has motor imbalances and low muscle tone, which have impaired her mobility. She takes slow steps and displays a wide bound gait. She has been receiving occupational and physical therapy at a school for blind children that she has attended since 1983. Jean is classified as an auditory learner and has satisfactory verbal skills. She appears most proficient at verbal tasks that require use of memory.

Jean, an only child, resides with her mother, a full-time homemaker, and her father, who is employed in a managerial position. Due to the father's scheduling conflicts and extensive travel, he was unable to participate in treatment on a regular basis.

## Presenting Complaints

A number of problems were related by Jean's parents during their initial interview. First, they stated that her communication skills had recently deteriorated both at home and in school. In addition, she had become increasingly argumentative with classmates and parents and had exhibited considerable difficulty initiating and maintaining any form of positive interaction. Third, she was described as tactually defensive to the extent that training in areas requiring manual guidance and physical prompting (e.g., dressing, washing hair) was problematic. Consequently, she required considerable parental and teacher assistance with most adaptive living skills. Finally, Jean's parents expressed their concern that there was an overall lack of open and effective communication in their family in general.

## Assessment

The presently employed strategies were part of a comprehensive clinical-research project designed to identify and remediate areas of social and emotional dysfunction in visually impaired youth and their families. The goal of the assessment phase was to empirically determine specific deficits in participants that would subsequently be targeted for behavior change. The assessment package included self-report measures of psychopathology, social adjustment, and family members' perceptions of the quality of family life. The parents also were asked about various dimensions of their marital relationship. In response, they indicated the need to spend more time together as a couple and felt that their ability to communicate effectively required some remediation.

Instruments administered to Jean and her family are described below.

The *Areas of Change Questionnaire* (ACQ) is a brief, easily administered self-report index of marital and family adjustment. It ascertains the amount of change family members desire from one another in 34 areas of interaction using a 7-point scale ($-3$ = desires much less change; $+3$ = desires much more change). Jacob (1980) modified the ACQ for use with children by developing two forms. The first evaluates the amount of change the child would like from his or her parents (e.g., "I want my father/mother to pay attention to me"). The second form is completed by each parent regarding the amount of change they desire from their child (e.g., "I want my child to take care of his/her chores").

The *Child Behavior Checklist-Parent Form* (CBCL-P) is a widely used measure of parent's perceptions of children's levels of social and emotional adjustment (Achenbach & Edelbrock, 1979). The CBCL-P is an empirically derived and standardized device that yields scores reflecting a wide variety of behavior problems including hyperactive, delinquent, somatic complaints, schizoid, uncommunicative, immature, obsessive-compulsive, hostile-withdrawal, and aggressive. A Social Competence subscale provides information concerning the interpersonal relations of children. The *Youth Self-Report Form* (YSRF) was designed as a self-report measure to be completed by children and adolescents regarding their own behavior (Edelbrock & Achenbach, 1984). The YSRF parallels the CBCL-P in form and structure and provides scores similar to those obtained with the latter instrument. Both measures were used with the present family.

On the *Marital Adjustment Scale* (MAS), each member of the marital dyad is asked to indicate his or her overall satisfaction with their current marriage (Locke & Wallace, 1957). The MAS is considered a reliable and valid index of ongoing fluctuations in the couple's degree of marital satisfaction. The *Family Assessment Measure* is a comprehensive measure of family adjustment (Skinner, Steinhauer, & Santa-Barbara, 1981). It evaluated each family member's perceptions of how he or she is functioning within the family system and examines the respondent's feelings about relationships with each of the other family members.

*Goal Attainment Scaling* is a rating procedure used for determining the extent of change exhibited in targeted behaviors as a function of intervention (see Steinbook, Jacobson, Mosher, & Davies, 1977). With this strategy, specific, operationally defined goals are agreed on by both therapist and family. Then, each goal is represented on a separate scale that includes a continuum of possible treatment outcomes. Each outcome is assigned a numerical value ranging from "most favorable" (+3) to "least favorable" (–3). The scale's midpoint represents the "expected level of treatment success" (zero) and four intermediate outcome levels. With the present case, goals were identified that would be feasible to accomplish within a 4-month period.

Of particular importance with the use of goal attainment scaling is the clear specification of each scale outcome so that previous progress can be clearly determined in each treatment session. Prior to intervention, baseline levels of functioning are established via repeated observation and ratings by the therapist. Progress (or lack of progress) is then examined through subsequent ratings conducted over the course of treatment.

## Selection of Treatment

Behavioral Family Treatment (BFT) (Rowley, Van Hasselt, & Hersen, 1986) was implemented with Jean and her mother. BFT was developed specifically to meet the special needs of disabled children and their families. This form of intervention emphasizes the amelioration of deviant behavior patterns in the disabled child as well as the entire family unit. It consists of a number of modules designed to provide information and teach requisite skills to participants in order to eliminate or diminish problems and enhance family adjustment. BFT consists of four stages: (1) family assessment (described above), (2) family treatment, (3) posttreatment booster sessions, and (4) systematic follow-up. Several behavioral techniques are employed, including: direct instructions, modeling, behavior rehearsal, performance feedback, and role playing. Booster sessions (i.e., periodic posttreatment reviews of material previously covered) are carried out to consolidate and maintain gains and to remediate any response decrements that may have occurred after formal termination of training. Follow-up evaluations are conducted at regular intervals (1, 2, 4, and 6 months) to determine treatment durability.

In BFT, attention is directed to the deficiencies and problems identified through assessment. The procedure and sequence for training is as follows:

1.  The therapist *describes* the skill to be learned in specific, discrete, and nontechnical terms to the family.
2.  The therapist *models* the skill.
3.  The family is provided the opportunity to *rehearse* the skill in the therapeutic context. *Role playing* is used as a vehicle for assessment and training with the family in each skill area. The therapist provides modeling and feedback on an ongoing basis as needed.
4.  The family is encouraged to use their newly acquired skills in the *home environment* to promote transfer of training effects. The therapist provides further support and feedback.

## Course of Treatment

BFT was applied to Jean and her mother on a weekly basis over a 4-month period. As had been previously mentioned, the father was unable to participate in treatment due to extensive work related travel 5 days during the week. Mother, however, assumed the responsibility to communicate with her husband on weekends what she learned weekly during BFT sessions.

During the initial evaluation, Jean's parents stated that they wanted her to listen more attentively and carefully to them and to respond more appropriately during family interactions. Specific treatment goals identified in the assessment phase were: (1) to improve Jean's listening skills, and (2) to increase family communication skills in general. These goals were determined on the basis of data obtained on the ACQ and the Family Assessment Measure.

For the first four sessions, the therapist worked on components of effective *listening*. This was defined as the ability to understand what another person is saying and to then accurately repeat or restate what was said. The goal attainment scale developed to evaluate progress in this area is provided in Table 16.1. Initially, Jean was extremely inattentive and frequently interrupted others during interactions. With frequent modeling by the therapist, role playing of parent-child interactions, and therapist reinforcement for "good listening," she was able to listen to the statement(s) of the other party prior to responding. Moreover, all family members then began to express themselves and listen more attentively to each other.

The next behavioral category targeted for modification was *communication skills*, specifically Jean responding impulsively to statements without any evidence of forethought. Functioning in this area was

**Table 16.1** Goal-Attainment Scaling for Listening Skills

| | |
|---|---|
| +3 | Jean hears what is being said to her and can repeat back what was previously said to her on speaker's completion of conversation or brief interchange. |
| +2 | Jean hears the other person speaking to her, yet is not able to repeat back the thought or content of the conversation. |
| +1 | Jean hears the other person speaking to her and appears to be listening, which is noted by the nonverbal signs she exhibits (smiles, laughing, serious look on her face). |
| 0 | Jean shows signs of listening and questions if she did not hear the entire thought. Not able to repeat back what was heard. |
| −1 | Jean talks throughout a conversation with another person with no idea of the other person's statements to her. |
| −2 | Jean talks and yells while others are speaking. |
| −3 | Jean has no identification with another person's conversation and shows this through her yelling, talking over others, and at times, screaming. |

assessed via the goal attainment scale presented in Table 16.2. Due to Jean's visual impairment, the importance of her attending to verbal components (e.g., voice tone, intonation) of social interactions with parents and peers was underscored. The purpose of work in this domain was, in part, to increase Jean's social perception skills. Such training was viewed as requisite to her accurate interpretation and understanding of feeling states in others. It was anticipated that greater social awareness would, in turn, improve the acceptability and desirability of her responses. Concurrently, mother was trained to more effectively monitor and identify verbal and nonverbal social cues that family members emitted during interpersonal exchanges. Through extensive behavior rehearsal and therapist-provided performance feedback, the mother reported fewer disruptions and interruptions and more attentive listening during parent interactions with Jean, as well as with each other on the weekends.

Intervention for communication skills also involved teaching Jean ways to express herself in an appropriate manner without hurting the other person's feelings. Using modeling, role playing, and performance feedback, Jean acquired more effective alternative interpersonal behaviors. At the same time, her mother was trained to positively reinforce her improved social responding in role-played parent-child interac-

**Table 16.2** Goal-Attainment Scaling for Communication Skills

| | |
|---|---|
| +3 | Mother and daughter (Jean) maintain a pleasant conversation with one another (in reciprocal process) without any episodes of arguing. |
| +2 | Mother and Jean begin to talk to one another reciprocally and respond to what had been a part of the proceeding conversation. |
| +1 | Jean and/or mother initiate a positive opening statement with the two listening to what has been spoken; no episode of interruption. |
| 0 | Jean or mother initiates one positive opening statement, one at a time to one another. (The beginning of a conversation; interruption is possible at this time.) |
| −1 | Jean and mother talk at the same time, such that one is talking or interrupting at the midpoint of the other's statement. |
| −2 | Jean does not hear or listen to what mother is saying to her. (On the other hand, mother does listen.) |
| −3 | Mother or Jean initiate conversations, with yelling at one another or with an argument. |

tions. In addition, her mother was given homework assignments to provide reinforcement for the same behavior at home. Areas that were targeted under the rubric of communication skills were: (1) Jean's ability to demonstrate her appreciation and regard for her parents through use of attentive listening; (2) Jean's use of questions with parents, peers, and teachers to clarify the meaning of verbal statements or requests; (3) each family member's increased efforts toward understanding and acknowledging another person's needs and feelings.

As part of the attempt to enhance overall family communication, Jean and her mother were taught to ask for clarification of the meaning or intent of another's communication when messages were unclear. Special attention also was directed to the couple's marital interactions, given their initial complaints of poor communication in recent months. This, as previously noted, was carried out in sessions alone with the mother.

At termination of BFT, Jean's mother reported improvement in her ability to listen attentively, communicate more clearly, and initiate more positive interactions with both parents at home. All family members also commented on being able to interact with one another without arguments or misunderstandings. These changes are reflected by the therapist's ratings on the goal attainment scales (see Figure 16.1).

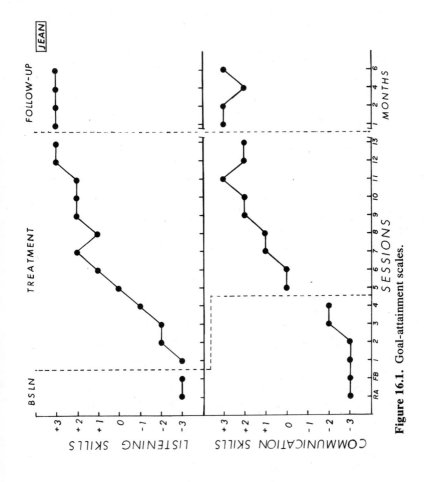

**Figure 16.1.** Goal-attainment scales.

**Table 16.3** Pre-BFT, Post-BFT, and Means of the 1-, 2-, 3-, and 6-month Follow-ups

| Measure | Pre | Post | Mean of the Follow-ups |
|---|---|---|---|
| *ACQ* | | | |
| (Mother re: child) | 33 | 25 | 17 |
| (Child re: mother) | 38 | 30 | 25 |
| *CBCL* | | | |
| (Activities) | 38 | 45 | 45 |
| (School) | 30 | 53 | 55 |
| (Anxious-obsessive) | 73 | 55 | 55 |
| (Somatic complaints) | 79 | 56 | 55 |
| (Schizoid) | 64 | 58 | 56 |
| (Depression withdrawal) | 74 | 55 | 55 |
| (Immature hyperactivity) | 68 | 61 | 58 |
| (Aggressive) | 67 | 56 | 55 |
| *YSRF* | | | |
| (Activities) | 35 | 45 | 53 |
| (Social) | 47 | 55 | 55 |
| *MAS* | 130 | 136 | 138 |

Results of a multiple baseline analysis across treatment targets indicates improvements in both listening and communication skills. Specifically, therapist ratings on listening skills increased from −3 at baseline, to +3 by session 12 of treatment. Similarly, ratings on the communication skills scale improved from a mean of −2.67 during baseline to between +2 and +3 by the end of formal intervention. Further, follow-up probes conducted 1, 2, 4, and 6 months after treatment revealed that gains had been maintained.

Pre- and post-BFT comparisons of scores on self-report indices also reflected improvements in child and family functioning (see Table 16.3). The data indicate that Jean and hear mother (family) made numerous adjustments in coping more adequately with problems presented in the preassessment. As changes were successfully accomplished it was evident that Jean's social interactions were improving both in the family and within the school setting. Indeed, her teacher observed that Jean engaged in more appropriate interpersonal behaviors and significantly fewer arguments with peers at school. In addition, she appeared to be more involved in classroom academic and social activities. Another positive change was the mother's report that the family was now engaging in more outside activities (e.g., drives, picnics, movies) together. She also related that communication now was better with her husband and that their relationship had improved.

Booster sessions were not required with this family given the durability of skill acquisition evident at follow-up evaluations.

## Overall Evaluation

The present case study involved a severely visually impaired child with mild mental retardation and deficits in interpersonal skills. These social skill deficiencies were apparent in interactions with parents as well as peers. Assessment of the child and family indicated that disruptive and maladaptive patterns of family communications characterized parent-child interactions as well as the marital relationship. Behavioral family treatment was implemented to improve areas related to interpersonal difficulties in the child and dysfunctional patterns of communication in the family system.

## References

Achenbach, T., & Edelbrock, C. (1979). The child behavior profile: Boys age 12-16 and girls age 6-11 and 12-16. *Journal of Consulting and Clinical Psychology, 47*, 223, 233.

Achenbach, T., & Edelbrock, C. (1983). *Manual for child behavior checklist and revised behavior profile*. Burlington, VT: University Association Psychiatry.

Ammerman, R. T., Van Hasselt, V. B., & Hersen, M. (1986). Psychological adjustment of visually handicapped children and youth. *Clinical Psychology Review, 6*, 67-85.

Biglan, A., Van Hasselt, V. B., & Simon, J. (1988). Visual impairment. In V. B. Van Hasselt, P. S. Strain, & M. Hersen (Eds.), *Handbook of developmental and physical disability*. Elmsford, NY: Pergamon.

Boyd, R. D., & Otos, M. B. (1981). Visual handicaps. In J. E. Lindemann (Ed.), *Psychological and behavioral aspects of physical disability: A manual for health practitioners*. New York: Plenum.

Cassin, B., & Solomon, S. (1984). In M. L. Rubin (Ed.), *Dictionary of eye terminology*. Gainesville, FL: Triad.

Dion, K. K. (1972). Physical attractiveness and evaluation of children's transgressions. *Journal of Personality and Social Psychology, 24*, 207-213.

Edelbrock, C., & Achenbach, T. M. (1980). A typology of child behavior profile patterns: Distribution in correlates for disturbed children aged 6-16. *Journal of Abnormal Psychology, 8*, 441-470.

Farkas, G. M., Sherick, R. B., Matson, J. L., & Loebig, M. (1981). Social skills training of a blind child through differential reinforcement. *The Behavior Therapist, 4*, 24-26.

Hoover, R. E., & Bledsoe, W. (1981). Blindness and visual impairments. In W. C. Stolov & M. R. Clowers (Eds.), *Handbook of severe disability*. Washington, DC: U.S. Department of Education, Rehabilitation Services Administration.

Jacob, T. (1980). *Modification of Areas of Change Questionnaire for adolescents and their parents*. Unpublished manuscript. University of Pittsburgh, Pittsburgh, PA.

Kleck, R. E. (1983). Physical stigma and nonverbal cues emitted in face-to-face interaction. *Human Relations, 21*, 19-28.

Locke, H. J., & Wallace, K. M. (1957). Short marital adjustment and prediction tests: Their reliability and validity. *Marriage and Family Living, 21*, 251-255.

National Society to Prevent Blindness. (1980). *Vision problems in the U.S.: Facts and figures*. New York: Author.

Richardson, S. A. (1969). The effect of physical disability on the socialization of the child. In D. Goslin (Ed.), *Handbook of socialization theory and research*. Chicago, IL: Rand McNally.

Rowley, F. L., Van Hasselt, V. B., & Hersen, M. (1986). Behavioral treatment of families with an adolescent with spina bifida: A treatment manual. *Social and Behavioral Science Documents, 16*, #2784.

Scott, R. A. (1969). The socialization of blind children. In D. Goslin (Ed.), *Handbook of socialization theory and research*. Chicago: Rand McNally.

Skinner, H. A., Steinhauer, P. D., & Santa-Barbara, J. (1981). The family assessment measure. *Canadian Journal of Community Mental Health, 2*, 91-105.

Steinbook, R. M., Jacobson, A. F., Mosher, J. C. & Davies, D. L. (1977). The Goal-Attainment Scale: An instrumental guide for the delivery of social reinforcement. *Archives of General Psychiatry, 34*, 923-926.

Van Hasselt, V. B. (1983). Social adaptation in the blind. *Clinical Psychology Review, 3*, 87-102.

Van Hasselt, V. B. (1987). Behavior therapy for visually handicapped persons. In M. Hersen, R. M. Eisler, & P. M. Miller (Eds.), *Progress in behavior modification* (Vol. 21, pp. 13-44). Newbury Park, CA: Sage.

Van Hasselt, V. B., Hersen, M., Kazdin, A. E., Simon, J., & Mastantuono, A. K. (1983). Training blind adolescents in social skills. *Journal of Visual Impairment and Blindness, 77*, 199-203.

Weiss, R., & Margolin, G. (1977). Marital conflict and accord. In A. Ciminero, K. Calhoun, & H. E. Adams (Eds.), *Handbook of behavioral assessment*. New York: John Wiley.

# Subject Index

# About the Contributors

**MICHAEL A. ALEXANDER**, M.D., is Chief of the Division of Rehabilitation at the Alfred I. DuPont Institute, Wilmington, DE, and Clinical Associate Professor of Physical Medicine and Rehabilitation at Jefferson Medical College, Philadelphia, PA. He has published widely in the areas of rehabilitation of children with varying neuromuscular disabilities and has research interest in the use of technology in augmenting the function of children.

**MARC S. ATKINS**, Ph.D., is Assistant Professor in Pediatrics and Psychiatry, University of Pennsylvania School of Medicine. His research interests include assessment of aggression and impulsivity in behavioral and pharmacological treatments for attention deficit disorder.

**FRANCISCO X. BARRIOS**, Ph.D., is Coordinator of Psychological Services at the Pain Evaluation and Treatment Institute at the University of Pittsburgh School of Medicine and Presbyterian-University Hospital, Pittsburgh, PA. His clinical and research interests include cognitive-behavior therapy, self-regulation and self-control, and the assessment and treatment of chronic pain, smoking, and obesity.

**FRANK P. BELCASTRO**, Ph.D., is Professor of Psychology and Education at the University of Dubuque, Dubuque, IA. His research interests include the use of behavior modification with handicapped populations, psychological assessment of the hearing impaired, and programs for gifted children.

**THOMAS L. CREER**, Ph.D., is Professor of Psychology in the Department of Psychology at Ohio University, Athens, OH. His research interests are focused on the application of behavioral procedures to asthma and other respiratory disorders.

**P. J. CUSHING**, Ph.D., is a clinical psychologist with the Carolina Institute for Research on Infant Personnel Preparation at the University of North Carolina at Chapel Hill.

**M. JOANNE DIXON**, M.A., is Assistant Director of the Attention Deficit Disorders Clinic at Western Psychiatric Institute and Clinic, University of Pittsburgh School of Medicine. Her clinical and research interests include behavioral assessment and treatment of children and families.

**JUDITH E. FAVELL**, Ph.D., is Clinical Director of Au Clair Palms in Mount Dora, FL, an educational and residential program for persons with developmental disabilities and severe behavior disorders. Her emphasis has been on the understanding and treatment of extremely challenging behavior, including self-injury, aggression, and pervasive noncompliance. In addressing these problems she has combined an interest in clinical treatment, systems of service delivery, and empirical research.

**GERALD GOLDSTEIN**, Ph.D., is Professor of Psychology at the Highland Drive Veterans Administration Hospital, Department of Psychiatry and Psychology, University of Pittsburgh School of Medicine. His main research interests include clinical neuropsychological assessment, cognitive rehabilitation of brain-damaged patients, and neuropsychological aspects of alcoholism and schizophrenia.

**BRUCE P. HERMANN**, Ph.D., is Associate Professor in the Department of Psychiatry and Neurosurgery at the University of Tennessee-Memphis and Neuropsychologist at the Epilepsy Center of Baptist Memorial Hospital. His research interests include the neuropsychological and behavioral aspects of epilepsy.

**MARY BETH JOHNSTON**, Ph.D., works at the Oaklawn Psychiatric Center in Elkart, IN. Her clinical and research interests are in the areas of cognitive and behavioral assessment, child therapy, and mental retardation.

**JOHN A. JUBALA**, Ph.D., is Chief of Psychological Services, Physical Medicine and Rehabilitation at Mercy Hospital, Altoona, PA. His primary clinical and research interests include the areas of adaptation to severe trauma, management of chronic pain, and the behavioral medicine of oncology.

**JOHN R. LUTZKER**, Ph.D., is a visiting professor at the University of Judaism, Los Angeles, California. His research interests are in child abuse and neglect, developmental disabilities, and behavioral medicine.

**MARTIN J. LUBETSKY**, M.D., is an Assistant Professor of Child Psychiatry at Western Psychiatric Institute and Clinic, Department of Psychiatry, School of Medicine, University of Pittsburgh. He is Module Director of the John Merck Multiple Disabilities Program. He is particularly interested in the assessment and treatment of multiply disabled children, and has conducted research in this area.

**ELAINE MALEC**, B.S., is currently enrolled in a Ph.D. counseling psychology program at the University of Pittsburgh. Her research interests are in memory and head injury.

**R. A. McWILLIAM**, M.A., is a research associate at the Frank Porter Graham Child Development Center at the University of North Carolina at Chapel Hill.

**LOUISE E. MOORE**, B.A., is a research associate with the Western Pennsylvania School for Blind Children. Her research interests include research statistics, behavioral assessment, and treatment of children and families.

**WILLIAM E. PELHAM**, Ph.D., is Associate Professor of Psychiatry and Director of the Attention Deficit Disorder Program at Western Psychiatric Institute and Clinic, University of Pittsburgh School of Medicine. He has written numerous articles and chapters on the effects of psychostimulant medication and behavior therapy in the treatment of ADD children.

**RUSS V. REYNOLDS**, Ph.D., is Professor of Psychology in the Department of Psychology at Baptist Memorial Hospital R.R.C., Memphis, TN. He is interested in a broad array of topics related to health psychology, particularly the development and evaluation of self-management and other coping strategies.

**THOMAS E. RUDY**, Ph.D., is Assistant Professor of Anesthesiology and Psychiatry and Associate Director of the Pain Evaluation and Treatment Institute at the University of Pittsburgh School of Medicine. His major research interests include cognitive-behavioral assessment and treatment of chronic pain patients, psychophysiological assessment in chronic pain, functional capacity and its measurement in chronic physical disabilities, and the application of multivariate statistical methods to behavioral medicine research.

**EDWARD S. SHAPIRO**, Ph.D., is Associate Professor at Lehigh University, Department of Counseling Psychology, School Psychology, and Special Education. His research interests and publications are primarily in the areas of behavioral assessment and intervention techniques for academic skills problems, self-management in classroom behavior change, and developmental disabilities.

**LORI A. SISSON**, Ph.D., is a Research Associate at Western Pennsylvania School for Blind Children, Pittsburgh, PA. Her clinical and research interests include behavioral assessment and treatment of problem behaviors presented by children with multiple disabilities.

**CHRISTOPHER STARRATT**, Ph.D., is Director of Neuropsychology at the Allegheny Neuropsychiatric Institute in Oakdale, PA. His major interests are in clinical neuropsychology and cognitive rehabilitation.

**PHILLIP S. STRAIN**, Ph.D., is an Associate Professor of Psychiatry and Director, Early Childhood Intervention Program, Department of Psychiatry, University of Pittsburgh. He is the author of over 100 scientific papers on the behavioral treatment of young children and he has received numerous grants from the U.S. Department of Education and the National Institute of Mental Health.

**DENNIS C. TURK**. Ph.D., is Professor of Psychiatry and Anesthesiology and Director of the Pain Evaluation and Treatment Institute at the

University of Pittsburgh School of Medicine. His major research interests include assessment and treatment of chronic pain patients, adherence to health care recommendations, cognitive-behavioral treatment approaches, the role of perceived control in adaptation to chronic physical disease and trauma, and clinical decision making.

**KAREN J. WHITE**, Ph.D., is Assistant Professor of Psychology in the Department of Psychology at the University of Notre Dame. Her research interests include peer relations, hyperactivity, and aggression.

**THOMAS L. WHITMAN**, Ph.D., is Professor of Psychology at the University of Notre Dame. His research spans a variety of areas, including applied behavior analysis, cognitive-behavioral instruction, parent training, self-regulation, and mental retardation.

# About the Editors

**MICHEL HERSEN**, Ph.D., is Professor of Psychiatry and Psychology at the University of Pittsburgh School of Medicine. He is past president of the Association for the Advancement of Behavior Therapy. He is the recipient of several research grants from the National Institute of Mental Health, the Department of Education, the National Institute of Disabilities and Rehabilitation Research, and the March of Dimes Birth Defects Foundation.

**VINCENT B. VAN HASSELT**, Ph.D., is Assistant Clinical Professor of Psychiatry at the University of California, Irvine, and psychologist at Fairview Developmental Center, and Associate Research Scientist with the State Developmental Research Institutes (California Department of Developmental Services). He is coeditor of the *Journal of Family Violence* and the *Journal of the Multihandicapped Person*. His major research interests are in the areas of behavior therapy for multihandicapped and behavioral disordered children and abuse of handicapped children.